HOW TO
BE, DO, OR HAVE
ANYTHING

A Practical Guide to

Creative Empowerment

LAURENCE G. BOLDT

TEN SPEED PRESS

Berkeley • Toronto

Copyright © 2001 by Laurence G. Boldt

Lightning Press
PO Box 91104
Santa Barbara, California 93190

Published by Lightning Press in association with Ten Speed Press.

Ten Speed Press
PO Box 7123
Berkeley, California 94707
www.tenspeed.com

Distributed in Australia by Simon and Schuster Australia, in Canada by Ten Speed Press Canada, in New Zealand by Southern Publishers Group, in South Africa by Real Books, in Southeast Asia by Berkeley Books, and in the United Kingdom and Europe by Airlift Book Company.

Cover and text design by Susan Shapiro

An earlier version of this book was published by Lightning Press as *Manifest Your Destiny: Life Planning with Punch*. Copyright © 1986 by Laurence G. Boldt.

Library of Congress Cataloging-in-Publication Data

Boldt, Laurence G.
    How to be, do, or have anything: a practical guide to creative empowerment/
    Laurence G. Boldt
        p. cm.
    Rev. ed. of: Manifest your destiny. 1986.
    ISBN 1-58008-308-0 (pbk.)
    1. Success. 2. Creative ability.   I. Boldt, Laurence G. Manifest your desinty. II. Title.
    BJ1611 .B65   2001
    158—dc21

                                                                2001000747

First printing, 2001

Printed in Canada

1 2 3 4 5 6 7 8 9 10 — 05 04 03 02 01

There is only one definition of success . . . .
to be able to spend your life in your own way.

—CHRISTOPHER MORLEY

Acknowledgments

To Ellen Marks

I want to thank several people whose help was instrumental in making this book a reality. First thanks to Susan Shapiro. In addition to typesetting the entire book, she deserves much of the credit for both the text and cover design. Beyond her hands-on assistance, she contributed in a variety of ways too numerous to mention. Susan is a human dynamo, a dear and loyal friend, and a pleasure to work with. Kim Grant's editorial contributions have improved every book I have ever written, including this one. She combines a subtle ear with a tenacious commitment to excellence. Thanks Kim, for all your help. Thanks to Tina Kolaas for encouraging me to revise and reissue this book and for her continued belief in and help with the project throughout. Special thanks to Rob Warner for his support.

I also want to thank the individuals whose personal stories appear in these pages. Though their names and some specific details of their circumstances have been changed in order to protect their privacy, they have added much in helping to illustrate the creative principles discussed in this book. Finally, thanks to Peter Beren for arranging the distribution of the book—and to Phil Wood, Kirsty Melville, Meghan Keeffe, and all the folks at Ten Speed Press.

Contents

✻

Introduction   ix

Chapter 1   The Creative Life: Yours for the Taking   1

Chapter 2   The Manifestation Formula: Understanding
the Creative Process   5

Chapter 3   Finding Balance: The Key to Personal Fulfillment   17

PART I: VISION

Chapter 4   Vision: Opening to a World of Possibilities   29

Chapter 5   The Vision of the Artist: Introspection   45

Chapter 6   The Vision of the Scientist: Observation   67

PART III: FOCUS

Chapter 7   Focus: Developing Your Powers of Concentration   87

Chapter 8   Decision Making: Establishing Your Priorities   105

Chapter 9   Motive Testing: Listening to Your Heart   127

Chapter 10   Goal Setting: Fixing Your Destinations   141

PART III: DESIRE

Chapter 11   Desire: Creating Lasting Motivation   161

Chapter 12   See It: Visualization   175

Chapter 13   Believe It: Affirmation   191

Chapter 14   Receive It: Act with Expectation   209

Chapter 15   Value It: Reward Your Progress   229

PART IV: COMMITMENT

Chapter 16   Commitment: Going the Distance   249

Chapter 17   Discipline: Mastering Distraction   263

Chapter 18   Daring: Overcoming Fear   285

Chapter 19   Diplomacy: Gaining Cooperation   311

Chapter 20   Detachment: Learning to Grow   335

Beyond Commitment   357

Appendix   365

Introduction

The thing always happens that you really believe in;
and the belief in a thing makes it happen.

FRANK LLOYD WRIGHT

The title of this book proposes to show you how to be, do, or have anything. At first glance, this seems an outrageous claim. While I admit to wanting to grab the reader's attention, there is more going on here than mere hyperbole. Of course, the "anything" referred to above must be something that is actually possible to realize or accomplish. Yet what is truly impossible is difficult for us to judge. In the course of our daily lives, we encounter as actualities things and experiences that only a hundred years ago would have seemed impossible fantasies—far beyond the reach of any reasonable expectation. The times we live in compel even the most pragmatic of realists to be very cautious about saying what can't be done.

I also want to make it clear that the "how to" in this book refers to general principles of the creative process. *How to Be, Do, or Have Anything* is certainly not an encyclopedic volume, exhaustively detailing the specific techniques involved in all of the arts and sciences, and I doubt any potential reader, even at first glance, would mistake it for such. When a French team under the direction of Denis Diderot, chief editor of the *Encyclopédie,* undertook such an effort in the mid-eighteenth century, the result was some seventeen volumes. Today, were a large team of experts to attempt a similarly comprehensive compendium of today's arts and technologies, the result would be many times that size and would already be out of date by the time it could be published.

My objective in writing this book was to present the principles of the creative process in a simple, step-by-step formula that could be easily understood and effectively used by virtually anyone. While some stumble upon it by accident, and a very few make a concerted effort to cultivate it, most go through their entire lives without ever coming to recognize, much less to consistently apply, the creative power they possess. It strikes me as a great failing of our educational system that we do not teach people how to create the results they want in their lives. Instead, we teach them that creativity is the private domain of uncommon individuals who work in special fields. Nothing could be further from the truth!

I have seen firsthand the transformative effect that using the principles in this book can have on even so-called troubled or difficult people. The material contained in this book was originally developed for a course on creative empowerment, called *Manifest Your Destiny*. In addition to being offered in college classrooms and in seminars for the general public, this course was given to "troubled" high school students and to prisoners in a federal penitentiary. It was particularly gratifying to see how participants in these latter two groups responded to this material. Many found the experience life transforming. They reported dramatic increases in self-confidence and a new sense of optimism about their prospects in life. This not only confirmed my faith in the innate creativity of all human beings but reaffirmed my belief that many good people go "bad" simply because they don't think they can do anything else. If this material can have this kind of effect on those society labels as incorrigible, how much more can it do for you? I am convinced that anyone who understands and consistently applies the principles described in this book will meet with success.

Application is critical. This book is meant to provide an interactive experience for the reader. While you will gain value from simply reading the material in the chapters that follow, you will gain much more by doing the accompanying exercises. The text of this book is meant to provide information and to serve as a catalyst and stimulus to action. The real value comes with doing the exercises, for in so doing, you'll begin to actively engage your own creative capacities in shaping your life. Reading about how to use a hammer and saw will not build a deck or a fence. To the get the finished product, you have to pick up the tools and use them. In the same way, learning about the tools with which you can change your life isn't the same as putting them to work. The creative formula presented in this book will work for you, but you will have to work at it. Don't confuse reading this or any other book with taking the concrete steps necessary to changing your life.

Getting the most from the principles in this book will take more than knowing about them; it will even take more than the personal engagement required to do the exercises. Above all, it will take passion. The poet Yeats said, "Education is not filling a bucket but lighting a fire." That fire is your creative passion. More than knowledge or even effort, it is your passion that empowers you to be, do, or have what you desire. In every child, the fire of creative passion burns bright. Yet if the bumps and bruises of life have dampened your flame, you must determine to stoke it up again. You fuel your passion by paying attention to what makes you feel alive and energized—to what interests and excites you. Passion cares; passion wants; passion ignites spontaneous action.

Resist the temptation to play it safe or hide behind cynicism. There is more to lose than win by holding back. After all, failure can be overcome, but if you lose your passion, you're beaten before you've begun. To lose your passion is to suffer the greatest defeat that any man or woman can ever know, for with it go confidence, beauty, and joy. Only those who keep the fire of passion burning bright have a chance of knowing what a grand and glorious thing it is to be alive. To live your passion, you must believe that something inside of you is stronger than any outer circumstance. You must eliminate not merely the words but the thoughts "can't" and "impossible." You must believe that YOU ARE THE ANSWER—that whatever the problems and challenges you may face, you have what it takes to master and overcome them.

*Knowing is not enough,
we must apply.
Willing is not enough,
we must do.*

GOETHE

Given these provisos, I stand behind the promise of the title. It can be logically derived from a simple set of axiomatic tenets, which I call "The Seven Principles of Creative Living." I believe that each of these tenets withstands the test of critical examination, as well as that of common sense. They are briefly sketched below and will be developed at length throughout the course of this book. The message of this book can be summed up in a few simple words: Live your passion. Activate your innate creative power. Best of luck in the creative adventure of transforming your most cherished dreams into living realities!

The Seven Principles of Creative Living

1. Among human beings, creativity is a natural, and not an exceptional, trait. Birds fly, fish swim, humans create.

2. For the individual, personal freedom and self-fulfillment depend upon the conscious expression of his or her innate creative capacities. Without such expression, one will meet with unhappiness and unnecessary limitation.

3. Social and psychological factors may limit or impede an individual's innate creativity. These factors can be overcome.

4. The creative process follows a definite pattern and is *essentially* the same for all outcomes.

5. The creative process is knowable and understandable. It can be taught and learned. (This process will be revealed and explained in this book.)

6. The more one creates, the more confident he or she becomes of his or her ability to create.

7. Experience gained in applying the creative process in one area of life can be transferred to other areas.

The Creative Life: Yours for the Taking

Every child is born a genius.

ALBERT EINSTEIN

I s it really possible for you to be, do, or have anything? Can you, in fact, create what you want in life? Once you have mastered the secrets of the creative process revealed in this book, you will be able to create virtually any outcome you desire. Of course, there are limits on what any one person can realistically do or accomplish in a lifetime. Yet the boundaries of these limits extend so far beyond what we typically imagine we can do, as to deserve little more than mention. What Thoreau said of the human race applies equally to us as individuals: "Man's capacities have never been measured, nor are we to judge of what he can do by any precedent, so little has been tried."

It is a fundamental premise of this book that we are all innately creative creatures. Simply put: To be human is to be creative. Yet in order for you to take full advantage of your innate creative abilities, it is vital that you see yourself as a creative person. In studies designed to uncover the critical variables that predict creativity—what makes one person more creative than the next—researchers looked at IQ, socioeconomic background, education, and a host of other factors. They were surprised to discover that the only variable that correlated with creativity—the only variable that could reliably predict whether or not an individual would demonstrate creative ability—was the individual's *belief* that he or she was a creative person. People who believe they are creative actually *are* more creative than others.

The first step, then, to unleashing your creative power is to accept—no—to affirm and celebrate that you are a creative person. Unfortunately, many of us (it is probably safe to say most) do not see ourselves as naturally creative. We often fail to recognize and appreciate our innate creative capacities because we hold limiting concepts about ourselves and about what it means to be creative. Many of us have come to believe that creativity is the exclusive domain of professional artists. Writers, dancers, painters, musicians, actors, and the like—these are creative people. For the rest us, creativity is something we are to admire from a distance, not something we are to know and live with as an immediate and familiar part of our daily existence.

In most cultures, including our own Western European culture prior to the eighteenth century, all of the practical arts of everyday living were considered equal in significance to what are today called the "fine arts." Before the era of machine manufacture, all of the practical arts from candlestick making to printing, from furniture making to blacksmithing and a host of other activities were recognized as vehicles through which individuals could express their innate creative abilities.

Whatever your vocation or calling in life, you can express yourself creatively through it. Moreover, opportunities for creative expression are not limited to your career. Whether you want to improve your personal relationships, furnish a new home, plant a garden, or cook a meal, you have the opportunity to express yourself creatively or to resign yourself to the tired habits of routine. Beyond the increased joy and beauty that specific applications of your creativity bring, your whole attitude toward life changes when you come to recognize that you have creative control of it. You come to recognize that you are the master of your own destiny.

The creative process is not something special or mysterious. This book will outline a simple, step-by-step formula that anyone can use to gain creative mastery in his or her life. One of the important things we will discover along the way is that developing creative power is simply a matter of gaining conscious, deliberate control over what are more typically automatic and unconscious processes. Gaining creative mastery is not so much a matter of doing different things as it is of becoming more aware of what we are already doing, and doing it more consciously and deliberately.

We can define creativity as "the process of bringing into form, ideas or ways of living that either previously did not exist at all or did not exist for an individual or group of individuals." Throughout this book, the term *manifestation* will be used to indicate the creative process. In this context, *manifestation* means "the process though which thoughts come to take concrete form in the physical world." Another definition of the word *manifestation* is "a materialized form of spirit." People in many traditional cultures throughout the world viewed the whole of the universe in just this way. They experienced the natural world as "a materialized form of spirit." They recognized that their own spiritual, mental, and emotional energies had a profound impact on the environment in which they lived. They understood that their thoughts and feelings played a critical role in creating their experience.

Throughout the nineteenth, and most of the twentieth, century, mainstream science rejected the natural philosophy of traditional cultures as mere superstition. Today, many people have come to recognize that traditional cultures have a great deal to offer in the quest to understand the nature of reality. Science, too, is coming to recognize that we cannot separate the spiritual, mental, and emotional from the physical. Research in the field of medicine in particular is helping us to better understand the complex nature of these relationships. In recent years, a

The future belongs to those who believe in the beauty of their dreams.

ELEANOR ROOSEVELT

host of studies have confirmed the role that thoughts, feelings, and life attitudes play in physical health. For example, the immune system, the body's first line of defense against disease, has been shown to be directly affected by our mental outlook and emotional state. These seeming intangibles actually alter our biochemistry.

If thoughts and feelings play an important role in creating health and illness, it is safe to assume that they play an equally vital role in shaping the entire range of our experience. By learning to gain mastery over our thoughts and feelings, we can take creative control of our lives and begin to actively shape our destinies. We can channel energies that are currently being wasted or scattered, and focus them into a determined effort to realize the life of our dreams.

Today, in an era of corporate down-sizing and increased environmental awareness, we hear a great deal about waste: wasted time, wasted money, wasted natural resources. Yet the greatest waste is unrealized human potential—the love, talent, and innate abilities within countless millions that never find their true expression. Above all, *this* is the waste we must address. This book is written in the hope of providing you with inspiration and information that will help you to realize your destiny and fulfill your dreams. Never for a moment underestimate what you can be or accomplish. The call to greatness, the challenge to be all we are, goes out to all of us.

In studying the lives and writings of the greats of history, be they artists, scientists, humanitarians, or exceptional political leaders, I have found a profound, almost uncanny consistency in their thoughts and attitudes toward life as well as in their belief in their own creative powers. Virtually without exception, and regardless of their personal backgrounds or the fields in which they excelled, they had somehow intuited or learned what I have come to recognize as universal principles of creative manifestation. Now, you too will have access to these principles, and with them, the keys with which to unleash your own creative powers. The rest of this book is devoted to revealing these principles and assisting you in making them come alive in your own life.

The Manifestation Formula: 2
Understanding the Creative Process

First say to yourself what you would be,
and then do what you have to do.

EPICTETUS

What do you want? You name it: an exciting new career, more meaningful relationships, spiritual enlightenment, optimal health, financial independence. Maybe you want to start a business, direct a film, establish a nonprofit foundation, or travel the world. Whatever it is, if your desire is strong enough, and you are willing to back it up with consistent and persistent action, you can have it. The Manifestation Formula described in this chapter will show you how. The Manifestation Formula is a clear and concise statement of the creative process, a step-by-step formula for translating thoughts into actions, ideas into results, dreams into realities. Once you understand, and begin to consciously and consistently apply, the principles in this formula, you will be able to create virtually any result you want.

The Manifestation Formula is such a potent tool for personal empowerment because it renders the mysteries of the creative process comprehensible and repeatable. Though you're probably unaware of it, you've been using it right along. Many times, it has brought good into your life. In fact, everything you've accomplished or created has come to you by means of the process it describes. Yet until now, you've probably been using it unconsciously. As a result, you may not have understood the role that universal creative principles played in the accomplishment of your successes, or how to apply them to achieve the results you want in other areas of your life. Even more to the point, as often as not, you have probably used these creative principles against yourself, creating situations and results that you did not want.

Now you have the opportunity to take conscious and deliberate control of your innate creative capacities and make them do your bidding. A thorough understanding of the principles, together with repeated practice of the skills discussed in the remainder of this book, will make you an expert in making things happen. As an expert, you will do in a deliberate way what most do in a hit-and-miss fashion. You will know how to get what you want.

The creative process described by the Manifestation Formula is value neutral. It works equally well in creating constructive or destructive, "positive" or "negative" results. It shows you how to make things happen, but it does not tell you what to create or what will make you happy. That's up to you. Of course, you will want to stay away from anything harmful to yourself or others.

What's it going to take to turn that idea of yours into a reality? The answer is: The same general ingredients that it takes to manifest anything, plus the particular ingredients that it takes to manifest your thing, the specific results you desire. The Manifestation Formula provides universal principles, a general outline of the creative process. You will fill in the specifics according to your unique desires. The critical components of the Manifestation Formula are:

1. The Vision
2. The Focus
3. The Desire
4. The Commitment

5. The Plan
6. The Execution
7. The Feedback
8. The Evaluation

Every created thing or event began as a Vision, an idea within some fertile mind or minds. Because one or more individuals repeatedly Focus(ed) their attention on the idea, it grew into a Desire, which is to say, they began to invest emotional energy (enthusiasm and longing) into the vision. When that feeling of desire became sufficiently intense, it reached a point of no return. This point, called "Commitment," is the point at which they determined to do whatever was necessary to realize their vision. Next, they in one way or another developed a Plan, or strategy of action, for its Execution. They took actions and received some kind of Feedback on them. Finally, they made an Evaluation of their efforts in light of their original vision or purpose.

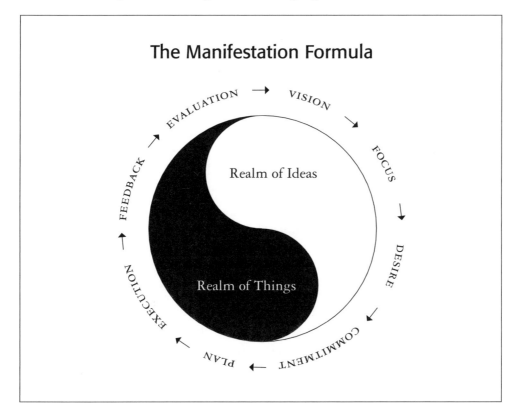

The Manifestation Formula

EVALUATION → VISION
FEEDBACK → FOCUS
EXECUTION → DESIRE
PLAN ← COMMITMENT

Realm of Ideas

Realm of Things

Anything Goes, and It Goes Like This. . .

The creative process described by the Manifestation Formula is a universal one that applies to the creation of all things and events. The significant steps in the process are the same, whether the result being sought is an artistic work, a scientific invention, a new product or service, or a social event. While all of the steps of the formula go into every manifestation and occur in the order given above, they may not always appear explicit and distinct. For example, some goals require complex and formal systems of feedback to ensure that efforts toward their accomplishment are yielding the desired results. For other goals, an individual may simply rely on her intuition to tell her whether or not the actions she is taking are yielding the results she desires. Some goals require extensive written action plans; others may only need a mental list of the steps involved.

The greater the scope of a vision, the more significant and distinct the steps to manifestation will appear to be. For example, in 1994, nearly two and a half centuries after the idea was first proposed, a 31-mile-long tunnel beneath the English Channel was opened to the public. Linking England and France by rail, the Channel Tunnel, or "Chunnel" as it is commonly known, is to date the largest privately financed infrastructure project in human history. This massive engineering feat cost 13.5 billion dollars and was seven years in the making. In addition to carrying 8.5 million metric tons of freight each year, the Chunnel made possible three-hour direct rail service between London and Paris. In an undertaking of this size, each of the elements of the Manifestation Formula is clear and distinct—many of the steps took years to accomplish.

Yet if we look carefully, we can recognize that the same steps occur in some way in every manifestation. In principle, the process of manifestation is the same for building a skyscraper, founding a company, throwing a party, or baking a pie. The same principles of manifestation used to create the Chunnel or put a man on the moon can guide you in creating a new career, launching a new business, or finding your dream home. Yet, if you want to consistently create the results you desire, it is important that you follow *all* of the steps in the Manifestation Formula—and in their proper sequence.

When we attempt only some of the steps within the Manifestation Formula, or attempt them out of sequence, we usually run into problems. For example, some people love to talk for hours on end—and to anyone who will listen—about their grand visions; yet they are unwilling to take any practical steps to make them happen. On the other hand, many people try to take action before they have a clear vision of the results they are after, let alone a plan for achieving them. Others start with a clear vision, make concrete plans, and enthusiastically take off after their goals; yet because they lack the commitment to follow through, they quickly give up when the going gets tough. Because it breaks down the creative process into its component parts, the Manifestation Formula helps you to understand where to put your attention and how best to marshal your efforts at every stage of the creative process. It will also help you to identify precisely where you are blocked when you are having difficulty accomplishing a particular goal.

By using the Manifestation Formula as a guide and asking yourself, "Is my vision broad and inspiring enough, my focus specific enough, my desire intense enough, my commitment strong enough, my plan clear enough, my execution effective and efficient enough, my feedback reliable enough, and my evaluation thorough enough to see me through?" you will avoid the problems described above. You won't put the cart before the horse, throw the baby out with the bath water, or get lost in the trees and forget the forest. You won't be hypercritical or detail oriented when you need to let go and dream your dream. Nor will you be dreaming when you need to be making realistic plans or taking immediate, effective action. You will recognize where you are in the creative process and what kind of approach will best advance your goals at any particular time.

Making the simple complicated is commonplace; making the complicated simple, awesomely simple, that's creativity.

CHARLES MINGUS

Transforming Thoughts and Feelings into Physical Realities

The Manifestation Formula describes a process for generating and transforming energy. We can think of a vision as a mental mold or form. To

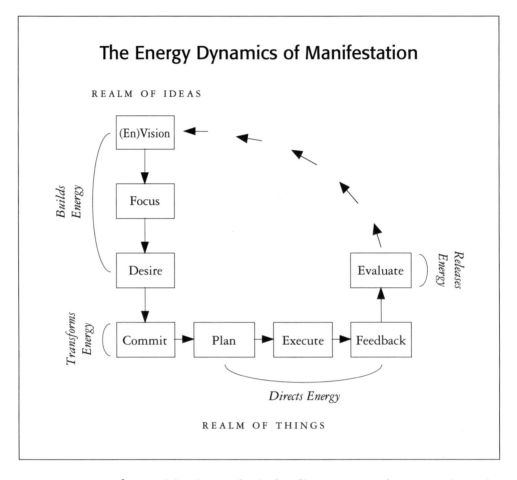

transform a vision into a physical reality, you must charge or animate its form with energy. The more expanded the scope or character of a given vision, the more energy will be required to bring it into the physical world. Initially, this energy is generated by concentrated mental focus and intense emotional desire. It is converted into a usable form in the physical world by means of commitment, the determination that you are prepared to do whatever it takes to make it happen. Commitment converts mental and emotional energy into physical force and action.

Commitment, then, is the critical step in the transformation of mental and emotional energy into physical energy. Planning, Execution, and Feedback manage and direct physical energy, which is finally released through Evaluation. Again, Vision sets the process in motion. Focus and Desire build the energy. Commitment transforms it. Planning, Execution, and Feedback direct it. Evaluation either releases or reinvests it.

As you can see from the diagrams on pages 7 and 10, the eight keys to manifestation can be divided into two groups: the "realm of ideas" and the "realm of things." The realm of ideas is the inner world of thought, imagination, and feeling. The realm of things is the physical environment in which we live, the world of actions, objects, and events. The first four keys: Vision, Focus, Desire, and Commitment—are in the realm of ideas. The second four: Planning, Execution, Feedback, and Evaluation—are in the realm of things. It should be noted, however, that Commitment and Evaluation serve as bridges between the two worlds and therefore can be thought of as residing in both.

In order for your intangible visions to manifest in the realm of things, you must cross the threshold of commitment, a point reached when you begin translating thought into definite action. Similarly, when you evaluate your efforts and results, you move back and forth between the realm of ideas and the realm of things, as you check the tangible results against your original intangible vision. The Manifestation Formula then seamlessly unites the world of thought with the world of action. It converts imagination, mental concentration, and emotion into practical, effective actions that yield definite results.

This book concentrates on the first four elements of the Manifestation Formula: Vision, Focus, Desire, and Commitment. The purpose of the information and exercises in this book is to help you reach the point of commitment, and develop a preliminary plan for achieving your objectives. Getting to commitment is vital because it's the pivotal make-or-break point in the manifestation process. It's commitment that propels you out of the realm of ideas and into the realm of physical action.

Each of the elements of the Manifestation Formula is important. Yet because the last four deal with the realm of things, they tend to be so specific to the individual situations in which they are being applied that there is little that can be said about them in general terms. These elements are addressed briefly in a section entitled Beyond Commitment which begins on page 357. While these elements are discussed only briefly here, keep in mind their significance to the overall process

To fulfill a dream..., to be given a chance to create, is the meat and potatoes of life. The money is the gravy.

BETTE DAVIS

11

Nothing splendid has ever been achieved except by those who dared believe that something inside them was superior to circumstance.

JOHN BARTON

of manifestation. (For examples of how all of the principles of the Manifestation Formula apply in creating specific results, see Appendix A.) By coming to understand, and more importantly, to consistently apply, the principles of manifestation, you are helping yourself to a lifetime of creative success in all your undertakings. You won't have to merely hope or wish that things will get better. You will know how to create what you want.

If I could give you a gift, it would be to endow you with unwavering confidence in yourself and in the creative process described by the Manifestation Formula. Assuming that you follow the formula laid out in this book, failing to achieve your goals will not be because of a lack of desire, talent, knowledge, or even because your goal was unrealistic to begin with. All these variables (and more) are factored into the formula. The two biggest reasons you will fail, if you do, are: (1) You will put off *applying* the principles. (2) You will become *impatient* and give up too soon. Your destiny is in your hands, and if you will unleash the full force of your own creative power, you will realize how strong and capable those hands really are.

What's Ahead in the Remainder of this Book

The next chapter introduces the Integrated Life Matrix, a tool you can use to look at your life in a balanced and wholistic way. It will aid you in constructing goals in all the areas that are important to you. The remainder of the book concentrates on developing the Vision, Focus, Desire, and Commitment you need to live your dreams.

Vision: This unit explores the critical role that vision plays in the creative life. It examines a right-brain approach to creative discovery, called the "Vision of the Artist," as well as a left-brain approach, called the "Vision of the Scientist." In the accompanying exercises, you will have the opportunity to apply both approaches as you set about identifying the creative visions for your life. Included are chapters entitled "The Vision of the Artist" and "The Vision of the Scientist." *If you want to come up with the inspirations, or solve the problems, that will transform your life, turn to the Vision section.*

Focus: The Focus unit begins with a discussion of the attention-selecting processes of the conscious mind. It goes on to show you how you can gain mastery of these processes, and in so doing, develop your powers of concentration. In the accompanying exercises, you'll have the opportunity to select the important priorities of your life and shape your visions into clear and definite goals. The Focus unit includes chapters entitled "Decision Making: Establishing Your Priorities," "Motive Testing: Listening to Your Heart," and "Goal Setting: Fixing Your Destinations." *If you want to increase your concentration, make decisions, or set realistic and attainable goals, turn to the Focus section.*

Desire: The Desire unit opens by considering the often overlooked role that the subconscious mind plays in goal achievement. You will learn a number of techniques to help you generate and sustain lasting motivation by enlisting the full support of your subconscious mind and its powerful inner resources. Included are chapters entitled "See It," "Believe It," "Receive It," and "Value It." These chapters discuss using visualization, affirmation, behavior modification, and reward reinforcement. *If you want to learn how to enlist the power of your subconscious mind to create the results you seek, with greater ease and speed than you ever thought possible, turn to the Desire section.*

Commitment: The final unit looks at commitment from two standpoints: the will to go for what you want, and the willingness to let go of things that keep you from getting it. You'll have the opportunity to realistically confront the costs of making a specific commitment versus those of not making it. You'll also have the opportunity to develop strategies for dealing with the four barriers that can keep you from realizing your dreams, namely: distractions, fears, the resistance of others, and the feeling of being overwhelmed. These obstacles, and the strategies to overcome them, are discussed in chapters entitled "Discipline," "Daring," "Diplomacy," and "Detachment." *If you want to overcome fear, master distraction, gain the cooperation of others, or learn to master new knowledge or skills with speed and confidence, turn to the Commitment section.*

Chapter 2 Exercises

❧

Create a Manifestation Journal

It's a good idea to create a manifestation journal. In it, you can record your answers to all of the exercises in this book, as well as any other ideas or plans that occur to you as you engage in this process. While it is not necessary to do so, there are definite advantages to keeping all of your work in one place. Reviewing your journal from time to time will help keep you motivated, stimulate new ideas, and remind you of all the work you have already done to achieve your dreams. Organize your thoughts in this way, and when you finish with this book, you'll have another to read—yours! Best of luck!

The Eight Steps of Manifestation

1. Recall some thing or event that you have brought into manifestation. Write out each of the eight manifestation steps for this thing or event (The Vision, The Focus, The Desire, The Commitment, The Plan, The Execution, The Feedback, The Evaluation).

2. Now follow the same process for some thing or event that you would like to bring into manifestation. Fill in each of the steps in the Manifestation Formula for this desired outcome. Refer to the examples in the Appendix to help you in this process. Note: you may have to do some research to complete this process, or you might want come back and fill it out after you have finished reading the book.

Unraveling a Negative Manifestation

The Manifestation Formula can be used to understand how we create negative as well as positive results. Of course, more often than not, negative manifestations result from an unconscious use of our creative powers. The purpose of this exercise is to help you to become aware of the role that the universal principles of creative manifestation discussed in this chapter play in these results. For example, you envision a negative outcome, which you keep replaying or focusing on in your mind. This produces an emotional reaction of fear or anger, which charges the image with energy. When the energy is sufficient, you become emotionally committed to this outcome. You begin to imagine (or plan) how it might come about, and take action (or avoid action) to ensure that it will. You get feedback along the way that this unwanted outcome is likely to occur. After it has, you evaluate the outcome and either decide to change the belief system that gave rise to the original vision or determine that this manifestation proves that it is true. Now try for yourself. Select a negative outcome you have brought into your life. Next, examine your role in creating it, by breaking it down into the steps of the Manifestation Formula.

Finding Balance: The Key to Personal Fulfillment 3

To every thing there is a season,
and a time to every purpose under the heaven.

ECCLESIASTES 3:1

You can, of course, use the manifestation principles detailed in the remainder of this book in any way you like. If you are eager to make a change in a specific area of your life, you may want to skip this chapter and move directly to chapter 4. Yet, at some point, you may wish to step back and take a look at your life as a whole. This chapter explores how you can balance your life by making sure your goals are in harmony with one another and that none of the important areas of your life are neglected.

If your life were a symphony, the different aspects of it could be represented by the different sections of an orchestra. All of the parts are complementary and work together to produce beautiful harmonies. In a good orchestra, the percussion section isn't in conflict with the wind instruments. In the same way, your career goals needn't be in conflict with your personal growth or family life. If you went to a symphony concert and heard only the percussion section or only the strings, you might feel as though you had missed something. In the same way, if your life is all work, or if your relationships aren't in some way informed by a sense of purpose or deep meaning, something is missing.

Too often we think in terms of this versus that. We tend to think in terms of conflicts rather than complements, as though the different roles we play are inherently at odds with one another. Much of this sense of conflict dissolves as you begin to assess your life as a unified whole with complementary parts, rather than as broken fragments competing for your time and attention. As you survey the whole of your life, you realize that you are not the various roles you play, that there is a center to your life—a core, or essential, Self. Ultimately, balance comes from living in full awareness of this Self. From your center, you can observe the different roles you play and make adjustments along the way. Instead of being pushed and pulled by various competing demands, you can create a balanced life, born from your essential Self.

Of course, there is no perfect model or example of what a balanced life looks like. It is something that each of us must endeavor to create for ourselves. How do you meet the many demands of life in today's fast-paced and chaotic world? How do you take control of your time and attention? No one has to tell you that you have many roles to play, many facets of yourself to develop, many responsibilities to take into account. While perfect balance is an elusive, perhaps even ultimately unattainable, goal, it is certainly one worth aiming for. It helps to take stock of your life on a regular basis and examine it in different areas.

To assist you in picturing and assessing your life as a whole, I've devised a tool that I call the "Integrated Life Matrix" (see diagram on page 19). Think of it as a road map to total life success. Within the Integrated Life Matrix are eight major life areas, including: Health, Lifestyle, Self-Development, Creative Expression, Career, Finance, So-

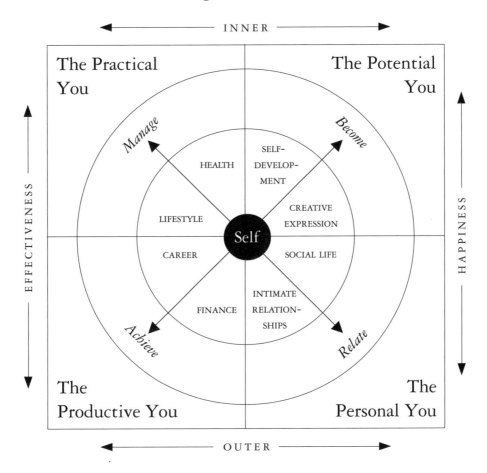

The Integrated Life Matrix

INNER

The Practical You

The Potential You

EFFECTIVENESS

HAPPINESS

Manage

Become

HEALTH

SELF-DEVELOP-MENT

CREATIVE EXPRESSION

LIFESTYLE

Self

CAREER

SOCIAL LIFE

FINANCE

INTIMATE RELATION-SHIPS

Achieve

Relate

The Productive You

The Personal You

OUTER

In the diagram above, you'll notice the terms *Happiness, Effectiveness, Inner,* and *Outer.* The Practical and Potential Yous have to do with your inner experience. The Productive and Personal Yous are primarily involved with your outer expression. The Practical and Productive Yous deal primarily with your effectiveness, while the Potential and Personal Yous consider your happiness. The Practical You reflects your inner effectiveness; the Potential You, your inner happiness. The Productive You reflects your outer effectiveness, and the Personal You, your outer happiness.

There is time for everything.

THOMAS EDISON

cial Life, and Intimate Relationships. In the Appendix, you will find a guide to help you determine where various aspects of your life fit within this eight-fold framework. Constructing an integrated life plan and updating it with periodic review will help to ensure that your life keeps moving in the direction you want. Beyond this, it will help you to see to it that all aspects of yourself receive the attention they deserve. To assist you in this wholistic planning process, the eight life areas are referred to in the exercises throughout the remainder of the book.

The eight life areas within the Integrated Life Matrix are universal elements of human life. They can be found in every human society, no matter how technologically primitive or advanced, how ancient or modern. In every human society, there is some consideration of health, for the care and maintenance of the human body. There is a lifestyle, or way of life, reflecting the values of the individuals within that society, and their relationship to technology and the natural environment. In every society, people make some attempt to understand the meaning of life, the relationship between the individual human being and the cosmos. All people in some way express themselves creatively, whether it be in the simple artifacts of everyday life, in grand architecture, in storytelling, or song and dance. In every culture, people do some kind of work and have some economic system for the exchange and distribution of goods. They have social relationships within the broader community and intimate relationships with some few others.

In our own lives, we each make decisions about our health, lifestyle, self-development, creative expression, career, money, and social and intimate relationships. Yet many of these decisions aren't the result of careful planning and conscious choice. They are decisions by default—choices made out of habit or instinct, or choices that result from making no choice at all. These default choices are unconscious capitulations to our social and physical environment and our personal history, not affirmative statements of what we can and will become. They are made haphazardly, without adequate consideration of their impact on the whole of our lives. Applying the eight life areas of the Integrated Life Matrix helps you to make *conscious* choices about the directions your life will take.

The eight life areas are complementary. Success in any one area increases opportunities for success in the other areas, while lack in any one area ultimately diminishes the whole. Though it may be necessary, and even wise, to choose to emphasize a particular life area for a period of time, you cannot neglect any major life area for an extended period of time without suffering an imbalance. Continued neglect of one area will begin to have a negative impact on even your strongest area. On the other hand, with a little creativity, you can find ways to use the success you've achieved in one area, to help shore up some of your weaker areas. It's all a question of maintaining awareness and making sure that all the important areas of your life get the attention they deserve.

The Four Yous

For the sake of simplicity, the eight life areas are grouped into "The Four Yous." The Practical You includes the areas of *health* and *lifestyle*. The Potential You considers *self-development* and *creative expression*. The Productive You includes your *career* and *finances*, and the Personal You focuses on your *social* and *intimate relationships*.

The Practical You is that within you that wants to *manage* your life. This is the part of you that decides how to best use your time, energy, money, and physical resources. It recognizes the primary importance of your physical *health* not only for its own sake but also for the role it plays in providing the stability and energy necessary for achieving success in the other areas of life. It is also concerned with establishing a *lifestyle* that reflects the values that are most important to you. Do you live in the city or the country? Are you seeking security or adventure? These are questions for the Practical You.

The Potential You is that within you that seeks to *become* your best self, to know and express the best within you. I call the knowing aspect *self-development,* and the expressive aspect *creative expression.* The Potential You seeks to learn and grow as a human being, to find meaning, and enjoy a fulfilling spiritual life. This is also the part that desires to express itself creatively. Whether it be through your vocation or avocation, whether it takes the form of poetry, gardening, music, cooking, or you name it, The Potential You seeks a vehicle through which to say, "This is me; I created that!"

The Productive You is that within you that desires to *achieve* a meaningful life's work, to share your unique gifts and make a difference in the lives of others. It's the part of you that wants a rewarding and challenging *career.* Giving your gifts brings rewards. Many of these are intangible, like self-esteem, inner peace, and self-respect—and some are very tangible indeed. The Productive You is also the part of you that is concerned with your *finances* and with achieving financial success, whatever that may mean to you. The Productive You wants to get down to business and make a difference.

The Personal You is that within you that wants to *relate* to others. The Personal You seeks a rich and rewarding *social life.* It's the part of you that wants to feel a sense of belonging and community, to enjoy the company of kindred spirits. It wants to share interests, activities, and ideas with others. The Personal You is also concerned with your *intimate relationships.* It's the part of you that yearns to know others deeply, to love and be loved unconditionally. It's the part that wants lifelong companionship, a rich and exciting sex life, and a rewarding family life.

We can see the factors of *becoming, relating, achieving,* and *managing* in terms of stages of human development. From infancy through early childhood, we are primarily involved in *becoming*—growing, developing, and learning. As we grow older, the issue of *relating* comes to the fore. By our early teens, we have learned empathy, the primary relating skill, and have become increasingly concerned with our social standings and influenced by peer pressures. Around the time we are ready to graduate from high school, the issue of *achievement* begins to dominate. Will we be able to continue our education? If so, at what school, college, or university? What our career and financial futures will hold become issues of primary concern to us. Achievement issues dominate from the late teens well into middle age. The issue of *managing* health and lifestyle first becomes a major consideration when the young adult leaves the parent's nest and begins to be responsible for him- or herself. This continues on into old age, when health and lifestyle issues typically dominate.

While it is important to recognize the relationship between the qualities (*becoming, relating, achieving,* and *managing*) and the stages of life, it is equally important to recognize that we don't have to let this relationship rule us. For example, we needn't wait until we are forced by old age to become concerned with our health; we can determine to care for our bodies while we are still young and vital. Nor do we have to become inflexible and set in our ways as we get older. We can determine to continue the process of becoming, by deliberately seeking out experiences that spur learning and growth. Many look back on their high school or college days with a certain longing and nostalgia because it was the last time they had a rich social life. Yet the opportunity to create one is available at any stage in our lives. The point is simply that while it will take more effort to cultivate the qualities that are not naturally dominant at a given stage in life, we are never too young or too old to enjoy any of these.

Seeing your life in terms of the eight life areas and the Four Yous is a powerful tool for promoting a balanced, full-bodied vision of the rich and varied possibilities for your life. Yet it is always important to remember that in reality, life is an indivisible whole that cannot be broken into neat categories or compartmentalized into sections. Everything affects everything else. For example, the way you manage your health and lifestyle affects the way you relate to others socially and intimately. Similarly, your ability to relate to others impacts your health, lifestyle, and career. What you become, that is to say, the degree to which you realize and express your creativity, impacts what you can achieve in your career.

The success you achieve in your work, and the financial rewards this brings, enable you to put greater energy into your relationships, personal growth, and creative expression. On the other hand, failure to achieve career and financial success can frustrate your self-development and creative expression and take a tremendous toll on your relationships. I could go on and on. The point is simply this: when you are developing a vision of what your life can be, consider all the important areas of life, and recognize how all the areas affect one another. The exercise that follows will help you to get a sense of what you would like to create in all the major areas of your life.

I take a simple view of living. It is, keep your eyes open and get on with it.

SIR LAURENCE OLIVIER

Chapter 3 Exercises

❦

The Whole of Your Life

Think about the next five years of your life (or, if five years seems too far way, substitute three years). You know they're going to happen. Even if you don't plan the next five years, you're still going to be five years older. But are you just going to be five years older, or five years better? Are you going to be in a rut, or are you going to use the next five years to develop yourself, to gain knowledge, wisdom, ability, skill, and character? Imagine yourself five years from now, and see the best you that you can be.

Health: Imagine yourself five years from now as the picture of health. How do you look? Notice your weight, shape, and energy level. What do you do for exercise, sports, and recreation? What do you eat? What do you avoid eating? What bad habits have you eliminated? What good habits have you incorporated? See these things and then write them down, along with anything else that occurs to you with reference to your health.

Lifestyle: Imagine the perfect lifestyle for you five years from now. Where do you live? What does your home look like? Do you travel? Where? How often? How do you manage your time? What's the level of stress in your life? How much time for recreation and rest is best for you? Describe your answers to these questions, and anything else that occurs to you with reference to your lifestyle.

Self-Development: Imagine yourself five years from now, developing yourself to your maximum potential. What qualities, attitudes, and emotions do you include or eliminate from your character? What spiritual qualities or strengths have you developed? What new knowledge or skills have you learned? Describe how you feel about yourself as you see yourself transforming and growing into a stronger and better person. Describe anything else that occurs to you with reference to self-development.

Creative Expression: Imagine your creativity coming through in exactly the way that's right for you, five years from now. In vivid mental images, describe what your unique creative expression looks like. How do you express? Is it through music, dance, poetry, hobbies, collections, or arts and crafts? Perhaps it's through writing, sculpting, gardening, or decorating? Describe the image of how you feel about yourself as you express your creative best—and anything else that occurs to you with reference to your creative expression.

Career: Imagine the career or careers that you're engaged in five years from now. See your responsibilities, the environments that you work in, the business and professional associations you participate in, the accomplishments that you've made, and the satisfaction that you get from your work. Describe these and anything else that occurs to you with reference to your career.

Finance: Imagine what you want your financial status to be in five years. What's your yearly income? What's your net worth? Do you have an investment strategy? If so, what is it? Do you have retirement plans? If so, what are they? Describe your answers to these questions, and anything else that occurs to you with reference to your ideal financial life.

Social Life: Imagine the social life you want to have in five years. In vivid mental pictures, describe the perfect social scene for you. Describe your friends, your standing in the community, your personal and professional associations, community service organizations, church group, and/or political groups. Who are your kindred spirits? How do you come across to others? How comfortable are you around other people? Where do you stand? How do you fit? Describe your answers to these questions, and anything else that occurs to you with reference to your social life.

Intimate Relationships: Imagine the intimate life that's right for you five years from now. Do you have a lover or a spouse? If so, describe what you want the relationship between you to be in five years. What about your friendship, communication styles, and sex life? Describe your relationships with your close friends, family, and children. How do you relate to the people with whom you want to share the deepest parts of yourself? Answer these questions, and record anything else that occurs to you with reference to your intimate life.

PART I

Vision

Vision: Opening to
a World of Possibilities

———

The Vision of the Artist:
Introspection

———

The Vision of the Scientist:
Observation

Vision:
Opening to a World of Possibilities

4

Imagination is the beginning of creation.
GEORGE BERNARD SHAW

Think of your life as a story. Doesn't the story of your real life deserve at least as much care and attention as a novelist gives a fictional story? Following the program in this book will help you craft the story of your life. Like an author, you'll start with a theme, a general idea of what the story of your life is about and where it is headed. Then you will work backwards to outline and flesh out the plot, determining the progression of scenes, turning points, and character developments that will make the story of your life the masterpiece it was meant to be.

The idea isn't to set up a rigid program for your life but rather, like an experienced writer, to let the story grab ahold of you, allowing it to suggest its own pace and direction. While crafting a general outline for the story of your life, leave room for spontaneity and serendipity. Give yourself the freedom to respond to new inspirations or intuitions, to adjust your plans as unexpected developments or new opportunities arise. Your objective in this, the Vision section, will be to get an outline of the important elements of your life's story down on paper. At this point, don't worry about the details or about how you are going to accomplish your objectives. We will get to that later.

For now, the idea is for you to become better acquainted with you—the main character of this story. What makes him tick? What turns her on? What are his innate talents? What are her natural interests? What values guide his or her life? In a good novel, the main character is transformed by the action of the story. By confronting and overcoming the obstacles that block the realization of some goal, the main character grows and evolves as a human being. So too in a good life. In fiction, as in real life, the significant turning points come when the character asserts who he or she is, in a new or more decisive way.

In addition to a strong main character, a good novel has an interesting plot. So does a fulfilling life. An interesting plot is one in which the main character faces a series of exciting and difficult challenges that test his or her abilities, character, and determination. These challenges force the protagonist to realize some latent potential, and in the process, to gain new confidence in his or her ability to successfully handle life. The question to ask yourself is, "Would anyone want to read the story of my life?" If the answer is yes, then how can you make the next chapter even more exciting than the last? If the answer is no, then perhaps your main character isn't growing enough or your plot isn't interesting enough. Come on author, get to work. Determine to make the story of your life all it can be. After all, isn't that what the rest of your life is for?

This chapter and the two that follow are designed to help you discover the central themes for the story of your life—in other words, your visions. Before getting under way, let's take a few minutes to consider: What is a vision? Why is having a vision so important? Where do visions come from? And how can you tap into the important visions for your life?

What Is a Vision?

We think in pictures, in images. To get an experience of this, pick a number from one to ten. Got it? You saw the number in your mind's eye, didn't you? You saw a picture. When I say the word *dog*, I'll bet you see a particular dog in your mind's eye. My dictionary defines the word *idea* as a mental image, and *thinking* as the activity of forming mental images. Though all ideas are mental images, all ideas are not visions. For our purposes, a vision is defined as "a mental picture of a future outcome, which inspires definite and sustained action toward its realization." A vision lies behind every creative manifestation. Everything around you—the book you are reading, the room you are in, the chair you are sitting on, the light you are reading by—began as an idea in someone's head. Come to think of it, every created thing began as an idea, a vision in some fertile mind.

What sets a visionary idea apart from the common run of ideas and, indeed, from imaginative fantasy is its capacity to inspire sustained action. *While fantasy uses the creative imagination to escape from reality, vision employs the creative imagination to transform reality.* A vision is an inspirational idea, one that motivates action. You'll know when a vision hits you by the energy and excitement you feel. A creative vision gets you going and keeps you going. The very thought of it charges you with energy and fills you with positive feelings. A visionary idea is pregnant not only in its capacity to motivate action but in its capacity to generate additional ideas that support its ultimate realization. A vision can be thought of as a seed idea, one which, when properly nourished, sprouts a host of root, stem, branch, leaf, and flower ideas.

Ideas are like rabbits. You get a couple and learn how to handle them, and pretty soon you have a dozen.

JOHN STEINBECK

Why Must I Have a Vision?

Your visions give you a sense of purpose and direction. They provide a sense of meaning and give continuity to your life. Your visions give you something to aim for, indeed, something to live for. They provide the motivation you need to transform yourself and your life. Without

All things are possible until they are proved impossible—and even the impossible may be only so as of now.

PEARL S. BUCK

visions, we are like ships without rudders, flailing about without purpose or direction, tossed this way and that by events and circumstances that seem to overwhelm us. When we are not reaching for the heights, we are settling for less; and as we settle, we begin sinking to the depths. At first, we may be merely bored; yet if we allow ourselves to continue to drift, we can become depressed or even destructive to ourselves and others. Finally, we go bitter and heavy-hearted to the grave, haunted by a powerful sense of regret, tormented by the knowledge that there was so much we missed.

Of course, life needn't be so dark and dreary. Hold your life up to the light of creative vision, and you'll soon begin to feel as though anything is possible. Creative visions rekindle the sense of wonder and exuberance for life that we all knew as children. They awaken latent powers and abilities that lie dormant within us. History is filled with examples of individuals who were, to all outer appearances, abject failures—until they were seized by some creative vision particularly suited to their unique abilities. What a shame it would have been had these people never tapped into the visions that drew their best out of them. What a shame it would be if you failed to take advantage of what a vision can do for you.

Vision sets in motion the creative process described by the Manifestation Formula. When you have a clear vision in mind, you have something to focus on, a basis for constructing definite goals. As you focus on your vision, your desire to achieve or realize the results it represents grows ever stronger. Putting your visions to work will help you realize that you are a stronger, more capable and talented person than you may ever have dreamed. As you discover, nurture, and activate your visions, you will find that they inspire, guide, and comfort you on your journey through life.

Beyond giving you a point of focus and an impetus to action, a creative vision provides you with a powerful planning tool. During the Cold War, the United States and the Soviet Union were embroiled in a fierce and highly competitive arms race. When one side got a technological edge in some kind of weaponry, the other side was desperate to get their hands on the item so they could give it to their scientists and have them "back-engineer" it. *Back-engineering* means taking a finished product and breaking it down into its component parts to determine how it was made, and thus, how it can be replicated. You can think of your visions as completed realities that you want to "back-engineer." Once you have a vision firmly fixed in your mind, imagine it as already achieved or realized, and mentally reconstruct the key steps that "went" into creating it. These will become the major action steps that represent critical landmarks on the road to realizing this vision. The steps to reaching each of these landmarks can in turn be further broken down. Before you know it, you have a clear, well-organized plan for achieving the results you desire. It all starts with a vision.

You Can't Take Constructive Action Without a Clear Picture

It's difficult to act without a clear picture of where you are going. For the sake of illustration, imagine jumping into your car on a cold and frosty morning. The windows are covered with ice. You can't see, so you can't move. You turn on the defrosters. You're in a hurry, so before the windows have entirely cleared, you cautiously pull out. Because your visibility is poor, you must go slowly. By the time the window has completely cleared, you're driving along at full speed and with complete confidence.

This little story illustrates several key points: if you can't see the road ahead, you can't move from where you are; if your vision is hazy, your action will be slow and cautious. A clear picture of where you are going puts you in the driver's seat, with an open road in front of you and plenty of gas in the tank. Vision gives you the confidence you need for positive, sustained action. You wouldn't think of building a new home without a blueprint. Yet many of us try to live our lives without a clear sense of the results we are after. Again, the clearer you are about what you are trying to create, the easier it will be to make it happen.

1. No picture   =   No action.
2. Hazy picture   =   Hesitant or cautious action.
3. Clear picture   =   Confident action.

Where Do Visions Come From?

All right, visions are important, but where do they come from? Henry Ford was once asked where his ideas came from. He replied, "The air is full of them. They are knocking you on the head. You don't have to think about it too much. You only have to know what you want, then forget it and go about your business. Suddenly, the idea you want will come through. It was there all the time."

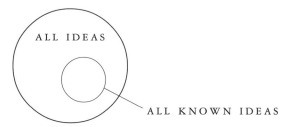

It was there all the time. Think about it. All ideas, even those that will not be discovered for hundreds or even thousands of years, already exist now. To help us understand how all ideas already exist, imagine a universe of ideas—a vast, timeless realm containing all possible ideas. Now imagine a subset within this broad universe, which we will call "all known ideas." These are the ideas that have been discovered. We could say that their time has come.

The right idea at the right time holds great power to transform the lives of individuals, communities, nations—indeed, the entire world. As Voltaire put it, "There is one thing stronger than all the armies in the world, and that is an idea whose time has come." How it is that an idea's time comes, we cannot say. The constellation of elements that create a perfect alignment of idea and circumstance are virtually impossible to predict or even to adequately comprehend in retrospect. Yet the power of such an alignment cannot be denied. We don't have to understand how this process works; we have only to recognize the trans-formative, truly life-changing, power latent in ideas. Truly, as Emerson said, "Thoughts rule the world." We need only look at how the ideas of Isaac Newton, Charles Darwin, Albert Einstein, or a host of others, have transformed the world. As great ideas possess the power to transform nations and societies, so a single visionary idea can completely transform your life.

When it comes to ideas, there is nothing new under the sun. The legend of Newton's discovery of the law of gravity while sitting beneath an apple tree is a graphic illustration of the point. The reality that lies behind the principle we call the "law of gravity" was operative, even before the fateful day that the apple came his way. Newton didn't invent or make up gravity; he simply recognized and articulated an already existing idea. In the same way, the principle that we call the "law of displacement" was operative before Archimedes discovered it while taking his famous bath. Long before primitive human beings began to use fire to provide heat for their shelters or to cook their food, the capacity for fire to do these things existed. In a sense, we could say that these uses were latent within the idea of fire. In the same way, the ideas for the uses and expressions of your life lie dormant within you. You needn't invent them; you have only to tap into them.

If visionary ideas exist before their discovery, they most certainly exist before their manifestation in the physical world. The vision of manned flight existed thousands of years before the Wright brothers made their first crude airplane. The vision of human beings landing on the moon existed centuries before the Apollo program made it a reality. Leonardo da Vinci envisioned the modern tank, submarine, and helicopter four hundred years before their actual manifestation in the physical world. In 1690, Denis Papin first proposed the idea of a piston-driven automobile. Yet over three hundred years passed before the first such motor car was built and tested. In much the same way, it may take you many years or even your whole lifetime to achieve an important vision for your life. Don't dismiss creative inspirations or visions for your life simply because they seem far off or out of reach. Indeed, these are often the ones that provide the greatest sense of fulfillment in their achievement and the greatest opportunities for growth in the process.

If all ideas already exist, what is the role of the genius? In its origin, the word *genius* meant "a channel." Those whom we call geniuses are simply those whose heightened receptivity or keen observational

I invent nothing;
I rediscover.

RODIN

35

skills have allowed them to discover previously unexplored or long-forgotten sectors of the universe of ideas. The great geniuses explore sectors that lie beyond the reach of ordinary awareness, then bring the ideas they find there down to earth by expressing them in ways the rest of us can comprehend. Einstein's genius lay not in the difficulty of his ideas (his theory of relativity is taught to many high school students) but in their potential to enlarge our understanding of the universe we live in. You too have the potential for genius, the potential to channel through the ideas that will expand your known universe.

Your Visions Await Discovery

We are all familiar with the great earth-shaking global discoveries. We know about the impact that the ideas discovered by Copernicus, Newton, or Einstein had in transforming our vision of the world. Yet equally important are the personal discoveries, the process through which each of us comes to discover for ourselves the answers to the age-old questions: "Who am I?" and "Why am I here?"

Imagine what wonderful inventions and strategies for living are yet to be discovered. These ideas exist now and await discovery, even as electricity waited for Ben Franklin, the light bulb for Edison, and relativity for Einstein. Like all ideas, the important visions for your life already exist, whether you have discovered them or not. Again, you do not need to make them up. You need only find a way to tap into them. You may be the next Copernicus or Einstein, with ideas latent within you that will shake the world. Yet even if you are not, the way in which you live your life is of great importance to yourself, your loved ones, and, in some significant way, to the world as a whole. Your creative visions hold the keys to the best use of your life.

Two Paths to Discovery

Creative visions are discovered or recognized in one of two ways: introspection or observation. The word *introspection* means "to look into one's

The Creative Process

THE VISION OF THE ARTIST: FROM IDEAS TO FORMS	THE VISION OF THE SCIENTIST: FROM FORMS TO IDEAS
1. What's going on within me?	1. What's going on around me?
2. Look for medium of expression.	2. Look for patterns, relationships.
3. Translate into form.	3. Develop system of images.
4. Communicate.	4. Communicate.
The artist interprets his inner reality through the medium of the outer world.	The scientist interprets the reality of the outer world by translating it into images.

own mind." Introspection is the intuitive path of discovery that I call the "Vision of the Artist." The artist sees what is going on within his or her imagination and develops forms or vehicles to express that vision in the outer world. As used here, the *Vision of the Artist* doesn't refer to the eye of a painter or architect, but to an intuitive way of experiencing the world, available to us all.

The word *observation* means "to become aware of, especially through careful and directed attention." Observation is the deliberate path of discovery that I call the "Vision of the Scientist." The scientist trains his mind to pay careful and focused attention to the world around him and to look for patterns that reveal the dynamics of the process under investigation. The scientist sees what is going on around him and develops a theory (or vision) to understand and interpret what he sees and make it known to others. Whether the path to discovery employs the "Vision of the Artist" or the "Vision of the Scientist," the final result is the same: Communication. (See the highlight box above.)

At the end of the chapters entitled "The Vision of the Artist" and "The Vision of the Scientist," you will find exercises. You may feel more inclined toward those that rely on the right-brain, intuitive style of the artist than those that use the more deliberate, left-brain style of the scientist, or vice versa. Work with the exercises you feel most drawn to, yet keep in mind that creative breakthroughs often come when we work against our dominant styles. Dr. Robert Ornstein of the University of California was the first to scientifically investigate the functions of the left and right brains. Dr. Ornstein found that when subjects in his experiments stimulated the "weaker" side of their brains and used its capacities in cooperation with those of their stronger side, they greatly increased their ability and effectiveness. In some cases, subjects' abilities increased as much as tenfold when they used both styles of thinking instead of relying solely on the one they were most comfortable with.

The *Vision of the Artist* and the *Vision of the Scientist* are meant to describe differences in methodologies, not to classify individuals. Most of the truly great geniuses have been highly developed in the use of both their left and right brains. Albert Einstein said that he discovered the theory of relativity not while wracking his brain over mathematical equations but while lying on a hill on a beautiful summer's day. The light streaming through his half-closed eyes seemed to break into a thousand sunbeams. Einstein imagined riding one these beams across the universe. But he didn't stop there. When he got up, he began working out the mathematics to support what he had seen in his imagination. Many artists have made prodigious use of left-brain thinking in the construction of their paintings. The notebooks of artists such as Leonardo da Vinci, Paul Cezanne, and Pablo Picasso reveal not only a keen eye for detailed observation but also a studied calculation of mathematical and geometric relationships in their use of line, form, and color. Make an effort to develop both sides of your brain, and be aware that experimenting with the "weaker" side will actually strengthen your dominant style. As the artist Henry Moore said, "To know one thing, you must know its opposite."

Expand Your Universe

A final word before you begin your vision quest: Think big, expand your horizons. Too often, people are shortsighted when considering visions for their lives. I would encourage you to take a look at the whole of your life from a "big picture" perspective. Focus on visions that are worthy of the important person you are. As someone once said, people tend to get in trouble in life NOT BECAUSE THEY WANT TOO MUCH, BUT BECAUSE THEY SETTLE FOR TOO LITTLE.

Who knows what tomorrow may bring? A self-educated farm boy and failed entrepreneur from the backwoods of Illinois held a nation together at the moment of its greatest crisis. His name was Abraham Lincoln. A patent clerk who flunked a college entrance exam changed our perception of the universe. His name was Albert Einstein. A nearly deaf man with three weeks of formal education invented motion pictures, the phonograph, and the electric light bulb—and changed the way we live. His name was Thomas Edison. A couple of struggling bicycle mechanics named Wilbur and Orville Wright inaugurated the era of manned flight. A vagabond drifter named Walt Whitman wrote some of his best poetry while in prison on vagrancy charges. A poor Scottish immigrant named Andrew Carnegie built a financial empire and a national system of libraries.

It would have been a mistake to count any of these giants out before they achieved recognition. It would likewise be a mistake to count yourself out. All you need is one good idea and the courage and determination to follow it through. It all starts with a vision. After all, you wouldn't be excited by a vision for your life unless you also have within you the power to make it a reality. Get the dreams of your heart and the visions of your creative imagination down on paper, where you can focus and reflect on them. Dare to record those positive mental pictures that come in intuitive flashes now and again, when you tune in to the Vision of the Artist or when you employ the Vision of the Scientist in the careful examination of an issue or problem. Now, let's turn our attention toward the Vision of the Artist.

If you refuse to accept anything but the best out of life, you very often get it.

SOMERSET MAUGHAM

The Process of Discovery
The Vision of the Artist

LEONARDO DA VINCI

What's going on inside me?
A vision of a painting "wherein the movements of the figures represent the passions of the soul."

Looks for medium.
A mural depicting the last supper of Jesus Christ.

Translates it into form.
Applies tempura to a base mixed on a stone wall.

Communicates the vision.
In 1498, Leonardo completes *The Last Supper*. It remains today the classic example of High Renaissance painting.

MICHELANGELO BOUNARROTI

What's going on inside me?
Sees within himself the image of David as a gentle warrior.

Looks for medium.
Selects marble sculpture.

Translates it into form.
Works to "liberate" the image from the stone. Chips off the ol' block.

Communicates the vision.
Completes the magnificent sculpture *David* in 1504. Tens of thousands view it each year in Florence.

The Process of Discovery
The Vision of the Scientist

JOHANNES KEPLER

What's going on around me?   What is the earth's relationship to the sun and the other planets?

Looks for patterns in data.   Reviews Tycho Brahe's data. Finds discrepancy for circular orbit of Mars.

Develops systems of images.   After four years and nine hundred pages of calculations, comes up with the elliptical orbit.

Communicates the vision.   Writes a scientific paper *Astronomia Nova* in 1609, in which he describes his findings.

JAMES HUTTON

What's going on around me?   How was the earth formed?

Looks for patterns in data.   Notes that the data do not fit the prevailing view that the earth is 6,000 years old and largely static.

Develops systems of images.   Develops the concept of uniformutarism, which states that the forces responsible for shaping the earth are still at work.

Communicates the vision.   Publishes his views in a paper entitled *Theory of the Earth* in 1785.

Vision

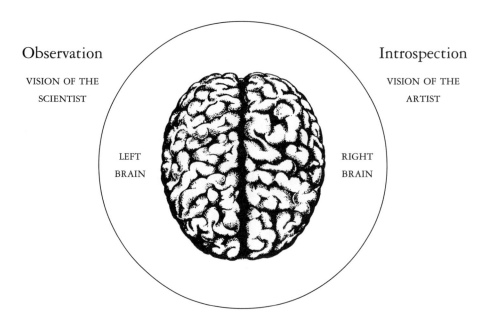

Observation

VISION OF THE
SCIENTIST

LEFT
BRAIN

RIGHT
BRAIN

Introspection

VISION OF THE
ARTIST

It's in the air. Frank Loesser of *Guys and Dolls* fame was quoted as saying he didn't know where his songwriting ideas came from. "They just pop into my head. Of course your head has to be arranged to receive them. Some people's heads are arranged so they keep getting colds; I keep getting songs."

Are you listening? Dr. Elmer Gates built a soundproof room he called his listening room. Here he would retire with the intention of "sitting for ideas." This strange practice yielded fantastic results. Dr. Gates came up with over two hundred patentable ideas in his listening room. Make you want to stop and listen?

There's nothing new under the sun. Emerson once lent a neighbor a copy of Plato's *Republic.* When the neighbor returned it, Emerson asked him if he had enjoyed it. "I did that," said the man, "This Plato has a lot of my ideas."

Chapter 4 Exercises

❧

Your Wish List

List below what you most want to be, do, or have in the next three to five years.

1. What do you want to be? Include new roles you want to play, states of mind you want to attain (e.g., greater self-confidence), states of body (e.g., health or strength), and emotional states (e.g., greater peace of mind, improved patience).

2. What do you want to do (e.g., change careers, travel, launch a business, get married, start a family, etc.)?

3. What do you want to have (e.g., possessions, financial assets, etc.)?

Until I Die

Imagine you have lived the life of your dreams and that you are now on your death-bed. Your family and friends surround you. You feel at peace with the world and ready to leave it. Now write your obituary. What was the message of your life? What do you want to be remembered for? What was your most important contribution? Why? What were your most meaningful experiences? Why?

The Vision of the Artist: Introspection 5

Look within. Within is the fountain of good,
and it will ever bubble up, if thou wilt ever dig.

MARCUS AURELIUS

Often we struggle to figure out what we want. We search outside for answers that lie within. Yet if we allow them to, our inspirations, intuitions, and dreams will guide us to the lives we were meant to live. The key is learning to attune our awareness to these inner messages, then trust what they are telling us, and act accordingly. This chapter will explore the "Vision of the Artist," the right-brained, intuitive path to creative discovery. In this chapter, you'll encounter a variety of ideas and activities designed to stimulate creative, right-brain thinking. In the exercises at the end of the chapter, you'll have the opportunity to apply these ideas as you sketch out the visions for your life.

The Father of Invention

If necessity is the mother of invention, then surely playfulness is the father. Playfulness is a roving, wandering, wondering, "What if?" It's following the lightning flash of insight, getting lost in the stream of consciousness, abandoning yourself to fantasy and play. Sailing through the cracks, creative visions come, free and unattached. The right-brain process hinted at here is not logical and measured but intuitive and spontaneous.

If all this sounds a little silly, it's important to recognize the creative power in it. Michael Faraday imagined living the life of an atom. He went on to discover electromagnetic theory. Albert Einstein imagined himself flying through space on a beam of light. Such play as this was significant in the development of the theory of relativity. As he put it, "Play seems to be the essential feature in productive thought." In the beginning, the telescope was just a toy for Galileo. Isaac Newton said, "I do not know what I may appear to the world; but to myself I seem to have been only like a boy playing on the seashore, and diverting myself in now and then finding a smoother pebble or a prettier shell than the ordinary, whilst the great ocean of truth lay all undiscovered before me."

The insights of Newton, Galileo, Einstein, and Faraday have, to a great extent, shaped our vision of the world. These giants of modern science weren't afraid to play. Unfortunately, many of us are. We don't realize that those who make the most important and serious contributions are often those who aren't afraid to look, or even be, ridiculous. We think it silly or undignified to really let go. We fear that others will think us foolish if we show too much of our joy, excitement, or playfulness. We keep a tight reign on our imaginations, lest they wander too far off the beaten path. Especially at work, we tend to take a serious, nose-to-the-grindstone attitude.

Our commercial culture with its bottom-line orientation has little use (or time) for play for its own sake. Our value as human beings has become equated with our productivity as measured in economic terms. To the extent that we value play at all, it is as an escape from the drudgery of the daily grind. Very seldom enjoyed for its own sake, play is more often seen as a reward for spending so much of our lives doing things we don't want to do. This tends to bring a goal-directed or driven quality to our play, which keeps it from having the refreshing and invigorating effect it otherwise might.

In countless ways, our daily routines tend to deaden and dull our senses. Yet creativity requires aliveness and spontaneity. Through play, we recapture the sense of wonder and the exuberance for life that we knew as children. In this spirit of wide-eyed innocence, we are able to see things in a fresh way, to make combinations and connections we might otherwise miss. To play in a childlike way is to let go of all self-consciousness, to drop the armor of our defenses, to give up our pretenses and be what we are, pure and simple. (While writing this chapter, I noticed the little boy who lives next door walking back and forth in front of my house with a stick in his hand and a box on his head. When I asked him what he was doing, he replied without missing a beat, "I'm an astronaut.")

It is this willingness to let go in fantasy and play that we must reawaken if we are to realize our full creative potential. Recent discoveries in neuroanatomy indicate that adult play may actually increase the number of glial cells, the connective tissue that links neurons within the brain. It has long been known that the number of glial, or connective, cells is a much better indicator of brainpower than the number of neurons themselves. By increasing our brain's connective tissue through play, we are enhancing our mental and creative capacities.

A long-term study found that children who spent more time playing had better survival skills and were more likely to succeed as adults than those who played less. One of the important habits acquired in play is that of taking risks. The capacity to take risks is the critical skill that creative people from all walks of life share. Creativity requires the ability to think independently and the capacity for bold, decisive action—and both of these demand that we take risks. We can think of ourselves as having a risk-taking muscle. The more we exercise it, the stronger it becomes. Anything you can do to strengthen your risk-taking muscle will help you to become a more creative person, and taking time to play is an easy way to get in shape.

Without this playing with fantasy no creative work has ever yet come to birth. The debt we owe to the play of the imagination is incalculable.

C. G. JUNG

Welcome to the Great State of Alpha

Scientists can measure the differences between the left- and right-brain modes of thinking in terms of the cycles per second generated on an EEG. Left-brain thinking is indicated by what are called beta waves, which run anywhere from fourteen to twenty-one or more cycles per second. The alpha state is indicated by cycles of between seven to fourteen per second. In the alpha state, the creative, intuitive right brain is fully functional. In the beta state, right-brain functioning is minimal. Left-brain or beta wave thought is best for taking in data from the physical senses; right-brain alpha states are better for the inner sensing necessary for a creative or imaginative style of thinking. To help you relax and tune in to your creativity, try the following exercise, "Entering the Alpha State."

Entering the Alpha State: Sit or lie comfortably. Close your eyes and roll them slightly upward. Now slowly count backward from fifty, visualizing the numbers inside your head as you count. Fifty, forty-nine, forty-eight, forty-seven, forty-six… When you reach the number one, recognize that you have entered the alpha state. Relax and sense what it feels like; learn to be at home in the alpha state. It's a rich source of creative ideas. To return to normal consciousness, simply count forward from one to five; at five open your eyes, and you have returned.

Practice this technique until you can easily go into the alpha state. Once you have, reduce the entry number from fifty to twenty-five, ten, and then five. Keep the exit number at five. Entering the alpha state will help you to relax and tune in. You may want to use this procedure before doing any of the right-brain processes throughout the remainder of this book, or anytime you want to relax and tune into creative ideas. This process is one of deliberate intervention. Yet there are more natural ways of inducing alpha. You may find yourself moving into the alpha state as you lie beneath a tree and watch the leaves move in the wind, or as you watch waves lapping up against a sea or lake shore. Listening to certain kinds of music, sitting in a hot tub or bath, or receiving a massage may also move you into the alpha state.

Relax and Tune You In

Ideas are like radio waves; they fill the air around you. All you need is a receiver set and an ability to tune to the proper frequencies. Your mind is the receiver set. The process of tuning it has more to do with relaxed, receptive openness than concentrated effort. Struggling and straining won't improve, and can only impede, your natural ability to receive creative ideas. The great and extremely prolific composer Wolfgang Amadeus Mozart was said to have written many of his finest works as if taking dictation. In describing the state of mind that best facilitated his capacity to receive ideas, he said, "[It is] when I am, as it were, completely myself, entirely alone, and of good cheer . . . that ideas flow best and most abundantly. Whence they come, I know not, nor can I force them."

Notice he said it was when he was "of good cheer" that ideas "flow best and most abundantly." Many people fail to recognize the importance of this emotional aspect of creativity. They readily discount their creative abilities yet fail to recognize how negative emotions block the natural flow of ideas. You're not going to be creative when you feel jealous, angry, or resentful. Nor is feeling worried, stressed, or depressed conducive to receiving creative ideas. These emotions block the flow of creative ideas, jamming our mental receiving sets and depriving us of the very inspirations that could turn our lives around. Often the way out of a rut begins with blessing and accepting things as they are. Condemning the situations we are in tends to lock us into them.

As William Blake put it, "Damn braces, bless relaxes." When we bless the world and all in it, when we feel of good cheer and at peace, we relax into the depths of our being, the fount of all creative ideas. Condemning situations, people, or events overloads the nervous system with stress, impeding our natural ability to receive ideas. A combination of energy and relaxation, of alertness and peace of mind, is most conducive to creative discovery. Scientists refer to this mindset as the "alpha state." It has long been known to be the mental state best suited for creative, right-brain thinking. (For more information on the alpha state, see the highlight on the previous page.) You enhance the

Every creative act involves . . . a new innocence of perception, liberated from the cataract of accepted belief.

ARTHUR KOESLER

49

power of your mental receiver set as you learn to relax without falling asleep. As Alfred Benit put it, "I find that images appear only if we give our minds uncontrolled freedom, when we are dreaming while awake." Visions germinate in a mind that is relaxed and alert, a mind that is dreaming while awake.

Learning to meditate can do wonders for your life. Meditating on a regular basis can lower your blood pressure, increase your energy, relax your body, and quiet your mind. Through its calming influence, meditation transforms your mind into a more sensitive and subtle receiver set, greatly enhancing your intuitive powers. In addition, meditation increases your powers of concentration and your ability to see things objectively. The philosophy behind the practice of meditation is simply explained by the Chinese Taoists. They tell us that in the normal course of events, energy is constantly being directed outward through the senses. It is thus depleted and exhausted. When we meditate, we reverse the flow of energy, directing it back within ourselves, where it rejuvenates and energizes our mental, physical, and spiritual capacities.

Be Open and Empty

A well-educated man once went to a Zen master to inquire about the meaning of Zen. After greeting him, the master instructed the visitor to be seated and proceeded to pour him a cup of tea. The cup was filled, and still he poured. Tea spilled over the sides of the table onto the floor, and still the Zen master poured. Finally, the visitor could contain himself no longer, "The cup is already full! It can hold no more!" The Zen master replied, "So it is. Just as you come to me so full of what you know that you can receive nothing new."

When empty and open, our minds are veritable magnets for creative ideas. Yet they are often filled with all we think we know, with the limiting beliefs and accepted opinions that we mistake for truth. We are so sure of the way things are, and we've lost the questioning spirit of the childlike mind. We think as we have been told to think, which, of course, is not thinking at all. This conformity of thought is how society maintains its traditions, on the one hand, and perpetuates its misconceptions on the other.

If you see in any given situation only what everybody else can see, you can be said to be so much a representative of your culture that you are a victim of it.   —S. I. HAYAKAWA

For example, just two hundred years ago, bleeding was an accepted form of medical treatment. George Washington was bled just prior to his death. At the time, medical doctors "knew" that bleeding was the most effective way of treating many diseases. Today, such a practice would be considered barbaric. In the nineteenth century, learned scientists "knew" that human beings could not survive traveling at speeds exceeding thirty-five miles per hour. It was thought that the pressure exerted on the body by such terrific speeds would crush the internal organs. Yet somehow today, we do survive. In the early twentieth century, scholarly papers were written, explaining why it was physically impossible for human beings to run a mile in less than four minutes. Today, high school kids do it. Yet all of these experts "knew" exactly what they were talking about.

Consider the following quote: "With reference to the electric light, much has been said for and against, but I think I may say without contradiction that when the Paris Exhibition closes, the electric light will close with it, and no more will be heard from it." This was the definitive conclusion of Oxford professor Eramus Wilson back in 1878. In the late nineteenth century, the head of the U.S. Patent Office declared that everything that could be invented had already been invented. While these ideas seem absurd, even laughable, to us today, we might pause to consider how primitive and absurd many of our commonly held beliefs will appear to generations to come.

Suspend judgment during your vision quest. Dare to be different, even a little crazy. Ask yourself strange "what if" questions. The idea is to break free of conventional, conformist thinking. For example: What if flowers could fly? What if you could understand languages you hadn't learned? What if there were no money or private property? What if your grandmother was younger than you? What if tomorrow was be-

Almost all really new ideas have a certain aspect of foolishness when they are first produced.

ALFRED NORTH
WHITEHEAD

51

fore yesterday? What if you could do whatever you want? What if all your dreams had already come true?

Dancing Outside the Lines

As a child, I began school at an early age. I had no difficulty adjusting emotionally and mentally, yet I did have a problem. When it came time to learn handwriting, I was unable to make the letters fit within the spaces of the ruled paper. Long after the other kids were writing with regular pencils on narrow-ruled paper, I was writing with a big, fat pencil on paper with huge lines. Even so, I found it difficult to stay within them. Yet as time went by, I learned that there are great advantages to moving outside the lines of accepted convention. In fact, I've found that all the creative, spiritual, and personal breakthroughs in my life have come from breaking the rules about what should be done. It's true that, as Katharine Hepburn put it, "If you follow all the rules, you miss all the fun." You'll also miss a lot of opportunities for creative thinking.

When looking for the creative visions for your life, give yourself permission to break the rules, to move outside the boundaries of your usual way of looking at, and thinking about, things. Forget about how practical or realistic your ideas are. There will be time for critical analysis later on. Most of all, go beyond the self-censorship that comes with concern for what other people will think. Follow your own heart and make up your own rules. Dare to dream the impossible.

Get In-Tu-It

When you have an intuition or hunch about a certain idea to pursue, a direction to take, or a person to contact, follow it! Trust yourself! We've all had the experience of saying to ourselves "I knew I should have done so and so. Why didn't I?"—or "I had a hunch that something about X just didn't feel right. Why didn't I listen to myself?" Why indeed. Because you were in hurry, distracted, or preoccupied;

because your intuition didn't fit with your habitual way of looking at or doing things; because you were seduced by the promise of some reward or influenced by someone else's opinion; or just because your intuitive hunch didn't make logical sense at the time.

The really valuable thing is intuition.

EINSTEIN

Learning to trust your intuition is a skill developed with practice. You'll master it more quickly if you pay attention to what happens when you do or don't listen to it. In time, you will discover that when you follow through on what your intuition is telling you, things work out well, and when you ignore it, you're headed for trouble. Follow your intuition in little things and you will be more willing to trust it with the big decisions of your life. When it comes right down to it, you can't rely on logic to decide the important things, like whom to marry or which career is the right one for you. Ultimately, you have to go with what your intuition is telling you.

Often following your intuition requires that you take a leap of faith. It demands that you act before you fully understand all the ramifications of your actions. When your intuition tells you to do this or that, it may not seem very important at the time. You might dismiss it by thinking it will not make much of a difference whether you do it or not, or whether you do it now or later. Yet one thing leads to another. Following your intuition even in little things can get you started down the road that leads to the best use of your life. On the other hand, ignoring your intuition can leave you hopelessly stuck in a rut. Often you can only understand the full significance of what an intuition was telling you *after* you have acted on it. If you set it up in your mind that you have to understand before you will act, you will miss out on a great many opportunities for creative breakthroughs.

Listening to your intuition can supply you with inspirations or solutions that you could never access through any other means. It can also provide shortcuts to solutions that could be worked out methodically, though at the cost of a great deal more time, energy, and expense. Your intuitions can also save you months, or even years, of struggle by steering you away from paths that will turn out to be dead ends or worse. Your intuition is there to guide you every step of the way—pay attention to what it is telling you!

Vision Questing

In many traditional cultures, it was expected that every individual would go on a spiritual quest or journey to discover his or her unique life purpose and the special gifts that he or she could offer to the society. Among Native American tribes of the Great Plains, the process of discovering one's purpose and gifts was called a "vision quest." Through fasting, solitude, trance dancing, chanting, and a variety of other means, they cultivated a breakthrough experience—one that would move them out of ordinary mundane consciousness and into a transcendent state of inspiration.

Virtually every traditional culture associates inspirations with some kind of divine intelligence or higher spiritual power. Look at the word itself "in-spir[it]-ation." It means "to be in the presence of, or filled with, the spirit." Whether we call it the voice of God or the Higher Self, the promptings of the muse or the whisperings of the conscience, there is a recognition that in dealing with inspiration, we are entering a realm informed by a higher order of intelligence than mere rational thought. In whatever way you conceptualize it, look to a higher power as the source of your inspirations. Pray for the revelation of your true purpose in life. Recognize all the inspirations that come to you as the touch of the divine; value the voice of the muse speaking in your life.

Many people will tell you that they are unclear about their goals, that they aren't visionaries and don't know what they want to do with their lives. Yet they may have discounted dozens of inspirations that have come to them over the years. I've found in my work as a career consultant that every person who claimed they didn't know what kind of work they wanted to do, had had inspirations over the years, which they had discounted. The point is, when inspirations hit you—pay attention. Treat them, not as your own personal property, but as sacred gifts that have been entrusted to you—and you will find increased motivation to see them through. If you want the muse to reside with you, show her that you are ready to put her inspirations to work.

In some way, make a mock-up or a record of your inspirations— something to anchor in the world of material things the visions and inspirations you encounter in the realm of ideas and dreams. Don't expect your initial representation to embody or do full justice to the inspirations you have seen. Just begin your sketch, no matter how blind or foolish you may feel. A journey of a thousand miles begins with the first step, no matter how awkward or tenuous that step may be. Just be sure to create some tangible reminder of the idea so it doesn't get lost in the hubbub of daily events.

Buckminster Fuller said, "I call intuition cosmic fishing. You feel the nibble, and then you have to hook the fish." The first step to hooking the fish is to get the idea down on paper. Francis Bacon, who advocated a new scientific method, had also the vision of the artist. He said, "A man would do well to carry a pencil in his pocket, and write down the thoughts of the moment. Those that come unsought for are commonly the most valuable, and should be secured, because they seldom return." That's good advice even today. Keep a notebook or journal with you and near your bed.

Dream On

Your dreams can be a rich source of creative visions. You can keep a dream journal and simply record what your subconscious mind is telling you through dreams, or you can use your dreams in a more focused and directed way. Before you go to sleep, ask your subconscious mind to reveal creative visions for your life. You may be surprised at the ideas you wake up with. Mary Shelly got the idea for *Frankenstein,* and Robert Louis Stevenson the idea for *Dr. Jekyll and Mr. Hyde* from dreams. Poets Samuel Coleridge, William Yeats, Goethe, and Voltaire all stated that they had seen or heard verses or entire poems in their dreams.

In addition to recording your dreams and the creative visions they inspire, you can also employ a technique called *lucid dreaming.* During a lucid dream, the person sleeping becomes conscious of the fact that she is dreaming. Even more exciting, a lucid dreamer can actually manipulate the content and flow of her dreams. In his book *Exploring the World of Lucid Dreaming,* Dr. Stephen Laberge, noted sleep researcher at Stanford University, outlines how you can learn this technique. Once

It is a common experience that a problem difficult at night is resolved in the morning after the committee of sleep has worked on it.

JOHN STEINBECK

*All life is an experiment.
The more experiments you
make, the better.*

EMERSON

you've mastered it, you'll be not only the star of your dreams but the screenwriter and director as well. You'll be able to use your dreams to experiment with life scenarios that you might like to incorporate into your waking life.

Charlotte Brontë, author of *Jane Eyre,* used lucid dreams to provide her with intimate details of experiences that she either couldn't or didn't want to experience in waking life. For instance, if she wanted to include in her story a description of someone taking opium, she would dream about taking opium. On waking, she could describe the experience in detail. By consciously directing your dreams, you will be able to try on new career hats, as well as new of ways of being and relating. Having lived them first in dreams, it will be easier for you to integrate these new behaviors, attitudes, and roles into your waking life. You can also eliminate or discard roles or behaviors that seem inappropriate for you, without having to spend valuable waking hours in experimentation.

You can use your dreams to come up with solutions to nagging problems or to overcome creative blocks. Simply pose a question in your mind before you go to sleep, and let your subconscious work out the answers while you sleep. Robert Penn Warren said, "I've dreamed many nights the next scene of a novel I've been working on, even dialogue and details." George Handel heard the last movements of his famed *Messiah* during a dream. Dreams have played an important role in scientific breakthroughs as well. Friedrich A. von Kekule credited a dream he had—of snakes whirling through space with their tails in their mouths—with assisting him in solving the puzzle of the structure of the benzene molecule. Kekule's discovery helped to revolutionize organic chemistry. After long hours agonizing over a way to classify chemical elements according to their atomic weights, Dmritri Mendeleyev saw the periodic table of elements in a dream. He recounted that upon waking, he "immediately wrote it down on a piece of paper. In only one place did a correction later seem necessary." Dreams have helped to solve many less earth-shaking problems. Golf champion Jack Nicklaus said that he broke out of a severe slump after a dream inspired him to change his grip on his golf clubs. There is no telling what your dreams can do for you in solving problems big and small. Since you spend roughly one third of your life asleep, it only makes sense to put this time to work for you.

Keep It Moving

Beginning writers often make the mistake of trying to edit or correct themselves as they go. They are too concerned with getting things exactly right the first time. In their efforts to maintain control, they dam the stream of consciousness, blocking the natural flow of ideas. They never know what it feels like to burn in the white heat of the creative fire, to be caught in a frenzy of inspiration, with ideas pouring forth faster than they can be recorded. If they ever get into it at all, they quickly shift out of the right-brain mode of free association and into critical, analytical, left-brain thinking. They forget that they can always come back later to correct and perfect what they have written. Don't you make this mistake when it comes time for your vision quest. Let go. Let the ideas flow without judgment.

The exercises at the end of this chapter are geared for right-brained, intuitive thinking. In order to stimulate this kind of thought, it is important that you move through the exercises rapidly. The idea is to answer so quickly that your conscious rational mind doesn't have the opportunity to evaluate, criticize, or censor the thoughts that come into your awareness. Don't be concerned about being exact. Go for quantity. Get down as many ideas as you can. If you start to slow down, you'll know you are in left-brain thinking, making judgments about the thoughts you are having. Remember, you can always come back later and weed out and correct what you have written. Just keep your pen or pencil moving as you proceed through the exercises.

The Vision of the Artist

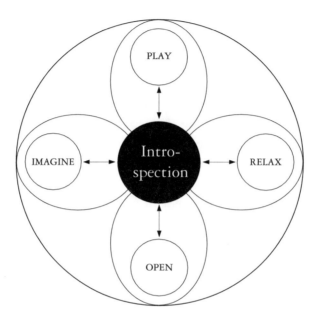

In every block of marble I see a statue as plain as though it stood before me, shaped and perfect in attitude and action. I have only to hew away the rough walls that imprison the lovely apparition to reveal it to other eyes as mine see it.

—MICHELANGELO

Art is not an end in itself, but a means of addressing humanity.

—M. P. MOUSSORGSKI

The artist does not see things as they are, but as he is.

—ALFRED TONNELLE

Art, as far as it is able, follows nature, as a pupil imitates his master; thus your art must be as if it were God's grandchild.   —DANTE

Chapter 5 Exercises

❧

These exercises, together with those at the end of chapter 6, provide the raw material from which to set definite goals. Remember, you're not writing goals now but simply exploring possible directions. Don't worry about committing yourself to anything. Just let yourself go. You needn't do all of the exercises. Yet it is easy and fun to do so; and by looking at what you want from a variety of angles, you may discover potential goals that might otherwise have eluded you.

Relax into a World of Ideas

The process of receiving ideas works best when you are totally relaxed. Make a tape recording of the following, in your own voice. You may want to play it before you do the exercises that follow—or any time you want to relax and open up to creative ideas.

Close your eyes. Begin to relax. Feel yourself totally at ease, at peace with yourself, the world, and everyone in it. Now, relax the tips of your toes. Feel a warm, relaxing sensation move into the balls of your feet and up into your heels. Now relax your ankles. Feel the soothing warmth move up your legs, as your calves and knees relax. All the muscles in your thighs are beginning to relax. You remain alert, but you are relaxing deeply. Now the soothing relaxation moves into your pelvis and up into your abdomen. All of your inner organs are relaxing. Your diaphragm is releasing and relaxing. Your chest is expanding and relaxing. Your hands and arms are feeling limp and relaxed. Your shoulders release and relax. Your neck lengthens and relaxes. The muscles in the back of your head relax. The muscles in your forehead, and all the little muscles around your eyes, relax. Even the tiny muscles around your nose relax. You're breathing calmly, easily, gently. Your mouth and jaw are releasing and relaxing. Your throat is relaxed and calm. You are alert and yet totally relaxed.

Reclaiming Your Dreams

Begin with the realization that in the course of your life you have had many inspirations. Some of these you may have brought into reality. However, if you are like most people, there are many that you have pushed to the back burner or discounted altogether. By taking these dreams out of mothballs and moving them to the front and center of your awareness, you can reclaim a vital source of inspiration and energy in your life.

1. Make a list of any and all inspirations you have had over the years that you haven't acted on or that you have given up on too easily.

2. Look over your list and choose the three that are the most meaningful to you. List these in order of priority.

    1._____
    2._____
    3._____

3. Now select the one that speaks most powerfully to you and list a number of specific, active steps you could begin taking immediately to turn this inspiration into reality.

Meeting Yourself

For the purpose of this exercise, imagine that you are meeting someone for the first time. Write your answers to the following questions posed by this imaginary (and rather forward) stranger.

1. Tell me about yourself. Who are you?

2. What do you want out of life?

3. What secret dream or ambition lies locked away in the inner recesses of your heart?

Value Identification

Your answers to the following questions will give you insights into your values and may suggest potential goals. (Allow two minutes to answer each question.)

1. Is there anything you would be willing to "risk it all" for? If so, what?

2. What is the most exciting thing you've ever done in your life, and why?

3. What do you consider to be the greatest accomplishment of your life? Why?

4. If you were going to produce an event, and money was no object, what kind of event would it be?

5. If you were given a gift of $10,000,000 tomorrow, what would you do with it? Briefly, why?

6. What historic figures do you admire most? Why?

7. If you were going to have a small dinner party, and you could invite anyone in the world, who would you invite? Why?

8. Complete the following statement: Something I have always talked about wanting to do someday is _____ .

A Flash from the Past

1. Recall a time when you felt especially creative, a time when you felt so absorbed in what you were doing that you lost all track of time and space. What were you doing?

2. Recall a time when you felt especially committed, a time when you were determined to stay with something even though it was difficult. What were you committed to?

3. Recall a time when you felt especially decisive, a time when you intuitively knew you were on the right track and no one could dissuade you. What were you decided about?

4. Do any of your answers suggest new goals to you? If so, write them down.

The Genuine Article

Imagine that a feature article about you or your work has just been published in a national magazine. Further suppose that this article describes how you accomplished or realized a lifelong dream. In what magazine would you want the article to appear? For example, you might want the article to appear in *Time*, *Newsweek*, or *People* magazine, in *National Geographic*, *Scientific American*, or *Success*. The magazine need not be a popular one. It could be a relatively obscure professional or trade journal in your field.

NAME OF MAGAZINE:

ARTICLE HEADLINE OR TITLE:

Now write the article. What does it have to say about you?

Your Life Mission

1. We are all here on this earth for some reason. You're here to be, express, and accomplish certain things. In other words, you have a mission in life. What is that mission? Write it down. (If you don't believe you have any particular mission to fulfill, imagine that you do, for the sake of this exercise.) (5 minutes)

2. Next, make a time line by drawing a horizontal line. The left endpoint of the line will represent the moment of your birth; the right endpoint, the time of your death. On this time line, mark your present position. In other words, where are you between your birth and the time when you expect to leave this earth? (1 minute)

3. Now write what you have already accomplished toward your mission. (3 minutes)

4. Next, write what remains to be accomplished. (3 minutes)

The Vision of the Scientist: Observation 6

A man of science doesn't discover in order to know,
he wants to know in order to discover.

ALFRED NORTH WHITEHEAD

Many people think of creative visions as the products of some mystical or otherworldly state, accessible to only a chosen few. Yet visionary ideas frequently result from confronting the very real and practical problems of everyday life. This problem-solving approach to creativity relies on the left-brain, or analytical, approach to discovery—the Vision of the Scientist. The Vision of the Scientist combines careful observation with objective analysis. Its metaphors are the microscope and telescope, symbolic of detailed analysis and detached, objective observation. In the exercises at the end of this chapter, you'll have the opportunity to observe the problems of your life with the detachment of distance, as if viewing them through a powerful telescope, and to scrutinize them carefully, as if examining them under a microscope.

The scientist collects data and then develops theories by observing patterns or relationships within this data. In its origins, the word *theory* meant "seeing" or "viewing." A scientific theory represents a vision of how things or processes work. This vision is a result of careful observation and astute interpretation. Like a scientist, you can develop visions, or mental plans, by examining the problems of your life with an objective, scientific eye.

Over two hundred years ago, Alexander Hamilton described the essence of the scientific approach to problem solving when he said: "Men give me credit for some genius. All the genius I have lies in this; when I have a subject in hand, I study it profoundly. Day and night it is before me. My mind becomes pervaded by it. Then the effort I have made is what people are pleased to call the fruit of genius. It is the fruit of labor and thought." The idea is to immerse yourself in a problem until the answers to it begin to present themselves to you. This is the approach to vision development that will be explored in this chapter. Below, you will find a formula for creative problem solving that you can apply to any area of your life.

Creative Problem Solving

1. Define the problem precisely, and frame it as a question.

2. Ask additional questions to stimulate the search for solutions, such as:

   • Have others had and solved this or similar problems?

   • If so, what strategies did they employ? Which were most effective?

   • How is this problem like other problems that I have solved?

   • In what ways is it different from other problems I have encountered?

3. Do research to answer these and other salient questions.

4. Develop a hypothesis, or strategy for addressing the problem.

5. Test this hypothesis in the real world.

Define the Problem Precisely
and State It As a Question

Visions arise as creative solutions to particular problems. Therefore, it is essential that you get clear on exactly what your problems are. Begin by making a list of the frustrations, or areas of stress, in your life, as well as places where you feel inadequate or unfulfilled. Try to be as objective as you can, and determine to overcome any resistance you may have to confronting your problems. It's only natural to fear problems and to avoid looking at the pain they bring to your life. Yet once you recognize that avoidance only perpetuates problems, you can begin to overcome your fears and face things head-on. You can learn to view problems as the raw material for the creative visions of your life. See problems and difficulties as interesting questions you've yet to answer. In what areas of your life are you hurting? Where are the sore spots, the places where you feel frustrated or in pain? If you're willing to confront them openly and honestly, you can turn pain into gain.

The treatment of a problem begins with its first expression as a question.

SUSAN LANGER

While it may be true that every cloud has a silver lining, you can't see that lining until you're ready to really look into the cloud. As a young man, Winston Churchill suffered from a speech impediment. Yet he went on to become one of the great orators of the twentieth century. Difficulty in speaking just didn't fit Churchill's vision of becoming a great statesman. The challenge of overcoming his speech impediment actually fueled his desire to speak in an impressive and distinctive manner. Needless to say, Churchill found a way. He could have avoided this problem, and in so doing, limited himself to a world in which he could comfortably move with the speech impediment intact. We all have the choice of avoiding our problems and staying within our comfort zones or expanding our horizons by confronting the painful aspects of our lives. Determine to identify, confront, and overcome the limitations that hold you back from the life you could be living.

Once you have a list of problems, begin framing them as questions: For example: "I feel tired, overwhelmed, and frustrated by the frenetic pace of my life" becomes "How can I achieve a greater sense of balance and harmony in my life?" "I hate my job" becomes "What work can I do that will give me the greatest sense of meaning and the deepest experience of joy?" "I am lonely and lacking genuine intimacy in my life" becomes "How can I deepen and enrich my relationships with others?" "I feel frustrated that I can't ever seem to get ahead financially" becomes "How can I earn more money and/or reduce my expenses?" "I feel empty inside. My life lacks meaning and purpose" becomes "How can I find spiritual fulfillment?"—and so on. Start with the subjective experience of pain and reframe it as a constructive, objective question.

Review your questions over and again, until you are sure you have penetrated to the essence, that you have defined your problem precisely. Take the time to get it right. As Albert Einstein put it, "The formulation of a problem is far more essential than its solution." This is because the way you frame a problem will both suggest solutions and limit available options. When people told Jonas Salk that he was wasting money on polio research, money that would be better spent on buying more iron lungs, he replied that what was needed was not merely a treatment for polio but a program for its eradication. Salk was trying to find the answer to a difficult and complex question, one that many of his contemporaries in the field were not ready to face. The same principle applies in facing the problems of your life. While there are times when asking limited questions will do, when you are seeking life visions, make sure you're asking questions that go to the heart of the matter. For example, the question "Where can I find a job I like better than my present one?" will yield a different set of answers than "How can I create the opportunity to do the work I truly love?"

Look at the word *question*—it is the quest-I-on. The questions you ask will determine the quests you are on—make sure they are worthy of you. Choosing the right questions and determining to stay with them until you have answers are the better part of wisdom and courage. They are potent keys to living the life of your true destiny. You don't have to accept the limitations that cause you pain. Whether your problem stems from being financially strapped, stuck in an unfulfilling job, trapped in a miserable relationship, or being painfully shy, there are things that you can do to improve the situation. Regardless of the circumstances, there are steps you can take to turn things around. You can find a way out if you are willing to keep looking until you can see solutions and then work to turn the solutions you see into realities. This sounds simple enough, and it is, but that doesn't mean it will be easy. Transforming our lives in any really significant way usually takes a great deal of work. Michelangelo said, "If people knew how hard I worked to get my mastery, it wouldn't seem so wonderful after all." Usually, we are only willing to work with this kind of dedication when we view it as a necessity.

The Mother of Invention

Over two thousand years ago, the philosopher Plato said: "The true creator is necessity, who is the mother of our invention." Surely this insight has stood the test of time, but just what did he mean by "necessity"? Necessity is a matter of perception. It's the perception that something must be done and that the perceiver is the one to do something about it. Necessity, like beauty, is in the eye of the beholder—your necessity is not my necessity. No matter how deplorable a situation may seem to an outsider, the individual involved finds no reason to look for a better way until for him it becomes a necessity.

Necessity has intensity and a sense of urgency about it. Without this sense of urgency, there is no drive to discover a better way. For example, 65 percent of all employed Americans report that they are dissatisfied in their jobs. This dissatisfaction, when keenly felt, becomes the necessity of finding a more suitable life's work. Most, however, never allow their dissatisfaction to reach a point where action becomes a necessity. They never know the kind of necessity that would prompt them to thoroughly examine their lives and discover a truer vision of their life's work.

Often, the greatest discoveries come to those who feel it a necessity to address the larger problems of humanity as a whole. Perhaps you are drawn to tackle some problem in your community, nation, or world. Buckminster Fuller, a true mathematical genius and the inventor of the geodesic dome, discovered that when he tried to work on

Necessity is the theme and the inventress, the eternal curb and the law of nature.

LEONARDO DA VINCI

You can observe a lot just by watching.

YOGI BERRA

his own problems, he met with little success. He failed miserably in business, drank heavily, and even contemplated suicide. Yet when Fuller shifted his focus to addressing global issues, his personal problems began to take care of themselves. He went on to make important contributions to architecture, engineering, environmental science, and a number of other fields. A college dropout, Fuller received thirty-seven honorary doctorates and was lauded by *Time* magazine as one of the most important minds of the twentieth century. If, in spite of confronting your problems and doing your best to solve them, they still persist, it may be that your life is intended for some higher purpose that you have yet to embrace. Step back and begin asking questions that address broader issues. You may want to ask questions like "What is the best use of my life?" or "What is my purpose for being here on this earth?"

Whether fueled by personal, national, or global problems, a sense of creative discontent is a key ingredient to scientific problem solving. When discontent reaches the point of necessity, you command of yourself and your world that a better way be revealed. Discovery of the electric light bulb was a necessity for Edison. His implacable determination proved it. His necessity to create was strong enough to carry him through more than a thousand failed attempts. He would have agreed with Terence who said, "There is nothing so difficult but that it may be found out by seeking."

One could say that it was a necessity for the Wright brothers to discover the secrets of manned flight, and a necessity for Alexander Graham Bell to invent the telephone. It was a necessity for Jonas Salk to save lives and alleviate suffering by discovering the cure for polio. What are your necessary discoveries? Perhaps it is necessary for you to discover a cleaner and more efficient source of energy. Maybe it's the cure for some debilitating disease. Perhaps it's simply the work you were born to do, or how to be the best parent you can be. Maybe your quest is for the meaning of life, the realization of mastery in your profession, or the keys to finding peace and balance in our stressful and highly competitive society. Whatever you are questing for, treat finding it as a necessity of your life.

Expect to Find Solutions

Once you have identified your necessary discoveries, begin the search for solutions. Start by affirming that there *are* answers; develop the confident expectation that you will find a way. One of the most important keys to finding anything is the belief that you will. Whether you're looking for a misplaced set of keys, a turn on a desolate rural highway, or the solution to an important life problem, it helps to expect that you will find what you are looking for. Before you do even one of the exercises at the end of this chapter, ask yourself if you really expect to discover solutions to the problems you face.

More than any lack of talent or ability, more than any external barrier—it is low expectations that prevent us from achieving our best. Of course we want to find solutions, but when what we want conflicts with what we expect, we get what we expect, not what we want. Expectation is the contextual filter through which we view the events and circumstances of our lives. Think of how differently we view the same set of circumstances and events, depending on whether we expect to overcome a problem or be defeated by it. Resist the temptation to fall into hopelessness and despondent resignation. Your expectation to succeed will attract the means to do it. Affirm your expectation that you will find answers, and begin to search for them in earnest.

Research How Others Have Solved Similar Problems

Ask yourself: Have others overcome problems similar to mine? This question moves you out of a subjective identification with the problem and into an objective search for solutions. When we look at things in a subjective way, we tend to feel that our situations are utterly unique, that no one has ever faced problems or challenges like these before. When we get out of ourselves a bit, we realize that we are hardly alone. There are, indeed, precious few issues or problems that others have not only faced but successfully overcome.

From this flows the next question: What solutions or strategies have others devised for successfully dealing with situations similar to my own? Let's say the problem you are facing is that you feel unhappy and unfulfilled in your work life. Moreover, you feel that your time and energy are so consumed by your current job that you haven't much left for making a transition into something that you would truly enjoy. This is a difficult problem, to be sure. Yet it is one that we can easily recognize many others have already faced and overcome. Do some research. Find out how others have tackled this problem. This will not only give you specific ideas that you can apply in your own life but will also strengthen your belief that it is possible for you to overcome this problem. As French writer Francois de La Rochefoucauld put it, "Nothing is so contagious as an example." Find examples through reading or, better yet, get to know others who have mastered and overcome problems similar to your own.

Learning about how others have dealt with similar problems is but one source of potential solutions. For some years, James Burke hosted a television series entitled *Connections*. (See the book of the same name.) In it, he demonstrated how many of the most important developments in science and technology were not the work of a single inventor or discoverer but were developed a piece at a time, until some bright mind put the pieces together in a way that yielded the innovation we are familiar with today.

Creative solutions often result from combining things or ideas from seemingly unrelated fields. The creative synthesis that results from combining two familiar ideas or things can yield something altogether new. For example, Guttenberg combined the technology for movable type with that of the winepress to create the printing press. The automobile or "horseless carriage" combined the carriage with the piston-driven engine. Consider how you can make connections you may not have thought of before to solve the problems in your life. Remember, you may be just one connection away from a brilliant solution.

Sir Joshua Reynolds wrote: "Invention is little more than new combinations of those images which have been previously gathered and deposited in the memory. Nothing can be made of nothing; those who have laid up no material can produce no combinations." This quote provides yet another key to creative problem solving: collect and input into your brain as much data about the problem as you can. The more facts you have to work with and the more you study them, the more likely you are to trigger a creative solution.

President Kennedy's goal of putting a man on the moon and returning him safely again would have been impossible in the few short years in which it was accomplished—if it hadn't been broken down into a series of problems that were simultaneously tackled by dedicated teams of committed individuals. While the issues in your life may not be as grand and complex as the historic moon landing, it's worth keeping in mind that most every major problem in our lives results from a number of contributing factors. Break down the problem and analyze the components that contribute to it. For example, if you are overweight, factors related to diet, exercise, stress, and emotional and physical health may be playing a role. Analyzing the problem in this way will not only make it seem less mysterious and overwhelming but will also help to ensure that you don't overlook any important aspect of it.

*It is only by risking…
that we live at all.*

WILLIAM JAMES

Develop a Hypothesis and Test It

Draw on the information you find, the connections you make, and the example of others to construct a vision, theory, or hypothesis of how to best solve your own problems. Then examine your hypothesis. Does it hold up under close scrutiny? Does it really offer a viable solution to your problem? Is there perhaps a better way? In the Focus section that follows, you'll have a chance to further test your hypotheses and shape them into definite, quantifiable goals.

Keep Your Mind Fit

A final word before you begin the creative problem-solving exercises: a creative life requires a mind that is strong and fit. When our bodies are out of shape, they tend to become lazy and sluggish. The same is true of our minds. A defeatist or negative approach to life results from mental

Iron rusts from disuse; water loses its purity from stagnation, and in cold weather becomes frozen; even so does inaction sap the vigors of the mind.

LEONARDO DA VINCI

laziness—from accepting, without examination, limiting ideas about life, ourselves, work, or others. In turn, negativity gives us an excuse to remain mentally lazy by discounting the value of searching for solutions. It simply requires less effort to bemoan or condemn a situation than it does to look for a better way. Then, because we haven't made the effort to find solutions, we can throw up our hands and say there aren't any. To a lazy mind, looking for solutions is often just too much trouble. Henry Ford said, "Thinking is the hardest work there is, which is why so few people do it."

Thinking to the best of your ability means thinking a lot. You wouldn't expect your body to stay in top shape without regular exercise, so don't expect your mind to perform to the peak of its abilities without regular exertion. The more you apply yourself to developing solutions to the problems of your life, the more easily, quickly, and naturally creative solutions will come to you. In fact, anything you can do to keep your mind fit will improve your problem-solving abilities.

Sharpening your observational skills helps tone your mental muscles. Leonardo da Vinci kept extensive notebooks on things he observed all around him. The detailed drawings he made of everything from human flesh to fish, from armaments to plants, from bridges to bees honed his observation skills. What he learned from these observations was of great benefit to him in his later inventions and artistic creations. The principle for the submarine (plans for which Leonardo first drew some five hundred years ago) is based on the swimbladder of a fish, which inflates and deflates by the infusion and release of gas.

This example reveals yet another key to creative problem solving. Pay attention to the world around you; observe things carefully—and keep learning and growing. The more information you input into your brain about a variety of subjects, the greater the resources you will have to draw upon when it comes time to develop creative solutions. Make a list of subjects you are interested in and develop a course of study. Pursue your interests, even if you can't see how they will immediately benefit you. Thinking and learning are their own rewards, and a fit and active mind is an added bonus.

In conclusion, we can say that creative problem solving is a natural result of keen and critical observation. It's the ability to perceive the essence of a problem, formulate a range of possible solutions, and select the critical criteria for determining which of these options will most improve the situation. Make the determination to confront the problems and sources of pain in your life—and to keep looking until you can see a better way.

The Doors of Perception

Have no fear if the Muse is not near;
There is another way to be clear.
Study well the problems of the day,
And visions will come to you without delay.
Careful observation is the door,
To discover what you are looking for.
Those who seek purpose in all they do,
Are sure to find visions true.

The Vision of the Scientist

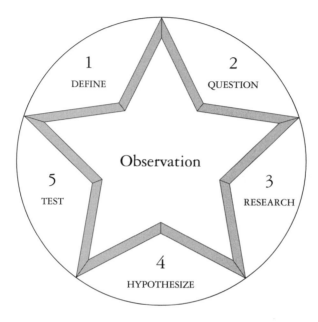

1 DEFINE

2 QUESTION

Observation

5 TEST

3 RESEARCH

4 HYPOTHESIZE

Sweet are the uses of adversity; which like the toad, ugly and venomous, wears yet a precious jewel in its head.
—SHAKESPEARE

All life is an experiment.
—OLIVER WENDELL HOLMES

The things we overcome in life really become our strengths.
—ANN BANCROFT

Science is nothing else than the search to discover unity in a wide variety of nature—or, more exactly, in a variety of our experience. Poetry, painting, the arts are the same search.
—JACOB BRONOWSKI

Chapter 6 Exercises

❧

The purpose of the exercises in this section is to give you the opportunity to examine real and potential problems until solutions (visions) arise.

Sources of Stress

List in rapid-fire succession all the sources of stress in your life, in each of the eight life areas. (Take three minutes for each area.) Some examples of sources of stress might include:

LIFE AREA	SOURCES OF STRESS
Health:	Poor diet, lack of exercise, low energy, illness.
Lifestyle:	Lack of free time, need for relaxation, tired of traffic or smog, cramped or inadequate housing.
Self-Development:	Low self-esteem, emotional problems, lack of education, lack of self-awareness, spiritual emptiness.
Creative Expression:	Suppression of the creative impulse, specific problems in a given creative work, lack of energy, lack of proper work space.
Career:	Lack of freedom and control, feeling your job is pointless or meaningless, job burnout, frenetic pace.
Finances:	Inadequate income, excessive debt, poor money management, lack of investments, lack of retirement planning.

Social Life: Lack of confidence, poor social skills, difficulties in relating to the opposite sex, problems with authority figures.

Intimate Relationships: Poor communication, negative patterns, lack of purpose in relationships, inability to forgive.

Next, review your list and identify the biggest source of stress in each life area. Then state the problem as a question. For example: How can I improve communication with my spouse? How can I create a work that reflects my values and allows me to express my unique talents? How can I eliminate excessive debt from my life?

HEALTH:

LIFESTYLE:

SELF-DEVELOPMENT:

CREATIVE EXPRESSION:

CAREER:

FINANCE:

SOCIAL LIFE:

INTIMATE RELATIONSHIPS:

Next, brainstorm a list of possible solutions. Examine your list, identify the best options, and construct potential goals based on these (see chapter 9).

The Time of Your Life

For each of the life areas (Health, Lifestyle, Self-Development, etc.), answer the following questions:

1. Briefly describe this area of your life as it is now.

2. Describe your life three years ago in this area.

3. What could you have done to make it better that you didn't do? Why didn't you do it?

4. Imagine yourself three years from now. What can you do between now and then to improve your life in this area?

Can You Feel It?

One way of stimulating your thinking about new goals is to take an inventory of your feelings. Maybe you don't have a clear picture of exactly what it is you want to be, do, or have, but you *do* have a feeling or a sense of what you are after. Maybe you want to feel more self-reliant. Perhaps you want to feel more confident. Maybe you want to develop a feeling of self-control. Look at the feelings you want, and write them down. Next, prioritize your list, indicating the top three feelings you want more of in your life.

Now begin to think of actions you can take to help you develop those feelings. Remember that what you think and do determines the way you feel. If we want to feel different, we need to think and do things differently. For example, Josh wanted to feel more confident. The action steps he chose were to take a public-speaking course, begin a regular exercise program, do some emotional-clearing work, and get going on projects he had delayed or abandoned because he had doubted himself. Now write at least three action steps for each of the feelings you wrote in the first part of this exercise.

Making Jealousy Work for You

We are often jealous when we see other people having enjoyment or pleasure that we are denying ourselves. Jealousy can be an extremely useful tool for increasing self-awareness, in that it often indicates what we really want, not what we think or hope we want, but what we actually *do* want. By exploring what makes you feel jealous, you can gain a clearer understanding of where you feel blocked or stuck in your own life.

1. Whom do you feel most jealous of? List the first three people that come to mind.

2. For each of these individuals, list three reasons why you are jealous of them. Pay particular attention to the qualities they exhibit or express that seem to be lacking in your life.

3. What can you do to bring these or similar qualities or aspects into your own life?

4. Write your response to what you learned from doing this exercise.

Now construct potential goals that will allow you to transform your feelings of jealousy into the expression of aspects of yourself which you may have blocked or denied.

Vision Summary

As a summary of the work that you've done throughout the Vision section, record any insights and perceptions that have resulted from completing the exercises in chapters 4, 5, and 6.

PART II

Focus

Focus: Developing Your
Powers of Concentration

———

Decision Making:
Establishing Your Priorities

———

Motive Testing:
Listening to Your Heart

———

Goal Setting:
Fixing Your Destinations

Focus: Developing Your Powers of Concentration 7

He who would arrive at an appointed end
must follow a single road,
and not wander through many ways.

SENECA

We all know people who are never at a loss for big ideas, yet can't seem to make even one of them happen. They lack the focus necessary to make their dreams come alive. Big ideas and grand visions are not enough. Having a good idea without the focus to make it happen is like discovering a vein of gold ore and leaving it buried deep within the earth. While still in the ground, the gold is worthless to you. In the same way, a great idea that you never put into action is of little value to you. Giving your visions sustained, focused attention is the first step to bringing them to life. It is not enough to have a vague idea of what you want—you must know exactly. Getting clear about exactly what you want, and keeping it in the forefront of your awareness, is what the Focus section is all about.

Those who reach greatness on earth reach it through concentration.

UPANISHADS

The Japanese have a saying: "The focused mind can pierce through stone." When you lack focus, your energy is scattered and dispersed. Focus concentrates your energy and magnifies its power. A laser can cut through a sheet of solid steel with the same amount of energy required to illuminate an ordinary light bulb. While the quantity of energy is the same, focus dramatically increases its effective power.

The power to concentrate or focus the mind is a skill that, like any other, is developed through understanding and repeated practice. Making the effort to develop this skill could spell the difference between success and failure in your efforts to make your visions come to life. As your powers of concentration grow, you reduce your mind's "down time," the amount of time given over to worry, preoccupation, or idle chatter. Just as an automotive engine can be tuned to perform more efficiently and thus get better gas mileage, so can you get more mileage out of the time you spend working on your goals by tuning up your concentration skills. When you've mastered your focusing skills, you will be able to spend more concentrated time working on your goals in a week than you could in a month with a scattered or distracted mind. It only makes sense that the more quality time and energy you invest in focusing on your visions, the sooner they are going to manifest.

In addition to helping you to reach your goals with greater ease and speed, there are exciting fringe benefits to increased focus. As you intensify your focus on your visions, you gain a sense of personal power, a feeling that you are taking control of your life. Self-respect and self-esteem get a definite boost as you learn to consciously choose your thoughts and stay focused on the positive results you seek. You'll also find that increasing your focusing skills has a positive effect on your energy level, and with it, your disposition. Focusing on constructive visions for your life tends to reduce stress, fatigue, and interpersonal conflict. Most of all, focus kills doubt.

Focus = TARGET + AIM

Focus can be defined as "the power to consciously decide where to direct your attention and the ability to hold it upon the objectives you have chosen." Imagine shooting an arrow into the air. The arrow soars for a time and then falls limply to the ground. Now imagine aiming at a definite target. Your sights clearly fixed on the bull's eye, you let go the arrow. You hear the satisfying thud as it slams into the target. Without a target, you have nothing to aim at, and without aim, you have virtually no chance of hitting the target. Focus, then, requires a target and concentrated aim.

 THE TARGET

IS YOUR GOAL

AIM IS:

Awareness

Intelligently

Maneuvered

Formulating definite targets or goals brings your visions into sharp focus. Goals provide a framework around which you can develop concrete plans of action. Chapters 8, 9, and 10 will address the goal-setting process, and the steps leading up to it, in some detail. They will help you to select well-defined targets. The remainder of this chapter is devoted to helping you improve your aim, or powers of concentration, and by so doing, increase your chances of hitting your target goals. If you are confident of your ability to concentrate, and are eager to turn your visions into goals, read the Focus unit overview on page 103, and then proceed to the exercises on page 104. If you would like a more thorough understanding of how you can improve your powers of concentration, continue reading.

Improve Your AIM

AIM is simply the ability to direct your conscious awareness toward predetermined objectives. AIM is an acronym for Awareness Intelligently Maneuvered. *Awareness* here means "consciousness," your attention. *Intelligently* simply means "thoughtfully," "with intention." *Maneuvered* means "directed," "placed," "positioned." AIM, then, is thoughtfully placed attention, the directed use of conscious awareness.

Awareness: Develop your ability to concentrate, to keep what you intend in the forefront of your awareness.

Intelligently: Understand the power of the life script and how the automatic selection process works.

Maneuvered: Take control of automatic selection process and use it to your advantage.

Conscious Awareness: A Matter of Selection

AIM is an acronym for Awareness Intelligently Maneuvered. The first step in learning to more effectively maneuver or direct your attention is to increase your understanding of how the conscious mind works. Conscious awareness is the result of a process of selection. You are constantly filtering out some of the data in your environment, while allowing other data into your conscious awareness. If you were hypnotized, you would be able to describe in minute detail scenes, events, and objects that normally remain outside your conscious awareness. These data are recorded in your memory (as hypnosis indicates), but they have not been selected for conscious attention. Your conscious mind selects particular aspects of your environment to focus upon, and ignores the rest.

To get an experience of this, look out a nearby window for five seconds. Next, look away from the window and take one minute to write down a description of what you saw. Now, look out the window again and check what you wrote against the scene before you. Did you describe everything? I'm willing to bet you didn't. Of course, it's difficult, if not impossible, for *anyone* to adequately describe in one minute what they can see in five seconds. Since you couldn't describe everything, you had to select the things that made the biggest impression on you. By necessity, we are always selecting. If you are married or have ever had a close friend, you know that two people can experience the same event in entirely different ways. Whether it's a movie, a meal, a party, or a concert, there are as many different experiences as there are people experiencing.

The difference in our experiences is a function of what we select to focus on. This applies not only to aspects of the outer environment but, even more importantly, to the thoughts we select. When Milton said, "The mind is its own place, and in itself can make a heaven of hell, a hell of heaven," he was reminding us that the better part of our experience of joy or suffering—of our success or failure, for that matter—is a function of what we choose to focus on. The fact that some people are bowled over by minor inconveniences while others persevere and overcome in the face of the most harrowing odds is, in large part, a function of the different kinds of thoughts they select to focus on. But how do we determine what to select for attention and what to ignore? We typically select material for conscious awareness by means of one of three distinct processes. The remainder of this chapter focuses on these processes and how you can use each to your advantage in achieving your goals. They are:

1. Deliberate Intention
2. Unconscious, or Automatic, Selection
3. Search Commands

Deliberate Intention: Aiming Your Mind

Deliberate intention means simply what it says—consciously selecting the object of your attention and holding it in your awareness. Deliberate intention is the ability to concentrate your mind on a given thought or object. In order to achieve your objectives, you'll want to keep your mind concentrated on them. The ability to concentrate is a function of motivation and skill. Motivation will be discussed at length in the Desire section. This chapter will explore how you can increase your focusing skill. The secret of concentration lies in what might be called "the mental law of displacement." Since the conscious mind can only focus on one thought at a time, to select and hold one thought in your awareness is to exclude or displace all others.

The yogis of India have been renowned for their powers of concentration. When the British first arrived in India, many were amazed at the feats these yogis were able to perform. It turns out that while Westerners had been busy for centuries learning to better dissect and analyze the physical world, the ancient masters of the East had been equally busy in their studies of mind science. In fact, the influence of yogic teachings on modern psychology and psychiatry has been profound and widely recognized by scholars in these fields. Patanjali was one of the first to systematically lay out the principles of yogic mind science. He likened the mind to a body of water.

If the water is still, as in a quiet, clear pond, one can see to the bottom. A wave made by throwing a stone in the water is clearly visible. However, if the water is choppy, with many waves on its surface, one cannot see the bottom nor easily detect a single wave. The waves, Patanjali compared to thoughts. The untrained mind is like the body of choppy water, tossed this way and that by waves of thought, most of which the thinker is hardly aware, much less in control of. The first step to quieting the pond and beginning to get control of the mind is to develop one's ability to concentrate, which is to say, to practice riding a single wave (thought). As one develops this ability, the pond, or background chatterbox of unintended thoughts, gradually becomes quiet. Thus, when you are intensely concentrating, you are not only temporarily displacing all other thoughts from your mind but also permanently removing the mental noise that disturbs your ability to focus. We could say that the more you concentrate, the more you can concentrate, and the easier it becomes to do so.

Yogis have employed a variety of techniques to assist them in developing their powers of concentration. Breath control and awareness

A man is about as happy as he makes up his mind to be.

ABRAHAM LINCOLN

Selecting Mechanisms

	DEFINITION	OPERATING PRINCIPLE
Deliberate Intention	The act of consciously selecting the objects of one's attention and holding them in the awareness.	The conscious mind can only hold one thought at a time.
Automatic Selection	The process through which the mind automatically selects the objects of its awareness, usually through unconscious association.	Dominant thoughts seek validating evidence in the environment.
Search Commands	Deliberate intention and automatic selection combine to produce a potent hybrid selecting mechanism.	The more you deliberately hold a thought, the more it automatically enters your awareness.

is perhaps the most widely known, although techniques involving light and sound were also common. Some yogis would focus their attention on the sounds and meanings of certain mantras, which they would repeat aloud or silently within their minds. While they believed that there are distinct energies, powers, and properties associated with particular mantras, from the standpoint of developing powers of concentration, the key factor is a single-minded focus that obliterates all other thoughts. If you can, like the monks of Tibet, hold your attention to the mantra *Om Mani Padme Hum,* you can just as easily hold your focus on the thought: I am accomplishing goal X, Y, or Z.

The point is simply this: the ability to concentrate is a transferable skill. Anything you do that requires you to concentrate will improve your ability to focus on your goals—or anything else, for that matter. Engaging in any of the following can sharpen your powers of concentration.

1. Rock climbing
2. Memorizing
3. Parachuting
4. Listening
5. Learning music
6. Juggling
7. Hang gliding
8. Planning
9. Archery
10. Writing
11. Flying an airplane
12. Performing arts
13. Target shooting
14. Photography
15. Calculating
16. Researching
17. Race car driving
18. Martial arts

Unconscious, or Automatic, Selection

Much of the time, the content of our "conscious" minds is not consciously chosen. Rather, it is comprised of a series of unconscious associations, strung together in a seemingly random fashion. More often than we may care to admit, the subject matter of our conscious minds is a result of automatic selection, not deliberate intention. Automatic selection brings things to your attention in two ways: through your survival instincts and through your unconscious mental associations.

Survival Instinct: When facing immediate danger, our instinctive survival mechanism kicks in, alerting our attention to significant factors in the environment. Imagine you are driving to work on a major freeway. You're mentally preoccupied, thinking about your plans for the day, when all of the sudden, a semitruck jumps a lane and comes bolting head-on toward you car. Your life depends upon on how quickly you notice and react to the danger at hand. Skip a meal and watch your attention move toward food. Miss a few more, and food you would never consider starts to draw you hither. In the highly complex and technologically advanced society we live in, survival instinct plays a minimal role in determining what we focus on. Unless you live in a dangerous neighborhood or frequently encounter life-threatening situations, this instinctively triggered focusing mechanism is typically dormant, though it is always available as a kind of emergency override system.

Unconscious Association: Most of what we automatically select to focus on comes to us by way of unconscious associations. Let's say you are watching television. A commercial comes on, asking you if you are hungry. Would you like a hamburger? All of a sudden, you are conscious of the leftover turkey in the refrigerator. You weren't intending to think about the turkey, but there you are, thinking about it. Let's say you're about to make an important presentation for a group of executives at your company. All of a sudden, you find yourself thinking about the time in third grade when all of the kids laughed at you as you stood in front of the class. You certainly didn't intend to think about your experience in third grade, but there it is, in your awareness. While reading a romantic novel, you suddenly recall an old flame. You do not intend to think of him, but there he is, in your awareness. He got there by means of unconscious association. While many unconscious associations are seemingly random and haphazard, others can be attributed to an organizing principle that psychologists call a "life script."

Who Is Screening Your Calls?

Alan was raised by extremely critical parents from whom he learned to focus on his shortcomings and inadequacies. In the course of a day, Alan might do a hundred things well before making a single mistake; yet his attention is trained to ignore the things he has done well and focus on the negative aspects of his performance. His mind has been conditioned to select data that reflect poorly on him. To better understand the filtering mechanism of conscious attention (which scientists have linked to the brain's reticular activating system), imagine that within Alan's mind, there is an executive secretary. It's her job to screen all of his incoming calls. These incoming calls represent data in his environment, seeking entrance into the field of his awareness.

Let's assume that Alan has just completed a difficult project at work. He did a great job and received kudos from his supervisor. A "call" notifying his awareness of this success comes in. The executive secretary screening the calls says, "I'm sorry, the boss is not in." Later in the day, an attractive woman gives Alan a sincere compliment on his appearance. The call with this data comes in. His executive secretary says, "Sorry, the boss is in a meeting; he can't be reached right now." That night, Alan makes an embarrassing slip of the tongue, in front of

It is not enough to have a good mind. The main thing is to use it well.

RENÉ DESCARTES

Life Scripts: Organizing Principles of the Switchboard of Your Mind

The diagram below illustrates how the life script determines which data from the environment will be allowed into conscious awareness and which will be rejected. At an early age, you began making generalizations about life, yourself, work, and others. These original decisions or "core beliefs" formed the cornerstones of your life script. Through automatic selection, your mind has been protecting and reinforcing the script ever since. Data in your environment that do not conform to the core beliefs in your script tend to be automatically filtered out of your conscious awareness. Meanwhile, data that substantiate your script are automatically sought after and admitted into your conscious awareness.

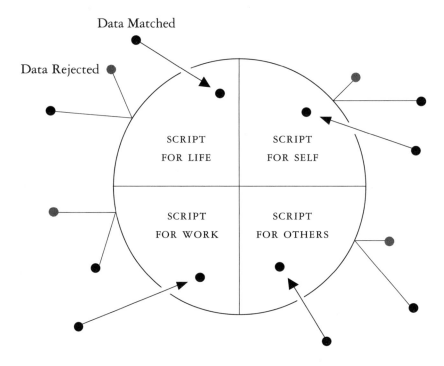

Data Matched

Data Rejected

SCRIPT FOR LIFE

SCRIPT FOR SELF

SCRIPT FOR WORK

SCRIPT FOR OTHERS

a date he is trying to impress. Again, the call comes in. However, this time the executive secretary says, "Thank you so much for calling. I'll put you through right away." It's as though the executive secretary had been given a script or set of criteria by which to screen the incoming calls. Alan's script directs his executive secretary to focus on data that support an image of him as incompetent.

Psychologists tell us that each of us has a life script. A life script works like this: Based upon your early conditioning, you internalized a vision of yourself and how your life would turn out. From that point on, you've tended to select out data that support your life script and to reject data that would challenge it. The supportive data are the calls that make it past your executive secretary.

What's in Your Script?

There is nothing inherently negative about a life script. The problem comes from the content of the script, which, for most people, is extremely limiting, and for some, downright destructive. Limiting life scripts sabotage our best efforts and seem to spoil our success at every turn. The more we try to run from them, the more our scripted programs seem to follow us. Our unconsciously conditioned beliefs wear us down until at last, defeated, we resign ourselves to our "fate." We can't blame it all on our parents either (not that it would do any good if we did). Psychologists tell us that we make most of our major unconscious decisions about life and the way it works by the time we are eight years old. Ask yourself, "Do I want an eight-year-old mind planning my life?" Of course you don't, but that's what you get if you don't consciously develop a plan for your life—your own life script.

Samantha came from an abusive home. Her father was an alcoholic and was often verbally, and occasionally physically, abusive. Some time before she was eight years old, Samantha decided, "Men hurt me." (The preteen mind is prone to sweeping generalizations.) The "logic" goes something like this: "Daddy is hurtful and abusive. Daddy is a man. Therefore, all men want to hurt me." The belief that her father is dangerous is grounded in reality, but to project that onto all men is to make an irrational and undiscriminating leap.

Your own mind is a sacred enclosure into which nothing harmful can enter except by your permission.

ARNOLD BENNETT

There is her belief, "Men want to hurt me," and there is reality. Most men are indifferent, some do want to hurt her, and some want to love and support her. In order to be effective in her dealings with men, she must be able to notice the difference on a case-by-case basis. Without this discrimination, she will project onto the indifferent men intentions that are not there, attract to herself men who do want to hurt her, or twist and distort the love of those who love her, to make it come out like hurt. Her belief about men is so powerful that it causes her to push away the men who truly do want to love her. Consequently, she feels rejected and hurt, and so confirms her original belief that men want to hurt her.

Since you did not consciously, much less rationally, choose the attention-selecting criteria associated with your life script, and since these were determined at such an early age, you're probably unaware of the power they have in shaping your life. You may think that because you have never actively developed a life plan, you have been merely drifting through life without direction. The fact is that all along, your life has been shaped and prescribed by the contents of your life script. Once you realize that you do in fact have a life script, and admit the power that it has in your life, you have an important choice to make. You can decide to continue operating from the life program determined by your conditioning, or you can consciously create a new vision for your life. Putting off the decision, of course, means signing on for more of the same. While it is easier to give in to your conditioned life script than to develop and affirm a new vision of your life, the latter option offers the possibility of exploring your full potential and realizing the most from your life.

When they first become aware of the powerful role that the internal "executive secretary" plays in their lives, many people say, in effect, "Thanks, but no thanks." They want to fire her. Of course, that isn't possible. Without a mechanism for screening incoming data, your conscious attention would be flooded with more information than you could possibly process. Your "circuits" would rapidly overload. Since firing your executive secretary is out of the question, the only alternative is to get her working *for* you. Once given a new set of screening criteria, your executive secretary will bring to your attention ideas, information, and contacts that will reinforce the positive results and experiences you are seeking in your life. While retraining her may require a considerable investment of time, thought, and effort, it's an investment well worth making. After all, she is going to be with you for the rest of your life. Besides, it's fun to experience yourself in control, consciously directing and shaping what were heretofore unconscious processes. In the Desire section, you will find a potent array of techniques you can use to begin retraining your subconscious mind. But for now, let's look at what a goal can do for you.

Search Command: Combining Deliberate Intention with Automatic Selection

Setting definite life goals changes your awareness by commanding your executive secretary to use new criteria for screening your calls or determining what will enter your conscious awareness. You've seen this principle in operation many times. Let's say you're driving on a long cross-country trip with the kids, so you make up a game of counting all the blue cars. Suddenly, everywhere you go, you see blue cars (or out-of-state license plates, or funny bumper stickers, or whatever it is that you've chosen to look for). They were there before, but you hardly noticed them. Establishing a goal changes your awareness. It's almost as though you had issued a "search command" to your mind.

The search-command principle is the third selecting mechanism of conscious attention. A search command takes advantage of both deliberate intention and automatic selection. *The more you deliberately look for something, the more you will find yourself automatically noticing it.* By issuing a search command, you help to ensure that the information that will assist you in achieving your goals will be automatically brought into your awareness.

Martin decided to become a real-estate investor. He had a goal to buy three residential income properties in his first year. Almost automatically, he began to approach his evening newspaper in a new way. Instead of turning to the sports page or headlines, he went straight

Man does not simply exist, but always decides what his existence will be, what he will become in the next moment.

VIKTOR FRANKL

The Answer's at Hand with Search Commands

SEARCH COMMAND · · · · · · · · · · · · · · · · IDEAS GENERATED

Marlene's original
$45,000 Goal

(Survival)

Holding onto a good,
steady teaching job.

Marlene's new
$150,000 Goal

(Greater Contribution)

Consult School Districts.

Conduct seminars.

Lecture for fees.

Write and sell a book.

Produce training materials.

---

to the classified section. "For Sale" signs that he had hardly noticed before began to jump out at him. Today, Martin can hardly drive down the street without sizing up properties in terms of market value, building or remodeling costs, and income potential. He does it automatically, as a kind of second nature. His goal has changed his awareness, and in so doing, his life. In his first year, Martin bought five properties, and he's working on acquiring more.

As you repeatedly train your attention upon your goals, you command your executive secretary to accept the new screening criteria that support them. You begin to automatically welcome the constructive calls that support a vision of you at your best and screen out the negative calls. All the data in your environment that fit with your new vision of your life will be rushed into your conscious attention, while anything that doesn't match will be rejected as insignificant. The more you focus on your goals, especially with intense desire, the more potent the search command becomes. Consistent focus on your goals will transform your experience until the outer circumstances of your life begin to match those you saw in your original vision.

As a dedicated teacher, Marlene had studied the role that self-esteem and goal setting play in learning. In fact, she had become something of an expert. Marlene was an award-winning teacher who had great success with her students. Still, she wanted something more. Marlene understood the principle of multiplication of effort. She realized that she was limited in the number of lives she could impact as a classroom teacher. After all, there is a limit to the number of hours in a day, and children in a class. She reasoned that by training other teachers in the techniques she had perfected, she could increase her impact geometrically.

She decided that she wanted to earn $150,000 a year as a private educational consultant rather than the $45,000 per year she was making as a teacher. Because Marlene now had a $150,000 problem, she realized she needed $150,000 solutions. Her $45,000 solutions just wouldn't work any more. By setting a goal and repeatedly focusing on it, Marlene was, in effect, issuing a search command to her mind to bring to her attention the data she needed to turn her dream into a reality.

Soon, she was noticing opportunities where previously she had seen problems. For example, principals and school administrators, whom Marlene used to view as "authority figures" who limited her creative freedom, became key allies in her plans for success. Today, she frequently lectures them on the role that self-esteem and goal setting play in learning. (By the way, her daily lecture fee is more than she used to make in two weeks as a classroom teacher, and that's doing great things for *her* self-esteem.)

In addition to generating the ideas that make possible the attainment of the goal, search commands attract the circumstances, people, and material resources needed for success. Setting definite, realistic goals and giving them consistent, concentrated focus sets in motion an automatic selection process that transforms the content of your mind, and in so doing, the quality of your life. The thoughts and images that you focus on are vitally important to your future. Be they conscious goals or the results of a leftover script, your dominant life visions anchor and magnetize your attention. Over time, you become

Nothing at all will be attempted if all possible objections must first be overcome.

SAMUEL JOHNSON

like that which you repeatedly focus your attention on—a point we will return to many times. Remember that to set no new goals is to accept the unconscious life script of your earlier life. Obviously, you want something better, or you wouldn't be reading this book. In the next three chapters, we will focus on converting the raw material of your visions into definite goals.

Focus: An Overview

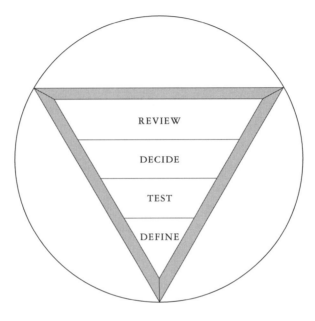

Review: Review the work you did in the Vision section. From a wide-angle perspective, consider all of the available options.

Decide: The exercises in chapter 8 will help you to develop critical selection criteria and determine which life areas and potential goals are priorities for you at this time.

Test: The exercises in chapter 9 will give you the opportunity to test your rational choices against the intuitions of your heart. Make sure the goals you have selected fit with what you want most and that they fit well with one another.

Define: The exercises in chapter 10 will help shape these choices into exact and definite goals that fit with the TARGET formula.

Chapter 7 Exercises

❦

Reviewing Your Visions

In the Vision unit, your purpose was to expand your horizons. Now, it's time to narrow your focus. The first step to focusing in on your goals is to review the raw material you amassed in the Vision unit. In order to shape these visions into definite goals, you must first get your attention riveted on them. That may sound simple—and it is—but it's not always easy. If you haven't already made a habit of setting personal goals, don't be surprised if your subconscious mind puts up some resistance when you begin. It may come up with any number of distractions or excuses to divert your attention. Now is the time to stay focused. PERSEVERE and you will break through to clarity!

With a notebook and pen at hand, take thirty to forty-five minutes of quiet time to review all of the exercises you completed from chapters 4, 5, and 6. Jot down the outstanding potential goals for each of the eight life areas. List your top three selections in each area. If you are interested in setting a goal in only a single life area, follow the same procedure for that area. Don't be concerned if, at this point, you have more than three potential goals in some, or even all, of the life areas. However, for the sake of clarity, do not exceed five potential goals in each life area.

Decision Making: Establishing Your Priorities

*Choose always the way that seems the best,
however rough it may be. Custom will soon render it
easy and agreeable.*

PYTHAGORAS

Assuming you have done the accompanying exercises, you have by now identified a number of important visions for your life. That's a great step forward and one you can take real pride in. Yet it also presents a problem. It's a wonderful problem, really, though one that must be faced head-on if you are to gain mastery over your own life. The problem is this: you have to make some decisions. You have to decide which of these wonderful visions are most meaningful and important to you and, among these, which you will choose to focus on first. This chapter and the one following will consider strategies for making effective decisions about life directions. Chapter 10 will focus on converting these decisions into definite and realistic goals.

Nothing is so exhausting as indecision, and nothing is so futile.

BERTRAND RUSSELL

How *do* you choose which visions to make the immediate priorities in your life? While it is exciting to consider the full range of possibilities, it's easy to see that you must make some choices. You recognize that, while your visions may be unlimited in number and scope, your time, energy, and attention are not. You will need to establish clear priorities and set definite goals. The American bald eagle provides an excellent metaphor for the attitudes necessary for effective decision making. This great bird flies high, spreading its enormous wings, gliding and circling, giving all appearance of ease and relaxation. Yet, within this calm flight, there is a steady concentration, an intense focus, as the eagle selects its prey—an unsuspecting fish, hundreds of yards away. Biding its time until just the right moment, the eagle swoops down, its entire being concentrated on the moving target below.

Some of us human decision-makers forget to soar, and some of us forget to focus and strike. Major life decisions should neither be rushed nor avoided. These two—impulsiveness and avoidance—are the major obstacles to effective decision making. You combat impulsiveness by taking time to deliberate, searching your values and motives, and identifying clear criteria on which to base your decisions. You overcome avoidance by accepting responsibility for your own life and recognizing that things do not improve until you decide and take action.

Don't Be Impulsive: Take Time to Decide

The calm, high flight of the eagle represents a wide-angle view, a detached and objective look at the situation before you. After all, the eagle cannot strike where the fish is; it must anticipate where the fish will be by the time it gets there. The eagle takes its time before making a decision, and so should you. Snap decisions often snap back. Major life decisions need time to incubate. This is one case where taking the time to get it right will save you a great deal of time and frustration in the long run.

Where you are now in life is a direct result of the decisions you have made or decided not to make. These decisions were based upon your awareness at the time you made them. *The quality of your decisions is no better or worse than the quality of your awareness.* We see so much better from hindsight because of the additional awareness we have gained. The question that occurs at this point is: "Is there any way I can improve my awareness before I make a decision?" The answer, of course, is yes. The remainder of this chapter will present effective decision-making tools you can use to increase your awareness before making major life decisions. Using these tools will increase your confidence that the decisions you make are the right ones.

The Elements of a Decision

The 1920s saw the dawn of a new era in American business, one in which professional managers would dominate. From that time to the present, those responsible for the management of large organizations have sought to better understand the decision-making process. After all, decisions are the lifeblood of management. The substance and timing of management decisions can often mean a difference of millions, or even billions, of dollars. Management decisions affect the quality of service experienced by hundreds of thousands of the organization's clients or customers, and the work environment of hundreds of employees.

Were we to ask an experienced management consultant questions like: "What is an effective decision?" and "What are the basic elements in the decision-making process?" she would tell us that there are three ingredients to effective decisions. First, an effective decision is one that recognizes that both opportunities and limitations are inherent in every choice. All decisions require us to make tradeoffs. Second, effective decisions are made in accord with relevant and clearly defined criteria. Third, effective decisions are consistent with overriding goals and values. Now let's explore each of these points in greater depth.

Choice: Opportunities and Limits

Decision making requires not only that we accept definite limitations but also that we consciously and willingly impose them on ourselves.

There are people who want to be everywhere at once, and they get nowhere.

CARL SANDBURG

There is a certain element of human nature that resists and resents limits of any kind. Yet if we are to enjoy and celebrate life, if we are to experience it as the creative adventure it was meant to be, we must learn to make peace with limitations. Indeed, we must embrace limits as the catalysts to growth that they really are. Every creative artist operates within definite limits of form. These limits do not impede the artist's creativity. Rather, they challenge him to shape his expression to both fit and transcend the confines of the form or structure with which he works. The limits of structure force the artist to make every line, every note, every scene or stroke, count. The creative tension between the vision of the possible and the limits of the physical world, challenges the artist to grow, both as a craftsman and as a human being.

When making decisions, you must leave behind the billowy clouds of vision and confront the practical limitations of space, time, energy, and matter. In other words, you have to put your visions to work in the real world. In this world, you can't do all things at once. You can't be all things to all people. You have to choose what is most important to you and establish the priorities of your life. Recognize that when you decide to focus on a particular vision, you must let go of one or several others, at least for a time. You have to make a choice.

By way of illustration, imagine that you are residing in Chicago, and your decision is whether to go to New York or Los Angeles. If you don't decide, you will stay in Chicago. You will remain where you are. If you choose Los Angeles, you cannot simultaneously go to New York. If you choose New York, you must let go of Los Angeles. The French philosopher and author Michel de Montaigne imagined a similar dilemma involving equal desires.

> *It is an amusing conception to imagine a mind exactly balanced between two equal desires. For it is indubitable that it will never decide, since inclination and choice imply inequality in value; and if we were placed between the bottle and the ham with an equal appetite for drinking and for eating, there would doubtless be no solution but to die of thirst and of hunger.* —MONTAIGNE

The same dynamics apply in making any choice. In order to make a decision, you must determine that something is more valuable than something else. This means, of course, that something will always be left out. No decision is perfect, and every decision requires that we make tradeoffs. Therefore, it is imperative that you establish definite criteria against which you can weigh the potential costs and benefits of any decision you make. Ultimately, you must go with decisions that support your highest priority values, even if they are imperfect (you can bet they will be) and even if it means giving up something else for a time.

Know Your Criteria

Okay, you must decide, but how do you decide? You start with criteria. Every decision is made on the basis of some criteria. The FDA has criteria for food and drug quality. The postal service has criteria for mailing packages. The office of immigration has criteria for entry into the country. Whether you are conscious of it or not, you also have criteria for every decision you make. From the kind of car you drive, to the kind of music you listen to; from the work you do, to the people you associate with—criteria determine your choices. Making your decision-making criteria conscious, explicit, and precise helps to ensure that the decisions you make are the right ones for you. Criteria that are explicitly stated can be checked for relevancy and kept up-to-date, while those that remain unconscious are likely to become outmoded. Consciously selecting your decision-making criteria helps to ensure that you bring maximum awareness to the choices you make. Again, it cannot be emphasized too strongly that anything you can do to improve the quality of your awareness will improve the quality of your decisions.

Decisions Further Goals

Generally speaking, effective decisions are made to further the accomplishment of specific goals or to eliminate problems in achieving them.

Without goals to serve as guidelines, decisions become random, haphazard, and sometimes—downright bizarre. To illustrate, imagine you have just built your dream home on the outskirts of a city in an unincorporated area that lacks any zoning ordinances. As the movers pull away, you suddenly hear the deafening roar of bulldozers, dump trucks, and graders. Much to your chagrin, you learn that an auto manufacturing plant is being built next door. It's not long before a gas station goes up across the street. You even hear that they're going to build a shopping mall in the next block. While this example may seem ridiculous, it is no more ridiculous than trying to make decisions without goals to serve as guidelines. Ambiguity in decision-making criteria often results from uncertainty about the goals they are meant to support. A city adopts zoning ordinances to ensure that its developmental goals are met. Just as the city's goals suggest the relevant criteria for making decisions, your goals will suggest relevant criteria with which you can make effective decisions about the use of your most valuable resources—your time and energy. Once your goals have been clearly established, it's relatively easy to make implementing decisions.

Yet when it comes to making major life decisions, we have a unique problem. We are attempting to make decisions without the benefit of goals to guide the selection of our decision-making criteria. We can hardly be guided by goals when we are still in the process of selecting them. So when it comes to making major life decisions, values replace goals in suggesting the key criteria for effective decision making.

Decision Levels

The elements of the decision-making process discussed thus far apply to all decisions. But all decisions are not created equal. Deciding whether to get married, to have children, or take up a new career are obviously decisions on a different order of magnitude than choosing which brand of milk to buy or which credit card to use. Again, we can learn from our management consultant.

She tells us that within large organizations, there exists a hierarchy of decision levels. The board of directors makes the value decisions; in

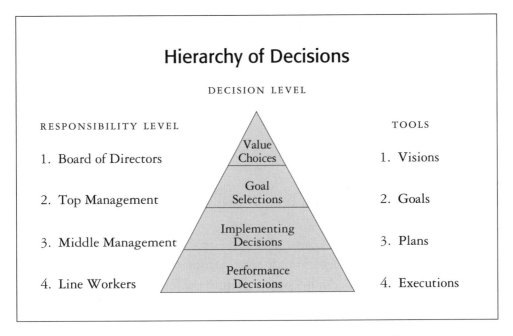

Hierarchy of Decisions

DECISION LEVEL

RESPONSIBILITY LEVEL | Value Choices | TOOLS

1. Board of Directors — Value Choices — 1. Visions

2. Top Management — Goal Selections — 2. Goals

3. Middle Management — Implementing Decisions — 3. Plans

4. Line Workers — Performance Decisions — 4. Executions

other words, they determine the philosophy, or values, that guide the organization. The chief executive officers and top management make goal decisions and issue policy directives. On the basis of these, middle managers make implementing decisions. In turn, the staff and line personnel make performance decisions in the course of carrying out these directives. Of course, most of us wouldn't want to run our own lives the way impersonal corporate organizations do. Nor would we want to adopt the single-minded corporate commitment to the profit motive as the central value of our lives. Nevertheless, the concept of a hierarchy of decision-making levels can be adapted to making major decisions in our lives. (See the diagram above.)

Part of the difficulty many of us face when we take on the challenge of life planning is that we are not accustomed to consciously making Level-One and Level-Two Decisions. Thinking of yourself as the visionary and value setter (the chairman of the board, if you will) and the goal and policy setter (or CEO) of your own life may be new to you. Many of us are accustomed to following the directives of others, but lack experience in determining our own values and goals. We're more familiar with playing the part of the middle manager (making mid-level implementing decisions) and/or the line worker, who makes the day-to-day performance decisions on the basis of the values, goals, and policies set by those above. When facing a decision, it helps to recall the Hierarchy of Decisions. Ask yourself what level the decision you are about to make is on. Is it a Level-One (Value) Decision, a Level-Two (Goal) Decision, a Level-Three (Implementing) Decision, or a Level-Four (Performance) Decision? Keep in mind that in selecting the visions you want to manifest, you are making Level-One (Value) Decisions.

Level-One Decisions: Calling a Director's Meeting

Value choices, or Level-One Decisions, are the most important choices we make. These determine the directions and outcomes of our lives. Everything we do, in one way or another, flows from the decisions we make about our values. Today, we have greater latitude in choosing the values that shape our lives than ever before in human history. We are free of many of the constraints that nature imposed on our ancestors. Most of us spend little time or energy on the primary pursuits of our ancient counterparts—namely hunting, gathering, or cultivating food; making clothing; and securing shelter. While today, the average person actually spends more time earning the money required to secure the modern equivalents of basic survival needs, she has far more freedom in choosing how to earn her living. Today, she can specialize in virtually any field she can imagine, something that would have been impossible for those living in more technologically primitive societies. In recent years, traditional moral and religious strictures have likewise lost their hold on us. Today, social "shoulds" and "should nots" are fewer in number, and the penalties for violating them less severe, than they were even thirty years ago. Stereotypical sex roles have fallen by the wayside, offering new possibilities for both men and women.

Greater freedom of choice has brought new opportunities, to be sure, but it has also resulted in a great deal of anxiety. If you are told what to do, you may resent it, but you don't have to worry about making the right choice. In response to this anxiety, some play victim, blaming society or their parents or mates for the choices they make.

He who wants to do everything will never do anything.

ANDRÉ MAUROIS

Others hide in groups that tell them what they should think and do. Still others succumb to alcohol or drug abuse or lose themselves in endless television viewing. Yet a growing number are ready to stand up and decide for themselves what their lives will be about. They, perhaps like you, are ready to embrace the new freedom of choice and make the most of it.

Again, because they determine the direction of your life, Level-One (Value) Decisions are the most important decisions you will ever make. They set the tone for your life and determine the parameters within which countless other decisions will be made. A change in values can bring a quantum leap in the quality of your life. These are the kinds of decisions you look back on and say, "That was a major turning point in my life!" The discussion that follows addresses five key steps to making effective Level-One Decisions.

Five Steps for Making Effective Level-One Decisions

1. Define your purpose.
2. Generate a wide range of alternatives.
3. Identify and rank critical criteria.
4. Match and rank alternatives to criteria.
5. Anticipate consequences.

Define Your Purpose: The first step is to define the purpose of the decision. What question or questions is the decision designed to answer? You can save yourself a lot of time, energy, and unnecessary struggle by being careful to pose the right questions from the start. Many times, people blame themselves for coming up with a "wrong answer," when it was, in fact, a perfectly appropriate answer to an ill-conceived question. Remember that the questions you ask define and limit the range of possible answers. In a sense, questions contain the answers within themselves, even as a seed contains the plant within itself. If you find yourself getting stuck during the decision-making pro-

*Life is the sum of all
your choices.*

ALBERT CAMUS

cess, go back to the beginning and reframe or repeat the basic question or questions you are trying to answer. For example: What work will enable me to make the best use of my talents and make the biggest difference in the lives of others?

Since you are reading this book, it is safe to assume that you recognize the importance of making a major decision in at least one area of your life. You are motivated by the fact that to fail to act is to remain trapped in an untenable position or to miss potentially golden opportunities. While the question can be defined broadly as "What do I want do, be, or have, in the area of life that I am now considering?" you will want to structure a more specific question. Make sure the question or questions that you settle on are the right ones for you.

Generate Alternatives: The next step is to generate a list of possible alternatives. You may not have been aware of it, but you have already done a great part of this work (assuming that you have done the exercises in the previous sections). A diverse range of questions was included in the Vision section in order to help you generate a host of available options. If you feel a measure of confusion about which way to go, don't be concerned. It's actually a good sign. Considering a wide range of alternatives before making your final selection will help you form a consensus. Let all points of view from within the "committee" of your mind be heard. It will actually help you to feel more decisive later on. Remember the eagle; it knows there are a lot of fish in the sea, but that doesn't stop it from being decisive and choosing one.

Identify and Rank Critical Criteria: The next step is to identify and rank the critical criteria for making your decision. Again, for a major life decision, these key criteria are your values. By making explicit your critical values, you are, in effect, identifying what you stand for. Now, let's take a look at how one person used this process in making a major decision in his life.

Peter was an engineer who for some time had felt extremely dissatisfied with his career. He decided he wanted to work in an entirely different field. In examining what he wanted from his new career, Peter identified three critical values. The first was making the greatest contribution possible by making the best use of his talents. The second was earning significant financial rewards for his efforts. The third was spending as little time as possible retraining for a new career.

Once Peter had identified these criteria, he assigned them relative values. Since using his talents in making a contribution was his first priority, he gave that a value of fifteen points. Since his second priority was being financially comfortable, he gave that a value of ten points. While he didn't want to spend any more time than necessary in retraining, this was relatively less important to him, so he gave it a value of five.

LIFE AREA: CAREER

Contribution	15
Financial Reward	10
Retraining	5

Match and Rank Alternatives to Criteria: The next step is to match each of the alternatives to the value criteria and rank them accordingly. List the top three visions that you identified on page 104. Next, match these visions against your key values. Give each vision a score based on how well it fulfills your critical criteria. (See the exercise on page 123.) To illustrate, we will again follow Peter in his decision-making process.

In the area of career, Peter had narrowed his options down to three. He was considering becoming a marriage and family counselor, an environmental lawyer, or a real-estate agent and investor. Once he had assigned values to the critical criteria, his next step was to rate each of his career visions according to these criteria.

VISIONS	#1 VALUE 15 POINTS	#2 VALUE 10 POINTS	#3 VALUE 5 POINTS	TOTAL POINTS
1. Psychotherapist				
2. Lawyer				
3. Real-Estate Investor				

There is no more miserable human being than one in whom nothing is habitual but indecision.

WILLIAM JAMES

Peter realized that he could express his empathic, verbal, and intuitive skills and make a real difference in the lives of others by working as a marriage and family counselor, so he assigned this option a value of fourteen out of a possible fifteen points. He determined that as an environmental lawyer, he could use his research and communication skills and make significant contributions to large numbers of people, but with less impact on each individual. After some thought, he assigned this option a value of thirteen. Peter decided that he could use his people skills as a real-estate investor and, through the large income he might ultimately generate, help others by donating a portion of it to charitable causes. He assigned this option a value of eight.

Peter knew that he wasn't going to get rich as a marriage and family counselor, but he realized he could make a comfortable living and have the things he really wanted, so he assigned this option seven out of the possible ten points. He realized that, while he might initially earn less as an environmental lawyer, eventually he would be earning as much, if not more, so he assigned this option a seven also. He decided that he could make considerably more money as a real-estate investor, so he assigned this option a value of nine.

Since Peter already had a college degree, but also had a family and financial responsibilities, he determined that it would probably take him from three to five years of evening classes and part-time work to become established as either a marriage and family counselor or a lawyer. Therefore, he assigned both of these options a value of three. Because he already knew something about real-estate investing, and already had one rental property, Peter felt he could become a full-time investor in three to four years. Consequently, he assigned this option a value of four.

Based on the value criteria that he had established, and their relative rankings, Peter decided to further research the option of training for a career as a marriage and family counselor. However, before making a final decision, he put this decision to the test of motives found in chapter 9. Note: The values expressed above were based upon a real-life case. They are not intended to suggest the relative merits of the occupations in question—only one individual's perception of them.

It is often necessary to do considerable research before you can determine how well potential options match your critical value criteria. For example, for seventeen-year-old Jerry, choosing which college to attend was a critical decision. Jerry identified academic excellence (15), personal attention from instructors (10), and a friendly, coeducational environment (7) as his top three critical values. He then spent many nights on the Internet and at the local library, searching for schools with the right mix to match his criteria. After careful research, he found five schools that suited his needs. He applied to these schools and was accepted at three of them. Before making his final decision, Jerry visited each campus, checking it against his criteria and getting a hands-on feel for each school. Finally, he was ready to make a choice. You will find an exercise in which you can match and rank your critical criteria against your alternatives on page 124.

Anticipate Consequences: Anticipate the consequences of your decisions. You can do this in any number of ways. One simple way is to draw a T-square on a piece of paper. On one side, list the benefits; on the other, the costs of making the decision in question. Again, recognize that there are always tradeoffs for every decision. Another simple exercise is to imagine that you have realized the vision you are considering. Ask yourself: Is this what I really want? How well does it fit with my goals in other areas of my life? What happens if it doesn't work out? Do I have a fallback position, or am I prepared to go for broke? Another tool to help you in anticipating the consequences of your decisions is "scenario building." For a given vision, you might build the best-case, mid-case, and worst-case scenarios. At the end of this chapter, you will find exercises to assist you in this process.

Life Decisions: The Choice is Yours

Many feel ill at ease when making major life decisions. Just when they most need to assert their own strength, they feel emotionally vulnerable and psychologically regressed. Out of a sense of desperation and neediness, they try to dump the decision—and with it, the responsibility for its outcomes—on others. They ask others to decide what they should do. Alternatively, they put off the decision by making it conditional on what someone else does. "After X does Y, then I'll decide." Another avoidance technique is to solicit advice from a number of sources and then play one individual off against the others. "Bill says do A. Mary says do B. Harry thinks I should do C. What do *you* think I should do?"

Remember, responsibility for the decisions you make is yours and yours alone. By all means, take advantage of the input of others, but maintain responsibility for your decisions throughout. You are the one who is going to face the consequences and reap the benefits of the decisions you make and the actions they inspire. When you ask for advice, present alternatives. Don't simply say: "What should I do?" You might say something like: "I'm considering making a decision with regard to ____. I've narrowed my alternatives down to A, B, and C. Which do you think would be the best course of action, and why?" Not only is it wise to seek the advice of others; it can be downright foolish not to. When asking for advice, keep in mind the guidelines that appear on the following page.

The Avoidance Trap: Indecision Hurts

You probably know people who seem unwilling to accept limitations and make decisions. Their fear of making the wrong choice deprives them of the greatest creative power that any of us possess—the power of decision. It is a horrible price to pay. Far worse than making the wrong choice is making no choice at all. As George Bernard Shaw put it, "A life spent in making mistakes is not only more honorable but more useful than a life spent in doing nothing." While mistakes can be corrected, inaction tends to compound problems. People who chronically shirk responsibility and avoid making decisions get trapped in self-created prisons, locked behind bars of fear and walls of doubt. They feel fragmented, torn by competing needs and interests. People who don't fight for something often end up fighting against everything. They appear as malcontents and complainers. These are not bad people but simply people without clear direction or priorities.

Human beings are volitional creatures. To deny the power of choice is, in a very fundamental way, to deny our humanity. It is to resign

He who hunts two hares leaves one and loses the other.

JAPANESE PROVERB

Guidelines for Seeking Advice

1. Do your homework first. Define your alternatives.

2. Seek out people whom you know to be responsible in their own lives (they tend to make good decisions) and whose opinions you respect.

3. Ask these people if they would be willing to offer their advice; don't unilaterally dump your problems or decisions on them.

4. Always maintain responsibility for your decisions.

5. Never blame others for the decisions you make.

ourselves to a sleeplike existence dominated by unconscious habits and conditioned responses. To abdicate the power of choice is to live as a stranger to one's own self. Camus said that to know yourself, you must assert yourself. By consciously choosing the values that will inform your life and determining the meaningful objectives you will pursue, you are affirming that you are a unique individual. You are reclaiming energy once bottled up in fear and doubt, and channeling it into constructive, creative pursuits. Your life is more than the sum total of your conditioned responses. You needn't succumb to the programming of your past or the circumstances of your present. You have the power to choose what you will be, do, and have.

You *always* have a choice. You are never in a situation that doesn't offer options and choices. The range of options available to you at any given point is a function of the choices you've made up to now. If you've made good choices, you have a wide range of options. If you've made poor choices or avoided choosing, the range is more limited. Still, you *always* have a choice. Regardless of your situation, there are decisions that you can make to improve your life. Determine to make them!

Mastery of effective decision-making skills will give you the confidence to confront the important choices and challenges of your life.

The exercises that follow will assist in you deciding which of your visions are the highest priority for you at this time. Just one more step is required before you convert these objectives into definite goals. The next chapter will explore how you can ensure that the choices you have made by means of the rational descion-making model presented in this chapter truly reflect the deepest desires of your heart.

DECIDE, DECIDE:
YOU HAVE NOTHING TO LOSE
BUT THE DOUBT INSIDE.

How to Avoid Making a Major Decision

1. Fail to recognize the need to make one.

2. Resist change (seek security in sameness).

3. Fail to adequately weigh the potential positive benefits.

4. Create distractions (or situational chaos).

5. Create conflict (or interpersonal chaos).

6. Get lost in detail (compulsive control).

7. Get lost in routine (structural control).

8. Dump responsibility on others (actively shift the locus of control).

9. Wait for permission (passively shift the locus of control).

10. Hide in depression, i.e., "nothing will work" (deny locus of control).

11. Escape into fantasy (avoid the limits of earthly existence).

12. Wait for the perfect time (deny the shortness of life).

13. Wait to perfect yourself (obsess on winning approval).

14. Wait for all the possible information and alternatives to be considered.

15. Deny your capacity to handle the consequences and demands of your decision (deny your abilities).

Decision Making

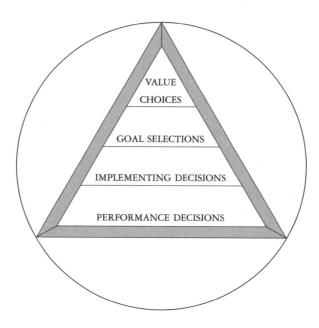

The opportunity is often lost by deliberating.

—SYRUS

The difficulty in life is the choice.

—GEORGE MOORE

The hardest thing to learn in life is which bridge to cross
and which to burn.

—DAVID RUSSELL

Things do not get better by being left alone.

—WINSTON CHURCHILL

Once a decision was made, I did not worry about it afterward.

—HARRY S. TRUMAN

Chapter 8 Exercises

❧

Identify and Rank Critical Criteria

Prioritize the eight life areas you identified in chapter 3, in order of their importance to you at this time in your life. Next, select one area. List your top three value criteria in order of importance, and assign each a numerical value. (See pages 114-115.)

LIFE AREAS

___ Health   ___ Career

___ Lifestyle   ___ Finances

___ Self-development   ___ Social Life

___ Creative Expression   ___ Intimate Relationships

LIFE AREA

1.

VALUE CRITERIA	NUMERICAL VALUE
1.	
2.	
3.	

Match and Rank Alternatives to Criteria

Divide a sheet of paper into four columns. Label the first column "Vision," and the second, third, and fourth columns "Critical Value Criteria 1," "Critical Value Criteria 2," and "Critical Value Criteria 3." Refer to the work you did in the previous exercise to match and rank the alternatives to the criteria you have chosen.

LIFE AREA #1

VISION	CVC #1	CVC #2	CVC #3
1.			
2.			
3.			

LIFE AREA #2

VISION	CVC #1	CVC #2	CVC #3
1.			
2.			
3.			

LIFE AREA #3

VISION	CVC #1	CVC #2	CVC #3
1.			
2.			
3.			

Anticipate Consequences

Imagine that you have achieved your goal. Is it what you want? Is it compatible with your goals in the other life areas that you have chosen to focus on? What happens if it doesn't work? Do you have an escape route, or are you going for broke? Write the best-case, mid-case, and worst-case scenarios for each potential goal you have selected.

BEST-CASE

MID-CASE

WORST-CASE

After you have answered these questions for one potential goal, do the same for goals in as many other life areas as you would like to consider at this time.

Selecting Your Potential Goals

Based on the analysis you have completed in the previous exercises, select, and list below, your major objectives in each of the life areas—or in as many as you would like.

HEALTH:

LIFESTYLE:

SELF-DEVELOPMENT:

CREATIVE EXPRESSION:

CAREER:

FINANCES:

SOCIAL LIFE:

INTIMATE RELATIONSHIPS:

Motive Testing: Listening to Your Heart

I need only consult myself with regard to what I wish to do;
what I feel to be right is right, what I feel to be wrong is wrong;
conscience is the best causist; and it is only when we haggle with
conscience that we have recourse to the subtleties of argument.

JACQUES ROUSSEAU

All right, you've done a good deal of focused thinking and made some decisions as to the objectives you want to pursue at this time in your life. Before converting these objectives into definite goals, put them to one more test, the test of your feelings. Good goals are not just well-thought-out; they represent things you deeply care about. They have emotional power, lasting motivation behind them. This final check on your potential goals will give you added confidence that they are the right ones for you at this time. Even more importantly, the questions in this chapter will help you spot when all the right reasons don't add up to caring.

Listen to Your Heart

*What you intuitively desire,
that is possible to you.*

D. H. LAWRENCE

The last chapter discussed decision-making strategies professional managers use when confronting choices. Managers have long tried to make decision making into an entirely rational and objective science. Of course, in practice, it isn't. In fact, recent studies indicate that professional managers make 80 percent or more of their business decisions for emotional reasons. While it's essential that you carefully think through your goals, don't neglect to take into account the emotional component of decision making. Make sure that your heart is really into your goals, that you have a burning desire to achieve them.

By carefully listening to your feelings before embarking on the path to your goals, you can save a lot of heartache and frustration later on. Your goals are the right ones for you when they reflect a balanced mix of intellect and emotion, head and heart. When your head and heart are working together, you have an unbeatable combination. If it comes down to a choice between the two, go with your heart. If your heart isn't really into it, chances are you will fail to accomplish your goal. Even if you do succeed, it will seem a hollow or empty victory. You don't want to spend your life climbing the ladder of success, only to discover that it was leaning against the wrong wall.

The Primary Motive: Now Is What Counts

To better understand your motive for selecting a particular goal, it helps to recognize the difference between primary and secondary motives. Primary motives are your current desires. You are free to act directly to satisfy them. Secondary motives originate from unresolved past experience, unmet needs from an earlier stage of development that one has not come to terms with and let go of.

Secondary motives are secondary in that they can't be satisfied directly in the present. They are attempts to satisfy, with present actions, unmet needs for love, recognition, and acceptance. They are unconscious attempts to heal old wounds from the past; yet because they are

Play for Happiness

Twelve-year-old Stephanie loves to play the piano. She has a genuine desire to play and to play well, a primary motive. She also has a secondary desire for her parents' approval. They have paid for several years of piano lessons and expect her to live up to what they need her to be, to feel good about themselves (in this case, the reincarnation of Frédéric Chopin). When Stephanie is playing for her own enjoyment and concentrating on the music, she plays well. When she is playing for her parents' approval, she tenses and makes a lot of mistakes. While her efforts are concentrated on controlling the piano directly, she is proficient. Her proficiency diminishes as she attempts to control what is outside her field of control, namely the happiness of her parents.

	MOTIVE	DOMINANT FEEDBACK
PRIMARY	Make herself happy.	Music. Direct control of instrument and her response.
SECONDARY	Make her parents happy.	Response of her parents. Indirect attempt to control the response of her parents.

The only real power you have is the power to make yourself happy. If you set it up that others must be happy before you can be happy, you give all your power away. Don't confuse expressing your desire to contribute with making other people happy. Expressing your desire to contribute is a necessary part of your happiness. Do it for you. It is the responsibility of others to make themselves happy. Your happiness or lack thereof is the most important feedback you have on how well you are playing the game of life. Of course, to be happy, you must want to be happy. As Abraham Lincoln put it, "People are about as happy as they make up their minds to be." The stronger your intention to be happy, the more willing you are to get what you want. The stronger your intention to be happy, the fewer conditions you place on being so. Deciding to make yourself happy then helps you to get what you want, by freeing you to directly pursue it, while at the same time helping you to better handle setbacks.

unconscious, they are more likely to recreate than to heal the original pain. Secondary motives often appear as a desperate need to prove that one is worthy of love or respect. I call primary motives "current wants" and secondary motives "leftover needs." Think of your current wants as freely circulating emotional energy. Leftover needs represent blocks in the spontaneous flow of this energy. There is a sense of struggle and inner conflict built into activities motivated by leftover needs. On the other hand, what you want directly for its own sake, you naturally move toward with confidence.

Leftover needs generate thoughts about what you should or must do; current wants flow directly from present desires. It is this sense of natural flow that gives your actions authenticity and power. A stage or film actor who is merely thinking about how her character feels will be unconvincing in her portrayal of that character. She may say all of her lines perfectly, yet something vital is missing. A good actor is not simply pretending to feel happy or sad or whatever emotion the scene requires—she *is* feeling happy or sad. In the same way, when our actions are motivated by what we think we need or what think we should do, they lack the authenticity and emotional power that comes from genuine desire. Remember, you will enjoy what you *feel* you *want* much more than what you *think* you *need*. Your energy is where your desire is. Follow it.

The questions in this chapter are designed to put you in touch with your emotional attitude toward your goals. Your feelings will tell you whether the motive for your goal is a current want or a leftover need. Logic is of little use to you here. Often we construct elaborate logical reasons to justify what we think we need. We may invent high-minded moral or philosophical justifications for what we are doing—or simply assert that it is the only practical alternative—but a need is still a need, and a want is still a want. Listen to what your feelings are telling you about the choices you have made.

If you want the new career, the beautiful dream home, or the expensive sports car because you will enjoy them, that is one thing. If you feel you need them to prove that you have made it, that you are somehow superior, or that you can keep up with the Joneses, that's a horse of a different color—and a disappointing and unreliable horse at that.

Claim what you want directly, for its own sake. Don't use your goals as an indirect means of satisfying leftover needs or settling old scores.

The Origins of Secondary Motives

Where do secondary motives come from? We all went through a period in our lives when we were totally dependent on others for attention, nourishment, and protection—in short, for survival. Though we are now adults, capable of providing these things for ourselves, we may not recognize this fact at a subconscious level. We are like the man who is begging for food while he has a hundred-dollar bill in his pocket. The money is there, but he doesn't realize it. In the same way, as adults, the power of choice is available to us, but we don't always recognize or use it.

A study done some years ago will help to illustrate. In the study, fleas were kept in a box. A lid was placed on the box—one that would allow the fleas to jump only six inches high, far below these fleas' maximum jumping capacity. After a period of time, the lid was removed. Even though the fleas could now jump to the full extent of their ability, they continued to jump only six inches high. They had become conditioned to perform at a level far below their natural ability. As adults, we are often like these fleas; we still think we are in the box of dependency, even though the lid has been removed. We remain psychologically committed to our conditioned limitations.

Criminologists and law enforcement officials recognize that an important contributing factor to criminal recidivism is the repeat offender's fear of living in the outside world. As strange as it may seem, many repeat offenders actually feel safer within the physical confines of the prison walls and the psychological confines of a totally regimented life. To a lesser degree, many of us have grown accustomed to our own self-imposed prisons. As much as we claim to want freedom, we must confront the parts within that actually prefer the prison walls of our familiar limitations.

When you step out of the box of dependency, you realize that it's up to you to decide how high you can jump. As you break through the walls of conditioned limitations, you confront your freedom to claim

The true worth of a man is to be measured by the objects he pursues.

MARCUS AURELIUS

Put Your Goal to the Test

Motive Test #1: Am I making this choice freely, or do I feel compelled to prove something?

Motive Test #2: Do I seem defensive about my choice?

Motive Test #3: Do I want it for me, or am I trying to please someone else?

Motive Test #4: Do I want it enough to do whatever it takes to get it?

Motive Test #5: Do I sound enthusiastic and excited when I talk about this goal, or do I sound half-hearted and flat?

---

what you want, and your innate ability to make it happen. At first, this new freedom can seem frightening. After all, embracing new freedoms means accepting new responsibilities. Launching a new career, moving to a new city, breaking off dead-end relationships—something must be done. It's up to you to decide and to act. Don't let what you think you need keep you from what you *know* you want.

It is vitally important that you understand your motivations for selecting any major life goal. Below are a number of key questions to ask yourself about the choices you made in the last chapter. They will help you to make sure that your choices are coming out of who you really are.

Motive Test #1: Am I Making This Choice Freely?

What you feel compelled to do out of a leftover need, you will do less well and enjoy less than what you do directly out of free choice. If you think you need something, part of you rebels against it. You end up fighting with yourself. Letting go of the need sets you free to either forget about the goal connected with it, or to choose it freely and go for it from a place of genuine desire. The road to happiness opens up before those who give up trying to rectify past feelings of hurt and disappointment through present means, and commit themselves to pursuing their genuine desires.

The past *is* past. What's done *is* done. Spending your time and energy trying to fix it can only slow you down. When we are honest with ourselves, we must admit that we know whether we *really* want something or are merely trying to prove something. Our feelings don't lie. It's useless to fake a desire your heart isn't into. Let's look at the difference between a primary and secondary motive, through the eyes of two individuals pursuing the same goal.

Bill and Ralph both have the goal of attaining a law degree—yet their motives are entirely different. Bill thinks he needs his because he comes from a long line of lawyers, and his parents, friends, and family expect it of him. Bill really wants to be a journalist and dreads the thought of years in law school. He tells himself how practical getting a law degree is, how glad he'll be some day to have it, and how much easier it will be because his father is ready to pay for it. When you talk to Bill about his plans, he sometimes becomes defensive and testy. At other times, he seems resigned and rather blasé about the whole thing. Bill is letting his need for approval dictate his career choice. He's acting on a secondary motive.

Ralph is a Native American who grew up on a reservation. He wants a law degree so that he can protect his tribal homeland from the abuse of lumber, mining, and power utility companies. For him, mastery of the law is a practical way of expressing his caring for his people and protecting the land he loves. When you talk to Ralph about his plans, he seems fired up and raring to go. He can hardly wait for law school's opening date. Ralph is into his goal, heart and soul. He's acting from a primary motive.

Often we do not really want what we say or think we want. We confuse what we want with what we think will please others, or with what we think we should want. This mistake can cost us years of our lives and bring a great deal of unnecesary suffering. Remember that, as Isidor Rabi put it, "life is too short to spend your time doing something because someone else has said it's important. You must feel the

The conclusions of passion are the only reliable ones.

SØREN KIERKEGAARD

133

thing yourself." As we saw with Bill and Ralph, the "correctness" or appropriateness of a decision is not so much a matter of what we choose but why we choose it.

Motive Test #2: Do I Seem Defensive?

Be careful. Your mind can trick you, justifying a secondary motive with an elaborate case for why you should do something. Yet the fact of the matter remains: no matter how well-thought-out the arguments or how well the case is made, you still care about what you care about and don't care about what you don't care about. According to French philosopher Jean Jacques Rousseau, it's only when we fail to listen to our hearts that we need to resort to "the subtleties of argument." Only then do we need to justify our actions with elaborate rationalizations. You may have developed wonderful arguments, but if your heart and soul aren't into it, it's all for naught. Rationalizations are like the showpieces in a furniture store window; they may look good, but you can't really live in them. If you listen, your heart will tell you what is right for you and what isn't.

One way that you can pick up on defensiveness is to listen to yourself talking about your goals. Are you making a case? Do you feel a need to prove what a great choice you've made? Are you constantly trying to win converts over to your side? Or do you feel a calm confidence that the choices you have made are the right ones for you at this time in your life?

Tony is a natural-born musician who is pretending to be an accountant. The act is killing him. Tony majored in music at college, sang and wrote songs in a band, but the people closest to him told him he needed "a real job." Over and again, he heard them say, "You can't make it as a musician." Tony believed them and stopped believing in himself. So he put away the music and went back to school. Tony set a new goal and, after a lot of hard work, became a CPA. He tried to tell himself how much more practical his new career was. But he wasn't happy. Behind the numbers and calculations, there were a lot of frustrations.

It got so bad that he couldn't look at a sheet of music without getting emotionally upset, almost physically ill. He hadn't practiced for six years. When I first talked to Tony about it, he was practically in tears. There was nothing Tony could do about the time he had lost. All he could do was start listening to his heart again and bringing the music through, day by day. All he could do was to start believing in himself again. Tony learned that if a goal is not what you really want, it is not going to make you happy, even if you get it. You're going to feel like something is missing. What's missing is the part of you that is yearning to express itself. Listening to your heart will help bring it through. Of course, you may have to do something else for a time to support yourself, but don't neglect your heart's desire. Keep at it, or you will lose something that no amount of financial success can ever replace.

Motive Test #3: Do I Want It For Me?

Charlotte got married when she was twenty-one. She didn't really know who she was or what she wanted out of life, but when all of her friends got married, so did she. Her dominant motive was her need to conform to peer pressure. Deep down, Charlotte knew she didn't really love her husband and that she wasn't committed to making the marriage work. She pushed her feelings aside and, in her drive to prove she could be the perfect housewife, postponed working on the rest of her life. It wasn't long before she was really miserable, and her marriage suffered for it. Just last year, her husband filed for divorce. Now she is twenty-six and in a fix, looking back on the past five years and wondering what *that* was all about.

Charlotte didn't take into account her feeling for her husband or her commitment to the marriage, which were the primary issues in this decision. Instead, she was more concerned with the secondary issues of what other people (who, after all, didn't have to live with the decision) thought. Charlotte was acting for the quick fix of the approval of her family and peers. Since she made an important decision without listening to her feelings, it didn't solve her problems. It only compounded them.

Fortunately, Charlotte is one of the lucky ones. She got the message: Don't make a major life decision without asking your heart how it

We do not wish ardently for what we desire only through reason.

FRANCOIS DE LA ROCHEFOUCAULD

feels. *When making a decision, you are not running for election; your vote is the only one that really counts.* Check your choice to make sure you're doing it for you, that you're not just trying to please others. It pays to do a little soul searching. You may be motivated by a leftover need without realizing it.

Motive Test #4: Do I Care Enough?

It doesn't matter so much that anyone else agrees with your goal choices, but it does matter that you agree with them—in your gut. To achieve your important life goals, you're going to have to take risks. If it's a gut goal, you will want to; if it's a head trip, you will find a hundred reasons not to. You owe it to yourself to attempt only those goals that are backed by the power of primary motives, the ones you have a real feeling for. Otherwise, you're likely to fizzle out along the way, with debilitating effects on your self-esteem.

Franklin's dream was to go into business for himself. A few years back, his dream got creamed when he was "shot down" on his financing scheme. Then he gave up. Too easily, he gave up. Today, he makes a living working for a large corporation, selling things he doesn't believe in. He's comfortable enough financially, but inside he's seething. Franklin is only forty-two, but he feels defeated, resigned to enduring his "fate." Meanwhile, his great idea is on the back burner. He's not working for this corporation because he believes in what he is doing but because he thinks he needs to, to avoid risking the rejection he might have to face to make his dreams come true.

Since he set a goal without caring enough to stick with it—and failed—he uses it as an excuse for being cynical about all goals and about life in general. He feels he's been cheated, but he cheated himself by only making a half-hearted effort. Franklin's lesson for us is not to launch ourselves into goals unless we are willing to go the distance. Ask yourself if you care enough about the choices you have made to go the distance for them.

Motive Test #5: Do I Sound Enthusiastic?

If the thought of your goal makes you moan and wince, find another goal about which you can be convinced. If, when you think about it, you feel heavy or fatigued, you're out of your league. The Desire section (chapters 11-15) will show you ways to increase and sustain your desire, but it should be strong at the outset. The techniques in the Desire section are for enhancing the desires you already have, not for creating new ones. Go for what you really want.

What we are getting at with all this talk about feelings is that the major life decisions you make ought to grab you in the gut. They ought to reflect the real you, your best self. They ought to excite and inspire you. If your desire to achieve your goal is not intense at the outset, your chances of success are limited at best. Don't expect your desire to get stronger later on. It may, but be aware that later on, you will have the difficulty of the obstacles that must be overcome. Now, before you've made even a single effort or had even one setback, your desire must be intense if it is to carry you through.

The reason it didn't work for Charlotte, Bill, and Franklin was that they weren't listening to their hearts. They tried to live as though they could put their feelings on a shelf, as though they could ignore what they felt, and somehow things would work out. But, of course, they didn't. It never works to ignore the things you care about or to fake it by building a case for why you need something your heart isn't into.

Before you set your goals, reexamine the choices you made in the previous chapter. Ask yourself which do you want strongly, unequivocally, and which do you want only half-heartedly? The exercises that follow are designed to help you test your motive.

Knowing what you want is the first step toward getting it.

MAE WEST

Motive Testing

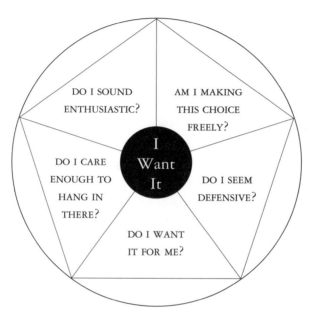

If you observe well, your own heart will answer.

—R. A. SCHWALLER DE LUBICZ

Back of every noble life, there are principles that have fashioned it.

—GEORGE HORACE LORIMER

One way or another, we all have to find what best fosters the flowering of our humanity in this contemporary life, and dedicate ourselves to that.

—JOSEPH CAMPBELL

The heart has its reasons that the mind knows nothing of.

—BLAISE PASCAL

Reason deceives us; conscience, never.

—JEAN JACQUES ROUSSEAU

Chapter 9 Exercises

❦

Give Yourself a Motive Test

Refer to the potential goals you identified at end of chapter 8. For each of these goals, ask yourself the following questions.

1. Am I making this choice freely, or do I feel compelled to prove something?

2. Is there anything I want more than this choice?

3. Do I want it for me, or am I trying to please someone else?

4. Do any of the following terms apply to the way I feel about to this goal: "I ought to," "I have to," "I should"?

5. Am I committed to following through with this goal, or am I likely to give up when things get difficult?

Getting Another Perspective

For this exercise, you will want to enlist the aid of a partner. Discuss your goal with your partner, and tell him or her why you want to achieve it. Ask your partner to listen to the energy level in your voice to determine whether or not your heart is really behind the choice you've made. When you finish your discussion, ask your partner to answer the following questions.

1. Do I sound enthusiastic and inspired when I talk about this goal, or do I sound blasé or lukewarm?

2. Do I seem defensive about my choice?

3. Do I sound like I want it enough to do whatever it takes to get it?

❧

Revising Your Potential Goals

If, after completing the motive evaluation process, you have determined that your goal was motivated by a secondary need, and not a present want, determine whether you will:

1. Release the need and select a different goal.
2. Release the need and determine to pursue the same goal from a different motivation.

Based on your answers, review the list of potential goals you selected on page 126, and revise them accordingly.

Goal Setting: Fixing Your Destinations

*We cannot seek or attain health, wealth, learning,
or kindness in a general way. Action is always specific,
concrete, individual, unique.*

JOHN DEWEY

Having explored the visions for your life, established priorities, and tested these against the desires of your heart, you are now ready to set goals. This chapter will provide you with the tools you need to construct realistic, written goals for the visions you chose and tested in the previous chapters. Some of you are familiar with the goal-setting process and have experience with writing and accomplishing definite goals. For you, the material in this chapter will serve as a review and as an opportunity to sharpen your focus and increase your motivation to set new goals. For the rest, which is to say for most of us, the material in this chapter will cover new ground. It may even provide the single most important key to realizing your dreams.

It's true, most of us have never learned how to set effective personal goals, much less to make goal setting a regular part of our everyday lives. We may even have some psychological resistance to doing so. How do *you* feel about setting goals? You have, no doubt, by this time heard that you *should* set goals. Goal setting is one of those things, like eating healthy foods and getting plenty of exercise, that virtually everyone pays lip service to—but few actually do. You may have said to yourself, "Yeah, yeah, I know I really ought to set goals," but then never gotten around to doing it.

Before you judge yourself too harshly, stop to consider that you may have only lacked the motivation that comes with understanding why something is important. Baron Von Stuben, the Prussian general who helped whip the ragtag band at Valley Forge into a disciplined fighting unit, said of his charges, "These Americans are different. In Europe I tell the troops what to do, and they do it. In America I tell them, and then I have to give them a reason." Before we get into the mechanics of goal setting, let's look at some reasons why it really *is* a good idea to set goals.

Why Set Goals?

Establishing meaningful personal goals for your life gives you something to work toward and look forward to, something to jump out of bed in the morning for—and each goal achieved stimulates you to do still more. It shows you what you *can* accomplish. Goal setting stimulates you to think big. It helps motivate you to make the most of your life. Once your goal is clearly fixed in your mind and written down on paper, you can begin to measure your progress toward that goal. Psychologists who have studied motivation in the workplace have concluded that feedback is the most effective way of improving motivation and increasing productivity. Feedback is most meaningful when it measures progress toward clearly defined goals.

Working toward your goals reduces stress and inner turmoil. It gives you a positive outlet into which to channel frustration and aggression. In his book *A Strategy for Daily Living,* Dr. Ari Kiev says, "In my practice as a psychiatrist, I have found that helping people to develop personal goals has proved to be the most effective way to help them cope with problems." Goal setting affords you the opportunity to take a constructive approach to your problems, to begin attacking them in a concerted and systematic way.

Creating definite written goals puts you into the top 5 percent. That's right. Only 5 percent of Americans have definite, clear, written goals. In major studies of successful, high-level executives, it was discovered that the sole characteristic that distinguished them from their less successful counterparts, and indeed from their subordinates, was the consistent use of definite, written goals. Think of all the artists, scientists, leaders, and achievers in every field who, though from humble beginnings, went on to accomplish great things. Their burning desire to achieve definite goals helped them to overcome amazing odds. They knew what they were after.

Developing clear goals puts you in charge of your life. You won't be a mere victim of fate, adrift in a sea of changing circumstance. You'll have direction; you'll know exactly what you want. Without goals, we tend to cling to the past and look ahead with fear and anxiety. With goals, the future becomes a creative challenge. You look forward to the coming years, because you know that you will progress— and how you will progress.

Yet, let's be honest, writing goals just isn't as much fun as dreaming about visions. A mental vision is complete within itself. Accomplishing a goal requires making considerable effort to achieve only a portion of the vision. In your imagination, you can experience the totality of a vision right now, with virtually no effort. On the other hand, achieving a goal takes a lot of work. It requires that we embrace a process that is necessarily fraught with frustrations. The primary frustration involves the limitation of time. A goal, to be a goal, must be accomplished within a specified time period. On the other hand, we can go on dreaming about our visions for the rest of our lives. Writing goals means putting yourself on the line. It means embracing the pressure of a deadline.

In order to convert your dreams into manifest realities, it's necessary to break them down into achievable steps, get these steps down on

If you cry "Forward," you must make plain in what direction to go.

ANTON CHEKHOV

paper, and then translate them into definite goals. Recall, from our earlier discussion of the Manifestation Formula, that visions require focus in order to manifest. Focus is a matter of bringing concentrated mental attention to a consciously selected target. If you have no goal, you have no target. Without a target, you have no place to fix your aim. You cannot employ the full power of your focus until you have selected definite goal targets. Goal setting, then, is an essential part of the Manifestaion Formula. Don't neglect it.

A Goal That's Writ Makes More of a Hit

Until it's written down, it's not a goal. It may be a wish, a dream, a vision, or a hope, but it's not a goal. A goal is a measurable written statement of a definite next step toward the realization of a particular vision. Getting your goals down on paper forces you to clarify and refine them. It helps you to spell out *exactly* what you want. As Francis Bacon put it, "writing [makes] an exact man."

A goal that is written down is much more likely to be achieved than one that is merely thought or talked about. In 1954, a survey was made of seniors about to graduate from Yale University. Only 3 percent of these students had definite written financial goals. Another 10 percent had a clear idea, but had not written it down. The vast majority, 87 percent, had no idea of their financial goals. Twenty years later, these Yale graduates were again interviewed. The results were startling. The 3 percent who had written financial goals had made more money than all the rest combined!

It's well known among financial planners and investment consultants that definite written goals play an important role in achieving financial success. What many people don't realize is that goal setting can be used with equal effectiveness in other areas of life. Armed with effective goal-setting skills, you become the captain of your ship, on your way to charting an exciting new course toward personal fulfillment in *every* area of your life.

Goal setting is easy to learn and apply. There is a formula, a kind of chemical equation to effective goals. Combine all the proper elements, mix with the catalyst of focused attention and a burning desire, and you *will* create the results you seek. There is no mystery in this, yet there is a kind of magic. Life itself becomes magical when you take control by determining your objectives.

Setting Your Goals: Making Level-Two Decisions

Chapter 7 discussed the formula: Focus = TARGET + AIM. We've already discussed AIM (how to increase your powers of concentration); now let's zero in on the target. The word TARGET serves as an acronym for an effective goal-setting formula. A well-stated goal fits all of the criteria below.

TARGET: Goal Formula

1. Time-Bound
2. Active
3. Realistic
4. Gradable
5. Exact
6. Tradable

Time-Bound

The first thing that sets a goal apart from a vision is that it is limited by time. We can't really think of goals without thinking in terms of deadlines. The sense of urgency and challenge that a goal provides results from the fact that it is limited in time. Goals must not only be achieved; they must be achieved within definite time constraints.

Don't confuse a goal with a purpose. A purpose is an open-ended intention without limitation in time and space. To become a better businessperson, artist, husband, mother, or gardener are all purposes. Conceivably, one could go on becoming better at these things indefinitely. Since a purpose is infinite, it is not achieved per se. A purpose is a direction. A goal is a destination. A goal is established for the sake of reaching a particular result, and it ends when the objective is met. A purpose goes on forever.

PURPOSE	GOAL
∞	A → B

NOT TIME-BOUND	TIME-BOUND
1. Sometime soon.	1. By June 1, 2004.
2. After I graduate.	2. By May 5, 2005.
3. In about five years.	3. By December 31, 2007.

Active

Use active verbs when stating your goals. Avoid passive "being verbs" or words that suggest participation rather than accomplishment. Below are action verbs you may want to use in writing your goals.

Accomplish	Develop	Inspire	Provide
Achieve	Direct	Invent	Publish
Acquire	Discover	Invest	Review
Build	Earn	Locate	Revise
Communicate	Establish	Manage	Revitalize
Complete	Evaluate	Manifest	Sell
Consolidate	Express	Master	Streamline
Consult	Exercise	Organize	Strengthen
Contribute	Forgive	Plan	Teach
Control	Illustrate	Practice	Train
Create	Improve	Present	Transform

Realistic

One the most common reasons why people fail to achieve their goals is that they start out with unrealistic ones. Remember that a goal represents only part of a vision. You don't try to eat a pizza in one gulping bite. You cut it into slices and chew it, one bite at a time. In the same way, move toward your vision in definite, well-measured steps, one at a time.

When I say that a goal must be realistic, I mean that, first of all, it must be possible to accomplish in the physical world. You're not superhuman; you can only do so many things at a time. A goal that might be realistic for a team of four or five to accomplish within a given time frame would most likely be unrealistic for a single individual within the same time period. Make sure your goals are realistic, given:

1. Your physical ability
2. Your knowledge and experience
3. Your other activities
4. Your self-image
5. Your material resources
6. The time you have allotted

Physical Ability: Take into account your physical ability and age. For example, if you're a thirty-two-year-old male, 5'5" in height, who played a little basketball in junior high—having a goal of playing as a star center in the NBA is certainly unrealistic. Similarly, if you're a woman in your late forties, who had a few childhood ballet lessons, and your aim is to become a prima ballerina with the American Ballet Theater—your goal is unrealistic. Sometimes, a goal that would be realistic for a twenty-year-old would be totally unrealistic for a forty-year-old; for other goals, the reverse holds true.

Relevant Experience and Knowledge: When setting your goals, evaluate your knowledge and experience in the areas you are considering. If you are noticeably lacking in either, you may need to allow additional time to achieve your goal. We often forget that it takes time and energy to learn. Consequently, we fail to take the learning curve into account when setting our goals. The learning curve is a simple concept that says that the more you do something, the better and faster you do it—up to a point.

For example, if your goal involves launching a new business, and you have never run one before, much of your energy in the first year or two will go into learning things that in later years will become more or less routine. If you work in sales, it may take you seven years before you are selling a million dollars worth of your product annually—yet only an additional year to reach two million dollars a year. What you have already gained in knowledge and experience speeds your progress toward steeper goals.

Time and Energy Commitments: In addition to your physical abilities and experiences, make sure that your goal is realistic in terms of your other goals and pursuits. For example, a goal that might be entirely realistic were it your only one, would probably be unrealistic if it were one of four challenging goals. The "realisticness" of a goal must be measured in terms of the time and energy you have available to devote to accomplishing it. When setting your goals, consider not only the demands of other goals but also those of your everyday commitments and responsibilities. Obviously, if you are a married person with young children, you have less available time for other pursuits than a single person.

Self-Esteem: Your self-esteem is yet another factor to consider when examining how realistic a goal is. Often, more than any lack of talent or ability, it's low self-esteem that holds people back. Your self-esteem affects not only your belief in yourself and your willingness to take risks but your ability to influence and motivate others. Ask yourself, "Is this goal within the range of what my present self-image will permit?" A short-term goal is probably unrealistic if it requires a significant number of behaviors that are incongruent with your current self-image.

Your self-image can, of course, be changed for the better. Indeed, one of the best ways of doing so is to set and accomplish goals that *are* realistic for you at this time. You needn't give up grand goals altogether. Just break them down into smaller sub-goals—and have at it! (Apply-

A straight path never leads anywhere except to the objective.

ANDRÉ GIDE

Overcoming Goal Phobia

As you begin to set long-term goals, you may experience a kind of psychic claustrophobia—a fear that you are somehow trapping, confining, or limiting yourself. Nothing could be further from the truth. In fact, it's more likely that the aversion you feel to setting goals is a defense mechanism for avoiding the pain you *already* feel about the limitations in your life. Setting and accomplishing meaningful goals will expand your horizons, options, and confidence. Don't let fear keep you from moving forward. You may feel intimidated by the prospect of taking greater responsibility for your life, particularly if you have long abdicated control. Acknowledge yourself for being willing to grow. You may feel frightened to look at your life in time frames that go out several years and, by extension, to face the fact that you have a limited time on this earth. Take pride in yourself for determining to make the most of the time you have. It may seem daunting to commit yourself to a path, the fruits of which you may not realize for years to come. Know that you can never go wrong by choosing to follow your heart, and nothing but good can come from the efforts you make to realize your dreams.

ing the techniques described in the Desire unit can also assist you in raising your self-esteem. Just don't plan on it happening overnight.)

Material and Financial Resources: When setting your goals, take into account your available financial and material resources. Some goals require significant financial investment. While there are many creative ways of raising money or using that of others, be realistic in assessing your financial wherewithal. If you are close to pauperdom, and your goal is to mastermind a hostile takeover of Microsoft in six months, your goal could be considered unrealistic. Again, recognize that what might be a realistic goal for you to accomplish in ten years could be entirely unrealistic if you expect to do it in two or three.

Estimating Time: Practice in setting and achieving goals will aid you in estimating time frames. It's worth noting that most people tend to allow too little rather than too much time. A good rule of thumb when estimating time frames is to calculate how long you think it will take to reach a goal and then add an additional 20 percent as a fudge factor. Of course, once you begin pursuing your goal, you can always change the time frame, should you come to realize that you have significantly over- or underestimated it.

Gradable

By *gradable*, I mean that progress toward your goal can be easily measured. Remember that one of the eight essential steps of the Manifestation Formula is feedback. Your goal should be stated in such a way as to suggest a feedback system, a way of monitoring progress toward the goal. If at all possible, it should be stated in quantifiable terms. Examples of gradable measures:

Dollars	Inches	Miles
Grade Point Average	Pages	Years
Hours	Percentages	Pounds

For many personal growth and relationship goals, empirical measures for grading progress are not readily available. In this case, use "percentage improvements," based upon intuitive perceptions. Here is an example of how it works. Imagine you have come to recognize the importance of increased emotional intimacy in your relationship with your life partner. You then indicate as one of your purposes: To become more emotionally intimate. A good intention—but let's make it gradable. Here is how you might do it.

To achieve at least 25 percent more emotional intimacy* in my relationship with my partner by March 15, 2003.

Attach to a goal such as this a clear definition of the term used. For example: As I define it, emotional intimacy means: . . .

While still subjective, putting a specific amount of improvement in writing clarifies the goal. With such a clearly defined goal, you can now develop a definite action plan. This plan might include things such as planning weekends alone together or attending relationship seminars with your partner, as well as scheduling regular uninterrupted times for dialoguing about your relationship. You will be delighted with the results you achieve as you apply the goal-setting process to areas you may have never thought possible.

NOT "GRADABLE"	"GRADABLE"
1. To golf better soon.	1. To achieve a handicap of three by January 1, 2003.
2. To lose weight next year.	2. To reduce my weight by twenty-five pounds by June 1, 2003.
3. To improve my grades.	3. To achieve a cumulative grade point average of 3.65 by June 1, 2004.

Exact

When writing your goals, spell out exactly what you want. Be *specific* and *precise*. A written statement of your goal ought to be clear enough that a total stranger could pick it up and know exactly what you mean. For instance, instead of saying that you want a new car, say that you want a certain model of Mercedes Benz or a Toyota. Instead of saying that you want to write a book, say that you want to publish a field guide to the birds of the Adirondacks, or the definitive guide to mushroom hunting. Instead of saying "get more exercise," say "jog two miles, four days a week," or "do weight training for thirty minutes, three days a week."

INEXACT	EXACT
1. To be making a lot more money.	1. To earn $175,000 a year by January 1, 2004.

2. To write a book.

2. To publish a field guide to birds of the Adirondacks by May 1, 2004.

3. To cut business costs.

3. To reduce marketing costs by 25 percent by October 1, 2003.

4. To buy a car.

4. To purchase a BMW two-door convertible by May 1, 2003.

Tradable

A good goal is one in which the trade-offs, or costs involved in achieving the goal, are explicitly recognized. When we take the time to consider and identify in advance what a goal is likely to cost us, we are helping to ensure not only that the goal is realistic but also that we are committed to seeing it through. Everything in life involves some kind of trade or exchange. You have to give to get. The emotional, financial, time, and energy, resources that you devote to any one pursuit can't be simultaneously channeled into something else.

For example, the pursuit of your goals may mean that you will have less time to spend with family or loved ones. It may mean that you will have to cut back on your social life or on certain leisure activities. Perhaps you'll have to cut back on some expenses in order to channel additional financial resources into your goals. Before you begin, take time to assess what it's going to take to achieve your goal. Include in your goal statement an estimate of what it is going to cost in terms of dollars and hours.

NOT "TRADABLE"

1. To earn a pilot's license by June 1, 2003.

"TRADABLE"

1. To earn a pilot's license by June 1, 2003, at a cost of $5,500 and 60 hours.

2. To get an M.B.A. by
   June 15, 2006.

2. To complete the M.B.A. course at
   Harvard by June 15, 2006,
   at a cost of two years and $50,000.

Long-Range Goals

Of course, goals come in all shapes and sizes. There are long-, short-, and medium-range goals. This chapter is designed to help you set long-range goals. I define long-range goals as those that will take you at least one year to accomplish. It's a good idea to set goals of one, three, and five years for each of your high-priority life areas. Good luck, and have fun setting the goals that will take you where you want to go.

Fix Your Target

The examples that follow will help you to see the difference between goals that fit the TARGET formula and those that don't. Make sure that your goals are on target.

NO GOAL	GOAL
1. To write.	1. To complete a manuscript of my first novel by June 5, 2004, at a cost of three hours per day.
2. To run more.	2. To complete the Boston Marathon in April, 2004, at a cost of $5,000 and twenty-seven hours per week training time.
3. To become more patient.	3. To achieve 20 percent more patience with my children by July 1, 2004, at a cost of three and a half hours a week.

Goal Setting

You give birth to that on which you fix your mind.

—ANTOINE DE SAINT EXUPÉRY

Our plans miscarry because we have no aim. When a man does not know what harbor he is making for, no wind is the right wind.   —SENECA

Go confidently in the direction of your dreams. Act as though it were impossible to fail.   —DORTHEA BRANDT

Life can be pulled by goals just as surely as it can be pushed by drives.

—VIKTOR FRANKL

Nothing is particularly hard if you divide it into small jobs.

—HENRY FORD

Chapter 10 Exercises

❧

Refining Your Potential Goals

Now it's time to convert your potential goals into definite goals that fit the TARGET formula. Refer to your answers to the final exercise at the end of chapter 8, and convert each of these *potential* goals into an *actual* goal, using the TARGET formula. See examples on pages 146–153.

1.

2.

3.

4.

5.

6.

7.

8.

Make Your Goal Hit the Target

On the left-hand side of a sheet of paper, state your goals. Next, divide the rest of the paper into six columns and label these as follows:

GOAL	Time-Bound	Active	Realistic	Gradable	Exact	Tradable
1.						
2.						
3.						
4.						
5.						
6.						
7.						
8.						

Place a check in the columns to signify that the corresponding criteria have been met. Completing this checklist will help to ensure that all your goals are hitting the TARGET formula.

Master List of Lifetime Goals

Record your goals on a master list. Keep them close at hand for easy reference. Post your goals on a bulletin board, refrigerator door, or wall, where you will be sure to see them.

1.

2.

3.

4.

5.

6.

7.

8.

Bringing It All Together: Values • Goals • Benefits

Here is an exercise that will help to remind you of what your goals mean to you—how they reflect your values and will bring you the benefits you desire. Complete the following statements for each of your goals:

Because I value _____

My goal is to _____

Achieving this goal will bring the following benefits into my life:

Reflect upon your answers to these questions from time to time for a motivational lift.

❧

We've Only Just Begun

Congratulations! You've set your lifetime goals. Give yourself a hearty and well-deserved pat on the back. I would love to tell you, now that you have made your selections and written them down as proper goals, that these goals will automatically and immediately manifest. But the truth is, that just isn't so. Getting from the goal to the manifestation is often a long row to hoe. Writing the goal down on paper is just the beginning, albeit an important one. To make your goals come alive, you must charge them with desire and maintain an unwavering commitment to their manifestation. In the Desire and Commitment sections, you'll have the opportunity to learn and apply principles that will significantly improve the quality of your life. Perhaps even more importantly, applying the material in the next two sections will help you reach your goals with greater speed and ease. You deserve the best, don't miss the rest!

PART III

Desire

Desire:
Creating Lasting Motivation

——

See It: Visualization

——

Believe It: Affirmation

——

Receive It:
Act with Expectation

——

Value It: Reward Your Progress

Desire: Creating Lasting Motivation 11

Nothing great was ever achieved
without enthusiasm.

EMERSON

To come to life, the creative ideas that you pictured in the Vision unit and refined into goals in the Focus unit must be charged with the energy of desire. It's desire that transforms sterile goals into living realities. Now that you know exactly what you want, the question becomes: How can you sustain the motivation necessary to reach your goals? How can you ensure that you will remain excited about achieving your goals long after the thrill of the initial inspiration has faded? This chapter, and the others in the Desire section, will provide the understanding and tools you need to develop and maintain a burning desire to see your goals through to completion. As we will see, enlisting the power of your subconscious mind is the key not only to staying highly motivated but also to bringing fun and a sense of ease to your efforts.

Desire Puts Life into Ideas

In much the same way that a seed requires water to germinate, visionary ideas require emotional energy to become active in the physical world. Without the infusion of the energy of desire, the exciting visions you hold for your life will remain as lifeless as the mannequins at Macy's. Desire provides the emotional energy necessary to transform thoughts into things and actions. Desire is the motor that propels you to act. It's born out of the creative discontent that arises as you compare your visions of how things might be, with the daily experience of how they are now. Standing on the foothill, looking at the summit, yearning to be, know, or achieve more—that's desire.

What You Focus on, You Want

Take a clear vision, give it persistent, focused attention, and it intensifies into a burning desire. Think of your vision as light. A magnifying glass focuses the light. The resulting fire is desire. You come to desire what you focus on. Remember: FIRST THE IDEA, THEN THE FOCUS, AND THEN THE DESIRE. First you see it (even if only in your mind's eye), then you want it. Food, sex, or a goal—first you see it, then you want it—that's the way it goes. People living in remote tribes in the Amazon jungles do not desire washing machines. They have never seen washing machines. Wanting them is not yet a possibility for these folks. We can only want what we have physically or mentally seen.

Consider this fact in light of our previous discussion of genius. The genius has a burning desire to translate a vision she has seen in her mind into form in the outside world. The reason she may seem a little crazy, especially at the start, is because no one else has seen what she has seen, and consequently, they can't understand what she is after. They don't understand her desire because they haven't seen her vision. Don't be surprised if, at times, others don't understand your desires. After all, they haven't seen your visions.

Fire Up Your Enthusiasm

Desire is both the product of focus and a power unto itself. The more you focus your attention on an object or objective, the more you want it. This is why it is so vitally important that you diligently guard what you put your attention on. Don't focus on things that you would rather not have happen, or your subconscious mind may begin attracting them to you. We can actually create situations we fear by repeatedly imagining them and charging these scenes with intense emotional energy. Focus on your goals, and your desire for them grows ever stronger. This is the passive, or indirect, way of exciting desire.

He did it with all his heart, and prospered.

2 CHR. 31:21

Desire can also be aroused in an active, direct, and assertive way. You don't have to sit around and wait for desire to hit you. You can determine to pour feelings of longing and enthusiasm into your visions. Pull your visions into reality by endowing them with powerful feelings of desire. Don't be bashful about wanting what you want—want it, want it, want it! Want it with unbridled passion and unmitigated zeal. Want it with such intensity that your socks start to steam. The stronger your passion for them, the quicker your desired results will manifest.

Many people hesitate to use this aggressive aspect of desire. Some have been taught that it is undignified, or even impolite, to get excited—to show much enthusiasm about what they want. Others have been repeatedly told that they can't have what they want. They have learned to mute their desires in order to avoid any frustration, disappointment, or embarrassment about not getting what they want. Still others think that it's just not cool to want anything intensely. And it isn't cool. Desire is hot, a blazing fire of emotional energy. It will get you fired up and raring to go—if you let yourself go with it. Don't hold back. Dare to get really excited about what you want.

How to Make Your Enthusiasm Last

In the remainder of this chapter, you'll learn about the powerful role the subconscious mind plays in desire, and how you can get this part of your mind working with you to achieve your goals. Desire is the engine that drives the process of manifestation, and your subconscious mind either fuels or cools the engine of desire. In the rest of this unit, you will learn how to get full power from your desire engine, how to keep it running well and avoid costly breakdowns. Release the abundant energy reserves of the subconscious mind, and you turn the key that ignites maximum motivation. Remember, the stronger your desire, the sooner your dreams become realities.

Subconscious Mind Power Is the Key

Again, focus creates desire, and desire turns thoughts into actions. As a result of the work you did in the Vision and Focus units, you now have well-stated goals that fit with your purposes in different areas of your life. Presumably, your conscious mind is now riveted on the goals. That's a wonderful and exciting step forward. Yet psychologists tell us that less than 10 percent of the mind's power and activity is conscious; the remaining 90 percent lies below the conscious level.

A study at the University of Minnesota concluded that 94 percent of all human activity is controlled, directed, or regulated by the subconscious mind. For example, most of the mental work of speaking, reading, and calculating takes place at an unconscious level, to say nothing of sitting and walking, much less breathing, digesting, and so on.

Your conscious mind is the decision-maker; your subconscious mind, the doer. These two aspects of the mind usually work quite well together. For example, your conscious mind decides to get up and get a drink of water. Then the subconscious takes over and instructs nerves to fire and muscles to perform. If you had to consciously think about all the things that the subconscious handles for you, you would get little else done. The subconscious mind is good at doing things, but it can't decide. The conscious mind is great at making decisions, but it can't carry them out without the aid of the subconscious. Working together, these two make a great team.

Your conscious mind has decided to achieve certain definite goals. Now, in order to actually accomplish these goals, you'll want to make sure that you have the full cooperation and active participation of your subconscious mind. The search-command effect of repeated concentration on your goals will help to bring useful data into your awareness, but in order for the subconscious mind to take over and do what your conscious mind is asking of it, it must be properly wired. Much like a computer, the subconscious mind can only do what it's programmed or "wired" to do.

The Subconscious Mind Can Only Do What It Is Wired to Do

To get an experience of the power of wiring, take out a piece of paper and a pen. Write your name as many times as you can in fifteen seconds with the hand you usually use. Next, take fifteen seconds and write your name with the other hand. Compare the results. You have just demonstrated to yourself the power of habit, of the way you are wired.

You can't effectively do what you haven't been wired to do. On the other hand, what you *have* been wired to do, you can do effectively, even after years of absence. When people say, "It's like riding a bike; you never forget"—they mean that you are wired for it. You are wired to read a book. It may have taken years to get the wiring, but now you just do it. You never think about it, but you are wired to speak in sentences. It probably took awhile to get that wiring down. (Remember Da-Da and Ma-Ma?) Most likely, you are wired to drive a car. Are you wired to dance the waltz or rumba? Learning the steps is getting the wiring intact. Once you are wired, you just go to it.

According to noted brain physiologist Dr. John C. Eccles: "When you learn anything, a pattern of neurons forming a chain is set up in your brain tissue. This chain or electrical pattern is your brain's way of remembering. The electrical pathways within the nervous system insure the repetition of habitual tasks. Typically, as the years go by, we become less adventurous. Becoming 'set in your ways' is, in a sense, an act of physiology. The resistance you may feel to doing different things

Only passions, great passions, can elevate the soul to great things.

DENIS DIDEROT

or doing the same things differently is a function of the additional energy required to establish a new electrical pattern of neuron firings."

Often, when an individual becomes excited about a new goal or direction for her life, she runs smack into the programming of her subconscious mind. That programming may run exactly counter to her stated goal (counter-programming), or it may simply lack the necessary information needed to execute her goal (insufficient programming). When Jeremy was in the third grade, his art teacher held up in front of the class a picture of a rabbit that he had drawn and said, "Class, look at how stupid this is. Does this look anything like a rabbit?" after which all the kids in class chimed, "Nooooo!" and began to laugh. From then on, Jeremy felt like he couldn't draw a straight line with a ruler. From then on, he had *counter-programming* for *any* artistic endeavors. When Gloria moved from Texas to Colorado, she decided she wanted to learn to ski. She had no negative conditioning about skiing; she simply hadn't been wired to do it yet. She had *insufficient programming* for skiing.

Typically, counter-programming is a more difficult problem to overcome than insufficient programming. This is because counter-programming often requires a transformation of core beliefs, while insufficient programming merely requires the development of new attitudes or skills. For some goals, you may have both counter- and insufficient programming. Todd Wilson wants to become a spokesperson for a cause he believes in. His conscious mind says, "Okay, Wilson, go out there and do it." Trouble is, his subconscious mind isn't properly wired for professional speaking. Todd has negative programming about his self-image and the way he projects himself to others. He also lacks skill and experience in the mechanics of organizing and preparing a speech. Todd recognizes that he has a good deal of work to do in terms of developing a commanding vocal presence and a polished professional delivery. In order for Todd to become a great speaker, he is going to have to do some major rewiring. That's the bad news. The good news is that there are definite, proven methods that Todd can employ to achieve the results he wants. We will discuss these at length throughout the remainder of the Desire section of this book.

Every time you do something, it becomes easier to do it again. This is a function of the wiring that occurs. Emerson said, "A great part of courage is the courage of having done the thing before." If we are to achieve our goals, we must get this power working for us. To accomplish this, it is essential that we recognize the following psychological truth: *The subconscious mind does not know the difference between what is real and what is imagined.* Let's explore some of the evidence of this.

The Subconscious Mind Doesn't Know the Difference Between What Is Real and What Is Imagined

A study was conducted in which the brain waves of subjects were measured as they responded to various stimuli—for example, the firing of a gun, a dog barking, a woman dancing. Next, the subjects' brain waves were recorded as they imagined the same events. There was no significant difference between the brain wave readings for the imagined and the real events. Individuals imagining a gun being fired generated brain waves similar to those produced in people who actually heard a gun going off. Likewise, with the other stimuli, there was no difference between the real and the imagined.

At the University of Chicago, an important study was done in which the effects of the imagined performance of a task were measured against actual practice. In the study, three groups were selected, and their ability at shooting basketball free throws was measured. Next, one group was told to practice shooting for one hour each day, for twenty days. The second group was told to imagine shooting baskets for one hour each day, for the same twenty-day period. The third group was told to refrain from mentally or actually shooting baskets for the duration of the experiment.

The researchers were astonished by the results. There was no significant difference between those who actually practiced and those who did so mentally. The performance of the first group improved 24 percent. The performance of the second group increased 23 percent, while

Sooner murder an infant in its cradle than nurse unacted desires.

WILLIAM BLAKE

167

the performance of the third group remained unchanged—again, evidence that the subconscious mind cannot tell the difference between what is real and what is imagined. Now, let's review what we have learned:

1. The subconscious is the most powerful part of the mind.
2. The subconscious can only do what it has been wired to do.
3. The subconscious mind doesn't know the difference between real and imagined experience.

Do these three facts give you any ideas? That's right. If you could trick your subconscious mind into thinking that you have already done what you want to do, then you could get it to cooperate with your conscious mind and its goals. The subconscious mind and the powerful 90+ percent of mind power it represents would perform as though new behaviors and attitudes were long established habits. Remember, your subconscious mind believes what it has seen, heard, and felt, but it doesn't know whether it was real or imagined. So long as the neuron chain has been established, or wired, you can act in a manner consistent with your goals. It doesn't matter whether that wiring comes by means of actual or imagined experience. The trick is to enter the behavior you want to manifest into your subconscious memory files. Then, when it comes time to do the task, you can do it with ease.

Subconscious Software

The universe is change; our life is what our thoughts make it.

MARCUS AURELIUS

Up to now, we've been focusing on how our mental hardware works. Now let's look at some software programs you can run to augment or transform your existing subconscious data base. I call these master programs "See It," "Believe It," "Receive It," and "Value It." They can be run to great effect, either alone or in combination. You are probably aware that there are a variety of specific techniques for altering the content of your subconscious data bank. These include (to name just a few): visualization, affirmation, subliminal programming, behavior modification, modeling, and hypnosis. What you may not know is that

Good Things Are Coming Your Way

Entering a vision into the subconscious mind reminds me of the time my little nephew sent away for a toy. It was one of those box-top deals, and he thought it was a big deal. His little heart was thumping as he dropped the letter in the box. He knew that any day, an exciting package would arrive. He could hardly wait; he just about drove his mother nuts. Yet his interest soon turned to other things, and he forgot all about it. The day the package arrived, he was surprised and thrilled at the results. Entering your vision into your subconscious mind is like dropping the letter in the box. It's nice to know good things are coming your way, isn't it?

all these, and many other techniques for transforming subconscious programming, rely in one way or another on the "See It," "Believe It," "Receive It," and "Value It" principles. Because every effective method for reprogramming the subconscious employs one or more of these principles, understanding how they work is imperative to obtaining maximum results. Each of the next four chapters is devoted to exploring one of these principles in depth.

Reading the material and employing the techniques in these chapters will give you the understanding and tools necessary to ensure lasting motivation. Doing the exercises in this unit will help you to: see the results you desire as already accomplished (See It), believe that what you want will come to pass (Believe It), act with the confidence that comes from knowing you will ultimately succeed (Receive It), and reward yourself for the positive efforts you make to achieve your goals (Value It). By making the future you want so vivid that you can see, feel, and hear it, you will convince your subconscious mind that the results you desire simply *must* manifest. As you train yourself to focus on and reward yourself for the constructive steps you take, your conscious, as well as your subconscious, mind will become pervaded with a growing sense of inevitability about your ultimate success.

Show Your Subconscious Mind Who's Boss

By doing the work in the upcoming chapters, you'll not only be feeding your subconscious mind with images, beliefs, and feelings of positive futures, but in effect telling it, "Look buster, I'm in control here. You're going to do what I want you to." Now, at first, your subconscious may put up a fight, but once it sees that you mean business and intend to "get with the program," it will relent and go along. It's much like taming a wild horse. At first, the horse will do anything to get you off of it. But once it is trained, it will easily and willingly do your bidding. Sound too good to be true? Well, it works, but you must take into account the overload barrier.

Watch Out for the Overload Barrier

We are constantly bombarded with stimuli that pull for our attention. Scientists have estimated that by the time the average person is thirty years old, he will have stored ten quadrillion (10,000,000,000,000,000) bits of information. In order to prevent overload and to protect the existing database, the subconscious mind erects a security barrier to deflect new data that is inconsistent with the original programming. This barrier must be penetrated if we are to gain the necessary access to the subconscious mind. In order to input new data on the "See It," "Believe It," "Receive It," and "Value It" programs, we must get past the security systems of the subconscious mind. See the material highlighted on the next page for keys to bypassing the subconscious security system. Keep these keys in mind as you apply the techniques outlined in the next four chapters.

Hacking the Subconscious Security System

To get your subconscious mind to accept new beliefs, attitudes, and behaviors, you must get them past its security system. Any good computer hacker knows that it is easy to bypass security systems if you know the right keys, the codes or passwords that will let you in. Here are some keys that will remind you of important methods for gaining access to the subconscious mind and inputting new data into its files.

Per Diem: By doing your subconscious programming exercises (for example, visualization and affirmation) every day, you help to ensure that the messages you are sending are making a deep impression on your subconscious mind.

Fait Accompli: Enter the new activity as though it has already been accomplished. For example, when you talk to yourself about your goals, talk as if you have already accomplished them. Visualize yourself already enjoying the results you seek.

Nocturnal: Work at night. Security is weakest when the mind is tired. Data slipped in just before you go to sleep is more easily accepted by your subconscious mind. In addition, you will be processing and integrating the new data while you sleep.

Alpha: If you are using the subconscious programming techniques by day, entering the alpha state before inputting new data into the subconscious mind will help to neutralize the mind's security system (see instructions for entering the alpha state, on page 48).

Multisensual: Engage as many of your senses as possible. The more of your senses that you employ in your imaginative rewiring, the better the chances that the data will "take" on the subconscious mind files. See, hear, touch, smell, and taste the results you want.

Reinforcement: You help to reinforce your rewiring efforts by keeping a record of them. Rewarding yourself for behaviors consistent with your goals has a similar effect.

Desire

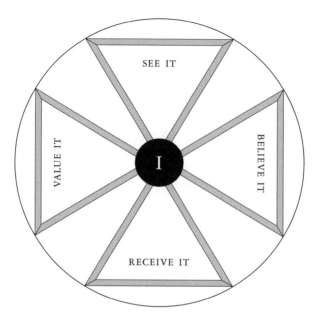

The Desire Formula

See It: Because you must have a picture to act.

Believe It: Because you believe what you hear repeated.

Receive It: Because how well you do depends on how you feel about it.

Value It: Because feedback is the strongest form of motivation.

Chapter 11 Exercises

❧

Evaluating Your Desire

The purpose of this exercise is to help you identify where you stand in terms of the four elements of Desire in relation to any particular goal. Below, rate yourself on a one-to-ten scale in each of the four categories. One indicates the lowest level of ability; and ten, complete facility. Then, as you move through the Desire section, pay particular attention to the areas you scored the lowest in, and think about how you can boost your desire quotient in that area.

1. State your goal.

2. Now ask yourself, "Can I see it clearly? Do I have a mental picture of the results I'm after? Can I visualize, step-by-step, the process of achieving this goal? Do I see myself in the picture with what I want?" Now rate yourself on how clear your vision is.

3. Next ask yourself, "Do I really believe I am going to achieve this goal? Do I believe I deserve to achieve this goal? Am I convinced that I am going to be, have, or do this?" Now rate yourself on how strong your belief is.

4. Now ask yourself, "Am I willing to receive it? Am I ready to seek out and ask for the help I need? Am I prepared to act as though this result has already been achieved?" Now rate yourself on how willing you are to receive it.

5. Finally, ask yourself, "Do I value the process of achieving this goal? Am I prepared to acknowledge myself for my efforts, or am I depending on others to validate them? Am I willing to establish a system to monitor my progress toward my goal?" Now rate yourself on how much you value it.

❧

A Final Note: Your Desires Change with You

As you grow and evolve, so do your desires. Desire is a tremendous power. Yet it is a neutral power. Just as fire may heat your home and cook your food—or burn your home and destroy your possessions—the power of desire can be used for good or ill. One could say that life is about learning what to want. Like a hero or heroine in a fairy tale who has been granted a certain number of wishes, you will gain in wisdom as you fulfill your desires. You learn what to want. By consciously using the principles of manifestation, you will realize your desires more quickly than you otherwise might. This will accelerate the evolution of your desires, leading ultimately to the greatest wisdom.

See It: Visualization

12

Vision is the art of seeing things invisible.

JONATHAN SWIFT

Creative visualization is an indispensable tool for achieving your dreams. It harnesses the awesome power of your creative imagination and puts it to work on your goals. Don't confuse visualization with the process of seeking a vision, which was discussed in chapters 4 and 5. When you're *seeking a vision,* your goal is to transcend the conscious mind and enter into the realm of deep intuitive knowing. When you're *visualizing*, you're consciously directing your attention to focus on specific images of the results you seek. This chapter will explore a variety of creative visualization strategies that you can use to turn your fondest dreams into living realities.

Another way of thinking of visualization is as a kind of mental rehearsal. As a Zen master once put it, "When the task is done beforehand, then it is easy." The task is done beforehand when it is first done in the mind. Remember, the subconscious mind doesn't know the difference between real and imagined experience. When you visualize yourself doing something in advance of actually doing it, you have, in a sense, faked out your own inner resistance to doing it. You have made what was unknown and unfamiliar into something known and familiar. When it comes time to actually do the activity in question, it seems easy because you *feel* as though you have already done it.

Visualization: It May Be Hurting You

Whether you realize it or not, you are already using visualization. Your subconscious mind is constantly imaging and rehearsing. If you could step outside of your head and objectively see the television screen of your own mind, you would realize that there is hardly a minute in your entire day when you aren't visualizing something. You would probably also be shocked to discover the negative character of much of what you are viewing. Social commentators frequently point out the adverse psychological effects of violent and fearful programming on our TV screens—how much more destructive to watch a steady stream of negative or fearful images on the TV screens of our own minds!

Too often, we picture less than the best for ourselves. You're running late and haven't had a chance to call home. You imagine your mate will be angry with you when you arrive. When you finally reach home, you are tense and defensive. Though your mate was not initially upset, he or she subconsciously picks up the messages you are telegraphing and soon becomes so. You assume that you were right all along to think he or she would be upset, and fail to recognize your part in creating the conflict.

While preparing for a job interview, you visualize yourself tensing up and becoming speechless or totally inarticulate when asked certain difficult questions. You hope the interviewer won't ask these questions, but continually worry that he will. Sure enough, on the day of the interview, the dreaded questions come, and you respond with a tangled tongue, just as you had visualized yourself doing. Instead, you might have thought out good responses in advance and visualized yourself giving them in a relaxed and masterful way.

Tita has long feared being abandoned by her husband Roger and consequently has become obsessively jealous. When Tita is not with Roger, she often visualizes him being with other women. Her visualizations make her extremely upset, destroy the fabric of trust in the relationship, and keep her from focusing on more constructive endeavors in her own life. While Roger has remained entirely loyal and faithful to his wife, her jealous accusations are beginning to drive them apart. Tita doesn't realize how her visualizations are helping to create the very thing she is afraid of.

If we want to enjoy life and achieve our goals, we have to stop letting our imaginations get the best of us, and start putting them to good use. If you find your imagination running away with you, say "STOP!" and immediately substitute a mental picture of something you *want* to manifest. Don't allow your attention to be drawn into negative pictures that run counter to your stated goals. Use your imaginative power to get what you want.

Man can only receive what he sees himself receiving.

FLORENCE SCOVEL SHINN

Visualization: It Is Already Helping You

You are already using visualization to help accomplish many everyday activities. We do this so naturally and automatically that we hardly realize we are doing it. Since Mike is familiar with his favorite food store, he mentally pictures himself picking up the items he wants, before he actually goes to get them. He ends up spending much less time at the store. When Maria plans her Christmas shopping, she makes a list, then mentally pictures where she will find each of the items and sees herself going to get them. Having chosen the perfect gift for each person on her list, she doesn't get drawn into a random shopping spree. Let's say you are planning to travel by plane to a familiar destination. You see yourself driving to the airport, parking your car, checking in, boarding the plane, arriving at your destination, greeting your loved ones, and so on. The ability to see things in advance of doing them is comforting and reassuring. This explains why some people become anxious when travelling to new places. They don't have a mental picture of where they are going or of what they will do when they get there. This applies to reaching any goal—the clearer your mental images, the less stress you will have about reaching your goals.

Over and again, throughout the course of the day, you are using visualization to help you accomplish a variety of tasks. Think of it! You imagine what you do, and then you do it. You imagine the image you project to the world, and that's the one you project. You imagine what you will say, and then you say it. You imagine how you are going to say it, and that's the way you say it. Again, all of this is usually happening so quickly and automatically that we scarcely even notice it.

Apply Creative Visualization to Your Lifetime Goals

The same tool that helps you do your grocery shopping or plan a trip can be used to speed and ease your progress toward the major goals of your life. The difference is that you will want to hold the image of a major goal in front of your awareness more frequently and intensely than you would a simple and familiar task like picking up groceries at the market. Since life goals often require overcoming limiting self-concepts and learning an array of new behaviors, they call for more frequent, intense, and persistent visualizations. Perseverance is critical. A random or half-hearted effort is unlikely to yield the results you desire. Continue picturing within your mind's eye the outcomes you seek, until they become visible in the outside world. Below, we discuss five different ways of using visualization to aid you in manifesting your goals.

Visualization Can Help You:

1. **Boost Confidence:**   Increase your confidence by recalling past successes.

2. **Plant Dream Seeds:**   Impregnate your subconscious mind with seed images of the outcomes you desire.

3. **Plan Ahead:**   Break down the activities needed to reach your goals into specific, concrete steps.

4. **Improve Performance:**   Increase your effectiveness in the performance of a variety of daily activities.

5. **Accelerate Learning:**   Speed the learning of new behaviors and attitudes.

Visualization Strategy #1: Boost Confidence

When you are about to do something new, particularly something you feel is risky, it's a good idea to spend some time picturing the positive results you desire. It is equally important that you be on guard against negative images that the new activity may trigger in your subconscious mind. Images of associated negative events from your past may begin to appear before your mind's eye. These negative pictures seem to provide "evidence" that you can't do what you're about to attempt, or that you'll do it poorly. They seem to say, "You screwed up before—so you'll probably do it again."

Counter this tendency by recalling past successes. Make a list of at least fifty things you have successfully done before. These successes can be small or large. Include everything from learning to ride a bike to graduating from college, from performing in a school play to landing your first job, from learning to play an instrument to asking for your first date. Include anything you have created, be it a poem, a song, or a company. Also include times when you demonstrated character strengths such as patience, compassion, or self-discipline. Recalling images of past strength or competence provides a positive emotional context for embracing new challenges. These images seem to say, "You were successful before; you'll be successful again."

Visualization Strategy #2: Plant Dream Seeds

While it's helpful at times to look back on past successes, in the main, you will want to use visualization to look ahead. Too often, we spend more time than is necessary replaying past events. We get caught up in "woulda, coulda, shoulda." Beyond learning from it, there is little we can do about the past. Don't let your imagination dwell on what might have been; keep it focused on what will be. Send it out in front of you to prepare and smooth the way. Give it a picture of what your ultimate success looks like, and let it go to work on creating it. Plant dream seeds in your subconscious mind.

When using visualization to plant dream seeds, see the outcomes you desire as whole and complete. Don't concern yourself with how you will accomplish them. For example, if you want to publish a book, don't look at images of yourself writing it; visualize yourself signing copies of it in the bookstores. If you want to open your own store, don't see images of yourself financing or furnishing it; see yourself going about your business in the already opened store. It's your consistent, focused attention on images of the outcomes you desire that impresses them on the subconscious mind. In time, it begins to accept these dreams as inevitable realities and so begins attracting into your world the connections, knowledge, and opportunities necessary to realize them. In ways that you could never have anticipated, your subconscious mind will transform the physical reality of your life to fit with the images in your mind's eye.

Of all the uses of visualization, planting dream seeds has the greatest power to transform your life. While this use of visualization seems almost magical, it has been proven effective time and again by those who dared to believe that they could make their dreams come true.

Long before he was elected, Abraham Lincoln repeatedly imagined himself in the role of President of the United States. Lincoln would mentally see himself carrying out the duties of the chief executive. Napoleon visualized himself as the Emperor of the French before such a position even existed.

Anyone who has ever had the pleasure of planting a garden knows that seedlings require greater protection, care, and attention than mature plants. So it is with your dream seeds. Give them the loving attention they need to take root and grow strong within your subconscious mind. Translate your lifetime goals into positive images or scenes that represent their completion or realization. Then, as often as you can, and especially before you go to sleep, visualize those scenes in your mind's eye. Water the garden of your dreams with regular loving attention, and watch the seeds bear fruit.

If you are having difficulty picturing these images in your mind, the following exercise can help. Buy a blank scrapbook or journal and designate it as your "See It Scrapbook." Fill this scrapbook with images that depict the successful completion of your goals. Draw them. Cut pictures out of magazines. Take photographs and paste them in. Be creative and have fun. Get out your scissors, drawing pencils, glue, tape, and paints; work in whatever medium most appeals to you. Write captions beneath your illustrations, referring to them as if they had already occurred. Once you have collected a number of images, look at them each and every evening before you retire. Then close your eyes, and see the image in your mind's eye, in exact detail. Be sure to put yourself in the picture with the things you want. Mentally rehearse the outcomes you desire. Then go to sleep and let your subconscious mind do the rest.

Make additional copies of your success pictures and hang them on the wall above your bed or on your bathroom mirror—wherever you will be sure to see them every day. By constructing the images you want, and holding them in the forefront of your awareness, you change your reality to fit the new pictures. Remember, the subconscious mind is much like a computer; the thoughts and images it is programmed to accept will eventually manifest in physical reality. In the end, what you see *is* what you get.

Your imagination is your preview of life's coming attractions.

ALBERT EINSTEIN

181

Visualization Strategy #3: Plan Ahead

Visualization is also a powerful planning tool. Once you have developed a clear image of the outcome you are after, you can use your mind's eye to scan the terrain from where you are to where you want to be. Identify the milestones, or critical steps, needed to accomplish this objective, as well as potential roadblocks that you are likely to meet along the way. You may be able to do this as a purely mental exercise, or it may be necessary for you to do research before you can identify the specific steps needed to realize your aims. In either case, it helps to send your mind out in front of you to prepare the way.

It may help to think of the goal you desire as the end of a movie, with the major action steps along the way as the critical turning points within this movie. Once you have identified these critical scenes, you can visualize them in sequence, as though you were running a movie on the screen of your mind. In addition to helping you to familiarize yourself with the territory ahead, repeated viewing of this mental movie will help you to create a momentum of success within your own mind. To use the example of opening your own store, you might visualize the successful completion of a business plan, the moment you secure financing, the moment you first take possession of the physical space, the day you are ready to open your doors to customers, and then the celebration of your first anniversary.

You can think of potential roadblocks as points of dramatic conflict within your movie. Anticipating potential roadblocks or difficulties helps you prepare for them. They will not seem to come upon you all at once; you will have plenty of time to react and develop strategies for going around, under, over, or through them. Using visualization to identify major milestones as well as potential pitfalls on the road to the realization of your dreams can save you a great deal of time and trouble and make the journey a lot more fun.

Visualization Strategy #4: Improve Performance

In addition to using visualization to plant dream seeds and to outline the specific steps to realizing them, you can use it as an aid to increasing your effectiveness in a whole range of everyday activities. Many top-level professional athletes use the power of visualization to improve their performance. Legendary golfer Jack Nicklaus has been quoted as saying that he never took a shot, not even in practice, without having a sharp, clearly focused picture in his mind's eye, of the result he wanted. Throughout the 1970s and the 1980s, athletes from the old Soviet Union dominated in Olympic competition. One reason they did so is that they began employing mind-power techniques like visualization well before their counterparts in the rest of the world had caught on. It was not unusual for Soviet athletes to dedicate 75 percent of their training time to techniques for mental preparation, including visualization.

If I see what I want real good in my mind, I don't notice any pain in getting it.

GEORGE FOREMAN

Pioneering sports psychologist Lars Erik Unastal conducted research on the top Swedish downhill skiers. He discovered that what the best skiers had in common was the habit of seeing in their mind's eye the kind of performance they wanted to give. Athletes use this flash-forward technique because it works. Yet it is not only athletes who have used the power of visualization to their advantage. The famous trial lawyer Clarence Darrow would paint mental pictures of his cases before he went into court, and he was a consistent winner. If your goal involves securing a new job, see yourself giving a great interview. If it requires public speaking, see yourself giving a terrific speech. Throw in a standing ovation just for fun.

Visualization Strategy #5: Accelerate Learning

You can use visualization to rapidly integrate new behaviors and attitudes into your personal repertoire. Carefully observe others while they are employing skills you want to develop or expressing attitudes you want to adopt. Then use these observations to inform your visualizations. See yourself applying the skills or projecting the attitudes with the same level of competence as those who have already mastered them. Again, the subconscious mind does not know the difference between real and imagined experience. Repeatedly visualizing yourself using new attitudes and skills will prewire your subconscious mind, making it believe these new attitudes and skills are old familiar ones.

How to Visualize

So far, we've looked at a variety of ways that you can use visualization. Next, we'll focus on the mechanics of visualization. Below is a list of seven keys to keep in mind when doing your visualizations. To aid you in remembering them, they are organized around the acronym DE-CIDES.

DECIDES: The Seven Keys to Effective Visualization

Deserve: Know that you can have what you repeatedly see in your mind's eye. Be willing to create the picture exactly as you want it. Focus on images that signify the completion of your goal. See it finished and complete. You may want to do a series of positive affirmations (see pages 194–200) related to your goals before beginning your visualizations. This will put you in touch with your desire to achieve your goals and will strengthen your belief that they will ultimately manifest.

Emote: Pour your feelings into the image. Let yourself feel an intense longing or desire for what you see. Emotion gives life to thought. You animate your images by pouring intense feeling into them. The stronger the feeling, the greater the likelihood that the image you see will eventually manifest.

Concentrate: Concentrate your mind. See the picture in your mind's eye and hold it there. Don't let your mind wander. If it begins to drift, return to the picture again and again. For some people, holding an image comes naturally. Others have to work at it. You can sharpen your visualization skills, and in the process, your will, by practicing looking at objects in the outside world and then closing your eyes and seeing them in your mind's eye. Visualization is a skill that, like any other, improves with repeated practice.

Include: If you want the object of your visualization, be sure to include yourself in the picture. It is not enough to see in your mind's eye the car or home you want. See yourself in the picture using and enjoying the objects of your visualization or the skills or attitudes you wish to acquire.

Detail: Step into your picture and see the detail. The clearer and more detailed the images you see, the faster and more powerfully they will come into manifestation. See the grain in the wood, the dew in the grass. Zero in on minute elements of detail.

Ease: Relax, don't tense or strain. Your subconscious mind responds better to suggestion when you are in a state of deep relaxation. You may want to enter the Alpha state (see page 48) or do muscle relaxation exercises first (see page 59). Don't strain to see or hold an image. If your mind begins to drift from the image, gently bring it back by focusing on some element of detail within it.

Savor: Savor the good feelings you have about accomplishing this goal. Express gratitude for receiving it into your world. Then completely release the image. Let it go. Know that it is done.

See It

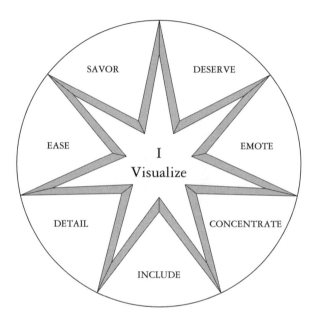

The real voyage of discovery consists not in seeking new landscapes,
but in having new eyes.   —MARCEL PROUST

The greatest achievement was at first and for a time a dream.

—JAMES ALLEN

So long as a man imagines that he cannot do this or that,
so long is he determined not to do it.   —BENEDICT SPINOZA

You imagine what you desire; you will what you imagine,
and at last you create what you will.   —GEORGE BERNARD SHAW

Chapter 12 Exercises

❧

"See It" Scrapbook

Use a blank scrapbook, photo album, or three-ring binder, to construct a "See It" Scrapbook. Designate a portion of your scrapbook to each of the life areas described in chapter 3. Next, for each of your goals, place visual images that you associate with the accomplishment of them. You can cut out photographs from magazines, or draw or paint your own pictures; just make sure you have an image that motivates you. Beneath each picture or group of pictures, briefly describe the goal as though it were already complete.

Visualization Strategies

1. Recall and visualize a number of past successes. Pay attention to the feelings you were having as you accomplished these objectives. Project these feelings onto one of your new goals. Repeat this process whenever you are troubled by doubts about your new goals. (See Visualization Strategy #1 on page 179.)

   GOAL:

2. For each of your goals, think of a scene that symbolizes its final and complete realization. For example, relaxing in your new home, signing your first published book at a bookstore, crossing the finish line of your first marathon. Repeatedly see these images in your mind's eye. Allow yourself to feel your excitement about achieving this goal. (See Visualization Strategy #2 on page 180.)

   GOAL #1:

   GOAL #2:

   GOAL #3:

   GOAL #4:

   GOAL #5:

   GOAL #6:

   GOAL #7:

   GOAL #8:

3. Select a goal you would like to focus on. Mentally review the process of achieving your goal, breaking it down step by step. Select four milestones or turning points en route to this goal. For longer term goals, divide into eight steps. (See Visualization Strategy #3 on page 182.)

GOAL:

MILESTONE #1:

MILESTONE #2:

MILESTONE #3:

MILESTONE #4:

4.   Identify skills you already possess that you would like to practice and perfect.

Once you have identified these skills, determine when and how often you will mentally rehearse them. Recall the example of shooting basketball free throws, discussed in chapter 11. Remember, the subconscious mind doesn't know the difference between mental and physical practice. (See Visualization Strategy #4 on page 183.)

5.   Next, identify new skills you would like to learn.

Ask yourself, "Who do I know who has mastered this skill? How can I arrange to observe them exercising this skill?"

Once you have a clear mental picture of what is involved in these skills, begin practicing them your mind's eye. (See Visualization Strategy #5 on page 183.)

Believe It: Affirmation 13

Man is what he believes.

ANTON CHEKHOV

et's say you can see what you want to happen. You can easily visualize the life you want to live. You have no difficulty seeing yourself with the new home, lifestyle, or career you seek. Yet it seems only a fantasy. A nagging voice from within keeps telling you it's not going to work. Sure, your vision is appealing. You just don't believe that it will really happen. Well, my friend, if you don't believe it, it won't happen. This chapter explores how you can tap the magic power of belief and develop a confident expectation of the fulfillment of your dreams.

Belief: The Power That Moves the World

The world belongs not to those with the most talent, brains, or skill but to those who believe in themselves and their dreams. Those who lack vision or are tormented by doubts can only stand on the sidelines and watch as those with faith in themselves and their dreams shape the world around them. Make no mistake—behind every social movement, technological breakthrough, architectural triumph, or creative life, you will find the power of belief. It built the pyramids, wrote the world's best music and literature, put an end to slavery, charted the oceans, and landed men on the moon. Where would we be today without the pioneers and innovators who believed in their dreams and kept on affirming them, even in the darkest hours? How often did those we remember today as great leaders and innovators demonstrate unwavering belief in their visions—often when all the supposed experts said it couldn't be done?

This kind of faith is a potent transformative power that you can channel into every aspect of your life. Believing in yourself and your visions gives you the courage to persevere at those times when it seems your visions will never manifest. If you want to see your dreams come alive, never give up on them simply because things look rough, and never forget that what you believe makes all the difference. As Henry Ford so aptly put it, "If you think you can or you can't, you're right." Right now, you are putting your faith, your power of belief, in something. Do you believe you will succeed or fail? Are you a prophet of gloom or a source of inspiration for all you meet? It all depends on what you believe.

You Believe What You Hear Repeated

You're probably familiar with the expression "garbage in, garbage out." Nowhere does this principle apply more than when it comes to the beliefs and attitudes that come to be accepted by our subconscious minds. What you believe—not what you assert with your conscious mind, but what you believe deep in your subconscious—is a result of what you have heard repeated. Unfortunately, most of it is probably negative. In a study conducted by a leading mid-western university, graduate students followed two-year-olds around and recorded every time their parents said something positive to them and every time they said something negative. The results were startling! On average, the children heard 432 negative and 32 positive statements per day, a ratio of fourteen to one.

Negative beliefs gained in early years are carried over into later life. In a study conducted at UCLA, incoming freshmen were asked to list their personal strengths and weaknesses. These were bright young students at one of the best universities in California, yet on average, their lists of weaknesses were six times longer than their lists of strengths. Most people are burdened by poor self-images and the negative beliefs that comprise and sustain them. Most could benefit from examining their inner attitudes and making some adjustments in their beliefs about themselves and the possibilities that life holds for them.

What Are You Thinking Anyway?

Throughout the day, you are constantly talking to yourself. (Don't worry, it's normal.) Psychologists have estimated that we hear up to five hundred words a minute in our "mind's ear." (To give you a frame of reference, a skilled typist types about one hundred words per minute.) That's a lot of talk. What you heard repeated over and over as a child, you came to believe and accept as fact. If your parents or teachers told you over and again, "No, you can't," you probably came to believe, "No, I can't." If you were repeatedly told that you were lazy or stupid, it's likely that you came to believe it. Once your subconscious mind accepts a belief through repeated hearings, it in turn begins to repeat that belief inside of your head.

Unfortunately, many of us are so accustomed to negative thinking that we don't even recognize it as such. It's simply a familiar and accepted part of our everyday thought processes. While most people hold negative beliefs of some kind, each person's package of beliefs is unique. For example, one man may hold a set of beliefs that support success in his career, while at the same time holding a set of beliefs that are ruinous to

As he thinketh in his heart so is he.

PROVERBS 23:7

193

his personal relationships. For another individual, this pattern may be reversed. It's probably safe to say that if you scratch just below the surface in those areas of your life that are not working, you will find negative, limiting beliefs. It is certainly worthwhile to take the time to identify precisely what these beliefs are. Awareness gives you the power to begin taking control. On the other hand, what you don't know *can* hurt you.

How to Change Your Mind

By now, you undoubtedly recognize that negative beliefs can hold you back. You may even be aware of what some of those beliefs are. You know it's difficult to move forward on your goals while being harassed by nagging voices of doubt from within your own mind. You're probably saying to yourself, "Okay, but what can I do about it now? How can I get my subconscious mind to cooperate so that instead of sabotaging my efforts to grow, it is encouraging and supporting me?"

To change your experience in any area of life, you can either change what you attract, change what you repulse, or change both. As the song says, "Accentuate the positive. Eliminate the negative." Affirmation is the mind's attractive force. What we affirm, we attract or pull to ourselves. Denial is the mind's repulsive force. What we deny, we repulse or push away from ourselves. You can change your mind and your life by affirming belief in what you want and denying thoughts of doubt about your capacity to get it. Now let's look at some specific ways that you can use the powers of affirmation and denial to transform your life.

Accentuate the Positive: Affirmation

It's not exactly going out on a limb to say that by thinking positive, life-affirming thoughts twenty-four hours a day, day after day, year after year, you could dramatically improve your chances of success in all areas of your life. Yet determining to think positively isn't enough. After all, most of your thoughts aren't under your conscious control. You have to find a way to make positive thinking as automatic as breathing. That's where affirmation techniques come in. You can use affirmations to alter your life script or to support specific goals. To alter your script, determine the core beliefs you want your subconscious to accept, and then repeatedly affirm these beliefs until they displace their negative counterparts. (See highlight on page 199.) In the same way, when you want to reach a specific goal, affirm that you will *and* displace, with positives, any specific negative beliefs that might slow your progress. In either case, repetition is the key. The more deeply ingrained the negative is, the more positive affirmations it will take to displace it. Once the new positive belief becomes accepted by the subconscious mind, it will work for you for the rest of your life. You won't even have to think about it again.

The greatest discovery of my generation is that a human being can alter his life by altering his attitude.

WILLIAM JAMES

As learning to effectively use the power of visualization means training your mind's eye to see what you want to manifest, so learning to effectively use the power of affirmation means training your mind's ear to hear the beliefs that will support you in what you want to manifest. The keys to this method are simple: (1) the affirmative declaration of clear, definite statements of what you want to be, do, or have and (2) the persistent spaced repetition of these statements to displace all beliefs to the contrary and to gain acceptance by the subconscious.

Now Hear This

All the negative beliefs that your subconscious mind eventually accepted came to you by means of repetition. If you want to change your beliefs, you must use the same method. The difference is that, while negative beliefs were acquired unconsciously, you must now consciously insert into your mind the new, positive attitudes you want it to accept.

While you may notice instant results in some areas, expect the transformation of deeply ingrained beliefs to be gradual and to require consistent attention over a period of weeks. It's easy to see why. Let's say the results of the study we sighted above are exaggerated, and the average child doesn't hear a ratio of fourteen to one negative to positive statements—but only ten to one. Still, that's hundreds of thousands of negative statements: "No, you can't! You're doing it all wrong!" or worse, "Boy, are you ever stupid! You'll never amount to anything!" It took you years to accumulate your negative beliefs. Don't be surprised if they don't disappear after a few days of using positive affirmations. Still, if you keep at it, you will soon see definite results.

While employed in a dull job with a utility company, Scott Adams dreamed of a career as a successful comic strip cartoonist. He took three important steps to realize his dream. He developed and drew his cartoon strip, "Dilbert"; he submitted his work to newspapers; and fifteen times a day, he wrote affirmations for his new career. As he observed in an article in *Newsweek* magazine, "The basic idea is that fifteen times a day, you write down whatever it is your goal is. Then you'll observe things happening that will make that objective more likely to happen. It's actually a process of forcing your environment to change." He began by writing fifteen times a day: I WILL BECOME A SYNDICATED CARTOONIST. Soon his strip was picked up by United Media. Once this goal was realized, he began writing I WILL BE THE BEST CARTOONIST ON THE PLANET fifteen times a day. Today, as this is being written, Scott Adams is indeed the best-selling cartoonist on the planet. Remember, as Adams observed above, when your subconscious mind accepts through repetition a new goal, it forces "your environment to change."

I Am: The Most Powerful Method: The most powerful way to use affirmation is to say the words "I am" before that which you want to be, do, or have. The words "I am" form the primary link to your self-image. Therefore, they should be used with the greatest of care. Remember, "I am" makes a strong impression. Be careful not to attach negative thoughts to the words "I am," "I," "me," or "mine," or these negative thoughts will attach to your self-image. Be sure to always follow these words with something positive and life affirming.

For example, if you repeatedly say, "I am too fat," your subconscious mind will believe it and proceed to make it a manifest reality, no matter how much you diet or obsess on losing weight. On the other hand, if you repeat, "I am trim and the picture of health," your subconscious mind will believe it and proceed to make it manifest. If you repeatedly say to yourself, "I am so scattered, I can never get focused,"

What You Hear in Your "Mind's Ear"
Gives You Confidence or Fear

AFFIRMATION	DENIAL
Say YES to:	Say NO to:

1. Belief in yourself.	1. Self-doubt and limitations.
2. Belief in the goodness of others.	2. Condemnation of others: it makes you feel low.
3. Belief that better ways can be found.	3. Dark or gloomy thoughts of any kind.

your subconscious mind will accept this belief and keep you distracted. On the other hand, if you repeatedly affirm, "I am focused. I know what I want, and I am doing what it takes to get it," your subconscious mind will accept the new belief, and you will begin to act accordingly. The more you repeat, the more you believe. Here are a few examples of positive affirmations addressed to different life areas.

I am now creating a healthy and balanced lifestyle, reinforced by complementary and harmonious goals.

I am now enjoying an exciting and fulfilling intimate relationship with the one I love.

I am now attracting an interesting circle of friends and enjoying a rewarding social life.

I am now earning lots of money doing the work I love.

Project Your Best: Second- and Third-Person Affirmations: Even as you have a self-image, so too, you have a public image, a mental image of the way you present yourself to others. For obvious reasons, your self-image is most important. As Seneca said, "What you think of

Our minds can shape the way a thing will be because we act according to our expectations.

FEDERICO FELLINI

yourself is much more important than what others think of you." If you don't believe in yourself, you will likely spend a good deal of energy trying to convince others to believe in you, or worrying about what they think of you. Your self-image is primary, yet your public image is also important. While you can't directly control what others think of you, you can change what you believe they think, and this, in turn, will affect what they think of you.

Darin believes that people think he is a dull wallflower. Consequently, he projects behaviors that match his belief. An acquaintance says to him, "What did you do this weekend, Darin?" and he says, "Oh, nothing much." In point of fact, Darin had a full and rewarding weekend; still, he projects dull city. The words "Darin" and "you," key what he believes others think of him, and he attempts to fill their "expectations."

Even when meeting new people who don't know what to expect, he projects Darin the Dull. The way Darin projects himself to the general public is keyed by the words "Darin" and "he." His negative beliefs about the way he comes across affect the way he carries and presents himself to the world. By using first-, second-, and third-person affirmations, Darin ensures that new, constructive beliefs are accepted by all levels of his subconscious mind. To improve his image of himself, Darin affirms, "I am an interesting and attractive person with many valuable things to share." To transform the way he projects himself one on one, he affirms, "Darin, you are an interesting and attractive person with many valuable things to share." To improve the image he projects to the world at large, Darin affirms, "Darin, he's an interesting and attractive person with many valuable things to share."

Using first-, second-, and third-person affirmations in combination is the quickest and most effective way to transform deeply ingrained beliefs and provide the motive power for accomplishing new goals. It's also best to write your affirmations down. Writing engages more of your senses than speaking and thereby makes a stronger impression on the mind. Set aside a few minutes each night (preferably just before you retire) to write your goal-related affirmations.

Here is an even easier method. After you have written down the positive affirmation statements of the outcomes you want to manifest,

Affirm Your New Life Script

As you may recall, the concept of a life script was discussed in chapter 7. Your life script has four major themes: the way you relate to life (your general outlook on life), the way you relate to yourself, the way you relate to work, and the way you relate to other people. The way you relate to each of these areas is determined by your core beliefs, your fundamental attitudes toward Life, Yourself, Work, and Other People. *You cannot alter your life script without changing your core beliefs*. The core beliefs you unwittingly accepted early in life formed the building blocks of your self-image. Ever since, they have circumscribed what you believe you can be, do, or have. Your subconscious mind has worked much like a magnet in sustaining and reinforcing these core beliefs. Like a magnet, it has attracted some things and repulsed others—only when it comes to the mind, it's "likes," not "opposites," that attract.

In your relationship with life, you attract happiness by embracing life as a gift and accepting responsibility to live it with joy, meaning, and purpose. You push away happiness and ease by believing that life is a burden or struggle, or that you are owed something from it. In terms of the way you relate to yourself, a fundamental belief in your own worth, dignity, and innate creative abilities attracts feelings of self-confidence and peace of mind. On the other hand, if you are given to chronic doubts, or if you judge yourself too harshly, you will find both peace of mind and genuine success eluding you. In your work life, you attract success by believing that you are blessed with unique talents and an important work to do on this earth, and that you will prosper doing the work you love. You push away career success by believing that you can't do what you really want or that you don't deserve to succeed. In your relationships with others, you attract love by believing that you are worthy and deserving of it. You push away love by believing that you will never find it or that people will never accept you for who you really are.

Affirmation is a powerful tool for transforming core beliefs and thus your life script. Take time to examine your core beliefs, identify those that hold you back, and then affirm a new life script. It will not only help you to achieve your goals but also make your whole life more rewarding and fun.

make a tape recording of yourself saying the affirmations, and listen to it several times a day. Play the tape over and over again, until you can hear the affirmations inside of your head, even when you are not listening to the tape. Remember, what you believe is what you hear repeated. Once your subconscious accepts a new belief, it will automatically create a new reality for you.

Another technique is to write your affirmation and then, next to it, write whatever comes into your head. To begin with, it will most likely be negative, but continue until what you hear in your head agrees with the affirmation. For example:

I am now enjoying a wonderful and exciting career as a successful writer.	Oh, yeah sure. What a joke.
I am now enjoying a wonderful and exciting career as a successful writer.	I don't have the discipline.
I am now enjoying a wonderful and exciting career as a successful writer.	I don't have anything worthwhile to say.
I am now enjoying a wonderful and exciting career as a successful writer.	It's too competitive. I can't make a living doing that.
I am now enjoying a wonderful and exciting career as a successful writer.	I do have a lot of good ideas.
I am now enjoying a wonderful and exciting career as a successful writer.	Maybe I could sell some things.
I am now enjoying a wonderful and exciting career as a successful writer.	I've always wanted to write.
I am now enjoying a wonderful and exciting career as a successful writer.	I really am a pretty good writer.
I am now enjoying a wonderful and exciting career as a successful writer.	Yeah, why not? I could do it.
I am now enjoying a wonderful and exciting career as a successful writer.	I am going to be so excited when my first book is published.

Eliminate the Negative: Denial

Once you have released your creative power into affirmative declarations of an outcome you desire, diligently deny all appearances to the contrary. Hold fast to your vision of success, by denying doubt an opportunity to take root in your consciousness. Don't think or say things you don't want to have happen. When negative thoughts arise in your mind, say, "STOP, not this" or "Cancel. Cancel." In so doing, you are commanding your subconscious mind to reject these thoughts and withdraw your creative energy from them. You are putting old patterns of negative thinking on notice that they will no longer be tolerated. Be vigilant and firm, and eventually they will get the idea that you mean business.

Speak the affirmative; emphasize your choice by utterly ignoring all that you reject.

EMERSON

"I say, I never!" No, I am not quoting a Victorian prude, but suggesting another way to alter your mood. If you want to overcome a habit or behavior that moves you away from your goal, try the "I never" approach. Let's say that one of your goals is to lose weight, and you realize that you have a tendency to blow your diet by eating large portions of the wrong foods. You find yourself saying things like, "I have a hard time resisting delicious deserts." Affirm that you enjoy healthy foods and that you are at your ideal weight. Also begin saying to yourself, "I never eat too much." Say it every time you eat, so that while you're eating, instead of thinking, "I can't resist certain foods," you are thinking, "I never eat too much." Go ahead and eat, just make sure you repeat, "I never eat too much." One day, you will discover, in the midst of feeding your face, that the new belief has come into place. Your subconscious mind, which now believes "I never eat too much" will stop you as you begin to reach for that second piece of cake. Here are a few examples of some "I never" statements applied to different life areas:

I never procrastinate.

I never settle for less than my best.

I never indulge in self-pity or negativity.

I never let fear prevent me from achieving what I've set out to do.

From Negative to Positive

Here is yet another technique you can use to root out deeply ingrained negative beliefs. Make a list of the recurring negative thoughts you have concerning a particular goal. List all your fears, doubts, and apprehensions. Next, make a positive affirmative statement for each negative one. For example, "I'm afraid I won't finish the project on time" becomes "I got it done with plenty of time to spare."

Next, make a tape recording in your own voice saying the negative statement in a dull monotonous tone; then, in a strong and decisive manner say the word STOP, followed by the positive affirmation. Say the affirmative statement with all the enthusiasm you can muster. Your tape might sound something like this: "I'll never get this done on time. STOP. It is done!" Repeat this exercise daily for two weeks, and you will notice your mind beginning to do the thought substitution on its own.

What to Do When It Isn't Working

Some people complain that even though they use them repeatedly, affirmations and denials just don't work for them (though this too is an affirmation). The problem may stem from the way they use affirmations. First, consider the frequency factor; make sure you are giving these new beliefs a chance, by repeating them often. Also, recognize that affirmation and denial are ongoing processes. It is not enough to merely affirm the good you want for a few minutes each day and then slip back into negative thinking for the rest of the day. If you want to succeed, keep constant watch on your thoughts and especially your words. The power of formal affirmations and denials will be diluted if, in your casual conversation, you allow yourself to dwell on doubts and negative thoughts.

Second, consider the feeling factor. Some people will say their positive affirmations in a monotonous or mechanical manner, only to then turn around and put tremendous emotional energy into negative statements about the same issue. Be it positive or negative, the belief with the strongest emotional charge dominates. If you can't immediately break the cycle of negative thinking, be dull while negative and energetic while positive. Simply by changing the emotional charge you put into your positive and negative statements, you will notice significant benefits. Our thoughts are the ideational forms with which we create our realities. Emotions animate these forms, bringing ideas to life. Feed positive thoughts with your emotional energy. Starve negative thoughts: don't give them your life-giving emotions.

Often, when we first begin taking control of our minds, there is a tendency to resist negative thoughts by becoming emotionally reactive when we observe ourselves thinking them. Yet this only intensifies the negative effect of these thoughts. Remember, the most powerful ideas in your life are those that you give the most emotional energy. If you want to reduce the influence of negative thoughts in your life, you are better off to ignore them than to react emotionally against them. Better yet, replace them. Stay with it. Patience and persistence will pay off.

Just as you can diffuse the power of negative thoughts and beliefs by withdrawing the charge of the negative feeling, you can increase the power of your positive thoughts by charging them with good feelings. Take advantage of times when you feel especially energetic and happy to repeat affirmative statements. Play with your affirmations. You may even want to sing them. Make the process of transforming your mind fun and exciting.

Make Friends with Believers: Affirm positive outcomes by associating with positive people. Deny negative outcomes by avoiding negative people as much as you can. Learn to guard your mind against the negative suggestions of others. Recognize that you are influenced, subconsciously as well as consciously, by those with whom you associate. For good or for ill, we pick up a lot by osmosis. If you want to achieve success, associate with those who have gained success. Stay away from negative people. Guard yourself against the negativity of family, relatives, business associates, employers, or co-workers. Don't share your dreams with those you can't trust to support them. Belief is a power so strong that it literally forces your environment to bend to its will. When you can clearly see what you want, and believe that you will receive it, you are well on your way to having it.

If you keep on saying things are going to be bad, you have a good chance of being a prophet.

ISAAC SINGER

Believe It

They conquer who believe they can.
—RALPH WALDO EMERSON

Always bear in mind that your own resolution to succeed is more important than any other one thing.
—ABRAHAM LINCOLN

They can because they think they can.
—VIRGIL

Nurture your minds with great thoughts. To believe in the heroic makes heroes.
—BENJAMIN DISRAELI

Our belief at the beginning of a doubtful undertaking is the one thing that ensures the successful outcome of our venture.
—WILLIAM JAMES

Chapter 13 Exercises

❧

The Three-Part Affirmation

For each of your lifetime goals, write first-, second-, and third-person affirmations. See pages 197–198. For example, if your goal is: To write and publish a best-selling book by January 1, 2004, write:

I, _____ , am now writing and publishing a best-selling book.

You, _____ , are now writing and publishing a best-selling book.

_____ is now writing and publishing a best-selling book.

Once you have constructed affirmations for each of your goals, write between five and twenty-five sets of each affirmation daily.

HEALTH:
1.
2.
3.

CAREER:
1.
2.
3.

LIFESTYLE:
1.
2.
3.

FINANCE:
1.
2.
3.

SELF-DEVELOPMENT:
1.
2.
3.

SOCIAL LIFE:
1.
2.
3.

CREATIVE EXPRESSION:
1.
2.
3.

INTIMATE RELATIONSHIPS:
1.
2.
3.

Affirmation and Response

Following the example on page 200, write an affirmation for a goal you would like
to manifest. Then, on the opposite side of the page, record the counter thoughts
that enter your head as you write each affirmation. Continue until you are consistently hearing positive self-talk in relation to this affirmation.

AFFIRMATION   COUNTER THOUGHT

1.   1.

2.   2.

3.   3.

4.   4.

5.   5.

6.   6.

7.   7.

8.   8.

9.   9.

10.   10.

Transforming a Negative into a Positive

Make a list of your biggest fears, doubts, and worries with regard to a particular goal. Be sure to be as honest as you can in admitting and recording your deepest fears. Next, convert each of these into a positive, affirmative statement. See page 202 for an example.

❦

Don't Buy It, Deny It

Make of a list of habitual activities or thoughts that might lead you away from your goals. Next, turn these into "I never" statements. See page 201.

Wheel of Fortune, Mandala of Balance

Draw a wheel of fortune like the one you see below. Place the words I AM on the hub of the wheel. Next, fill in each spoke of the wheel with a descriptive adjective that encapsulates your path to growth in each of the life areas described in chapter 3. Along the outer rim of the wheel, write a positive affirmation that corresponds to your general purpose in each of the life areas. Refer daily to your Wheel of Fortune for inspiration and reinforcement, as you strive to realize these qualities ever more fully in your life.

Receive It: Act with Expectation 14

If you wish to live a life free from sorrow, think of
what is going to happen as if it had already happened.

EPICTETUS

The two previous chapters examined how what we see (imagine) and believe shapes our experience of the world. Perhaps the most obvious way in which the images and beliefs of our subconscious minds control our experience is in the effect that they have on our actions. What you imagine and believe determines what you do and don't do and, perhaps just as importantly, *how* you do what you do. Visualization and affirmation are powerful methods for creating the mental and emotional environments necessary to attracting and sustaining success in the outer world. These are methods for creating success from the inside out. This chapter explores another method, one with which you can create success from the outside in.

Our deeds determine us, as much as we determine our deeds.

GEORGE ELIOT

Even as your thoughts and feelings influence your behavior, so your behavior influences your thoughts and feelings. Simply put: *What you do affects what you think of you.* These two principles tend to reinforce one another. What you think affects what you do, and what you do affects what you think of yourself. Each of these principles may be employed as an effective strategy for personal transformation. Yet for maximum results in the shortest period of time, it's best to apply both methods simultaneously. After all, you can only integrate a higher level of success when your thoughts and actions consistently match that new, higher level. As you change the images (through visualization) and beliefs (through affirmation) within your mind, you change the way you act. You can also CHANGE YOUR BEHAVIOR SO DRAMATICALLY AND CONSISTENTLY THAT YOUR MIND IS FORCED TO CHANGE ITS PERCEPTION OF YOU.

How Changing Your Behavior Changes Your Mind

The subconscious mind is constantly observing and recording events. Clearly, one of the things it observes is your actions. This raw data is passed on to an internal command center for interpretation and analysis. The subconscious then proceeds to do everything within its rather substantial power to make sure that you receive what it determines that you deserve—as indicated by the actions it observes you taking and its analysis of them.

Your subconscious mind analyzes your actions by the same standards that it does anyone else's. When it observes you acting like a success, it concludes that you deserve the rewards commensurate with success. It proceeds to do everything within its power to ensure that you get them. If, on the other hand, it observes you acting like a failure, it concludes that you deserve a failure's rewards. Again, it does everything it can to make sure you get them.

Some years ago, a film called *Trading Places* explored the power of this principle in dramatic terms. In the film, a poor con man living in the streets of Philadelphia changed places with a high-level business executive. As the poor man observed himself acting responsibly, surrounded by the comforts and luxuries of wealth, and receiving the dignity and respect due an important person, his perception of himself began to change. He came to believe that he deserved what he was getting. Similarly, as the executive observed himself acting in a degrading fashion, being treated with contempt, and left to fend for himself without position, shelter, or friend, his perception of himself began to change. He, too, came to believe that he deserved what he was getting, and, incidentally, so did everyone else.

The essence of the "Receive It" principle is to act in ways that convince your subconscious mind that you deserve and are prepared to receive the results you seek. To achieve your goal, receive your goal by acting in accord with it. In other words, *act like you know it will happen, act as though it is already happening,* and *act calmly, with positive expectancy.* Demonstrate to your subconscious mind that you expect the result you seek, by acting accordingly. Just as you can learn to direct what you see in your mind's eye, and what you hear in your mind's ear, you can deliberately transform your behavior to fit your goals. The rest of this chapter will explore a variety of techniques you can use to begin "acting into" your goals.

Three Keys for Receiving Your Goals

1. Act like you know it will happen.
2. Act as though it is already happening.
3. Act calmly, with confident expectancy.

"Receive It" Key #1:
Act Like You Know It Will Happen

The first way to act accordingly is to act like you KNOW it will happen. We have all heard people say, after they have achieved some measure of success, that they knew it was going to happen all along. You act differently when you *know* you will achieve a result than when you are merely wishing or hoping for it. Imagine that the results you seek are already accomplished and complete. What can you do now to show yourself, when you look back over your actions, that you knew it was going to happen all along? As a practical matter, acting like you know it will happen means plunging into the new and letting go of the old.

Dig Your Ditches: Often we wait for conditions to be perfect before we act, when the situation demands that we take immediate action under less than favorable circumstances. A story from the Old Testament of the Bible provides a classic illustration of this principle. In the story, a prophet told his people to dig ditches in preparation for catching the waters of an impending rainstorm. The only problem was, the people had long been suffering from a serious drought, and there wasn't a rain cloud in sight. They were being told to act as though the result they desired would occur, even when there was no indication that it would. They did, and sure enough, the rains came.

When you act into your goals, you demonstrate to your subconscious mind that you are serious about attaining them—and that you expect you will. If you want to be a writer or a painter, begin writing or painting, even if you can only do it part time. The body of work you amass will convince your subconscious mind that you are serious about being a writer or painter. If you want to start a business of your own, put together a business plan, even if you don't know where you are going to get the start-up capital. If you always go as far as you can with what you have, you will find that you can always go further. As the German poet Schiller put it, "Who dares nothing need hope for nothing." Dare to begin taking immediate action toward the results you seek. Dig your ditches, and trust that the waters of success will soon rush in to fill them.

Ask for What You Want: Another way you can act as though what you want is going to happen is to ask for it. Often what keeps us from receiving what we want is the simple fact that we don't ask for it, or we don't ask enough (that is, until we get it). Every time you ask for what you want, you are acting on the belief that you will get it. You are translating belief into action. Ask for what you want, and you may be surprised at how often you get it, especially if you keep on asking.

Christopher Columbus dared to ask. Having been rebuffed by, among others, the King of Portugal and the King and Queen of Spain, Columbus would not be denied. In fact, he was so confident that it was his mission in life (he thought he was divinely inspired) to chart the Western Passage and find "those lands which were still undiscovered," that even after their repeated rebuffs, he arranged yet another meeting with Ferdinand and Isabella.

This time he didn't plead for permission; he boldly laid out his price. Under his terms, Columbus was to be knighted, made Grand Admiral and Viceroy, and receive a 10 percent commission on all transactions within his jurisdiction. The King and Queen were shocked by the audacity of these outrageous demands. They refused. Yet Columbus held firm. This upstart Italian navigator simply wouldn't back down. In the end, it was Ferdinand and Isabella who gave in, yielding to all of his demands.

Ask and it shall be given unto you.

LUKE 11:9

> *I finished my first book seventy six years ago. I offered it to every publisher on the English-speaking earth I had ever heard of. Their refusals were unanimous: and it did not get into print until, fifty years later, publishers would publish anything that had my name on it.*
>
> —GEORGE BERNARD SHAW

Nineteen-year-old Rick Little designed a course called *The Skills for Living* in response to educational needs of high school students, which he felt were being neglected within the traditional curriculum. He approached nonprofit foundations with a request for a grant of $55,000 to launch his program within the local public schools. His request was repeatedly rejected. In fact, he went to more than 150 organizations before the Kellogg Foundation finally accepted his proposal. They surprised him by offering, not the $55,000 he had requested, but $130,000. At this writing, this program is being taught in over nine hundred high schools, with five hundred thousand students receiving benefits they might never have had, had Little not acted on his belief by asking and asking and asking yet again for what he wanted.

It has been reported that Richard Bach received dozens of rejection notices before his book *Jonathan Livingston Seagull* was finally published. No one could have blamed him if he had given up after rejection number eight, twelve, or twenty. Yet his willingness to persevere resulted not only in a highly successful writing career for himself but many hours of enjoyment for his readers. To keep on asking for what we want, like Columbus, Little, or Bach, we must overcome the fear of rejection. By continuing to ask for what we want, we are demonstrating to our subconscious minds that our desire for a result is stronger than our fear of looking foolish. We are also affirming our belief that we will in fact get what we want, by refusing to give up until we do.

Burn Your Bridges: Burning your bridges to the past can provide the needed impetus to put yourself totally into your goals. When we close the back doors of escape, we open the front door of total commitment. Successful people know that if they try to play it safe and fail to take calculated risks, they will hold part of themselves back—often the very part needed to accomplish their goals. The average millionaire goes broke three and a half times en route to achieving his or her millions. In any field, the people who win big are the ones who aren't afraid to take chances and put it all on the line.

In the early 1980s, a couple of young entrepreneurs named James Calano and Jeff Salzman decided to get into the business of putting on seminar trainings. They committed themselves to risking it all on their first seminar, "Image and Self-Projection," investing everything they had and more into getting it off the ground. They went out on a limb and came back with a win. In their first outing, they received three times the standard response for seminar mail promotions. They made a large profit and launched what became the most successful seminar company in the world, CareerTrack.

Act in a way that demonstrates to your subconscious mind that you know the results you seek are going to happen. Show it that, as far as you are concerned, you have passed the point of no return. There is no going back; your goal must manifest. Throw out the old furniture to make room for the new. Break off old, unsatisfying relationships in order to make room for new, rewarding ones. Take decisive action that demonstrates that you fully expect your goal to manifest. Of course, use common sense. You can be decisive without being reckless.

"Receive It" Key #2:
Act As Though It Is Already Happening

At the turn of the last century, the noted American philosopher and pioneer psychologist William James advocated the "act as if" principle as a powerful tool for transforming consciousness. According to James, it is easier to act your way into a new kind of thinking than to think yourself into a new way of acting. Few people realize what a malleable thing the personality really is. The word itself comes from the Latin *persona* and means "mask." By changing the masks you wear, you elicit new responses from others. The change in the perception of others, in turn, helps you to change the way you see yourself.

The famous and highly successful play *My Fair Lady*, based on George Bernard Shaw's *Pygmalion*, was a dramatization of this principle. In it, a young cockney girl was coached on how to act the part of a well-bred lady. Acting as if she was what she wanted to be, worked for her, and it can work for you. In the play, Liza Doolittle had a coach, Professor Higgins. You too may want one or more coaches to help you transform your act. One important kind of coach is a mentor (for more on selecting a mentor, see chapter 19). In addition, there are professional coaches who will teach you everything from how to walk, to how to breathe; from how to speak, to how to dance; from how to sing, to how to sink a putt; from how to hold your fork, to which wine to have with pork. Professionals will teach for a fee all that dear Liza learned for free. Examine yourself and ask: "In which areas of my life can I make improvements by myself, and in which would a professional's help be appropriate?"

Today, teaching people how to act the part has become a booming cottage industry. Media consultants, voice coaches, publicists, agents, psychologists, and others coach their clients to act in ways that ensure they will receive the responses they want from others. Certainly, if the salaries of these coaching professionals are any indication, the way we

If you want a quality, act as if you already had it.

WILLIAM JAMES

215

How to Be Your Own Coach

Think of yourself as your own media consultant. Size up your client. How can you highlight his or her strengths and shore up some of his or her weaker areas? First, take an inventory of yourself. If your goal involves your people skills (and how many goals don't?), pull out the home video camera or go and rent one. Get someone to point the camera at you. Stand and look into the camera. How do you feel about the person you see in the monitor? What is this person saying to the world? Do the same while walking and sitting. Get comfortable with the camera and with the person on it. Next, begin to experiment with playing different roles. For example, if you tend to play shy and withdrawn, try wild and outrageous. Experiment with a wide range of behaviors to demonstrate to your subconscious mind that you can play a variety of roles and that you aren't limited to your old standbys.

act makes a big difference in the response we get from others. When seeking out professional coaches, make sure you check their credentials and interview some of their clients.

How would you walk, talk, and dress if you were a millionaire? A creative genius? How would you act as a loving and supportive marriage partner? As an involved and concerned parent? Observe the behavior of others and note attitudes, demeanors, verbal styles, and specific actions you would like to incorporate into your own repertoire of behavior. Notice how others project confidence, warmth, authority, or whatever qualities you have chosen to integrate into your own personality. Identify the specific behaviors that will assist you in meeting your goals, adapt them, and begin to act accordingly.

Don't wait until you feel like it. Overcome the inertia of conditioned habits, and force yourself to act the new part. If you persist, you may be surprised at how quickly the new chosen behaviors will begin to seem as natural, easy, and automatic as the old, conditioned ones once did. If you begin to look, act, and feel like a million dollars, your mind will start to believe that you are worth a million. If you start to act the part of the gracious host or hostess, your mind will start to believe that you are a social dynamo. Act confident and you feel confident. Act like you make a difference and you will begin to feel like you do. Now and again, check your language, posture, dress, and attitudes. Ask yourself, "Would a person acting the part I want to play, act the way I am acting now today?"

Remember, the way you act and appear determines how you are perceived by others and what you receive from them. In the minds of most people, "how you do it" is at least as important as what you do, and often spells the difference between success and failure in getting what you want. In his book *Live For Success*, John Molloy reported on a study that demonstrates how the way we act influences how others perceive and treat us. In the study, actors were placed in professional business settings and were instructed to use differing communication styles. The same individuals, dressed identically, were perceived and treated in markedly different ways, depending on the vocabulary and communication styles they employed. By verbal clues alone, people made judgments about the educational and professional levels and socioeconomic status of these individuals and treated them accordingly.

Your image of yourself is influenced by the way others see you. Subconsciously, we pick up on impressions that others have of us. By adopting the "act as if" principle, you are making this power work for, rather than against, you. As you act the new part, people around you begin to respond to you in new and exciting ways. Don't tell them what you are doing, just go on acting accordingly. Often the trick among advertisers, agents, and public relations specialists is to make their clients appear successful, before they actually are. They know that nothing succeeds like the appearance of success. This principle works for them and can work for you.

Beyond the exciting benefits of the new behaviors themselves, and the wonderful changes they bring in your perception of yourself and in the perceptions that others have of you, the experience of breaking out of the conditioned personality is liberating in itself. It is extremely empowering to realize in a deep, experiential way that you are not the conditioned creature of habit you may have thought you were. Just as you can change the images you see in your mind's eye and the voices you

We cannot put off living until we are ready.

JOSÉ ORTEGA Y GASSET

217

hear in your mind's ear, so you can change your personality and its long-standing habits of behavior.

Fake it 'til you make it. "Sounds good," you say (and you know it works), "but if I fake it, won't I be a phony?" When you automatically act insecure and shy, it is every bit as much an act as when you intentionally act confident and outgoing. The difference is in your behavior and in the results that you get. You are altering your behavior, not your soul. You're changing the masks you wear, not who you really are. As Thomas Jefferson put it, "In matters of principle, stand like a rock; in matters of taste, swim with the current."

"Receive It" Key #3:
Act Calmly, with Confident Expectancy

So far we have discussed two ways to act accordingly. First, act like the result you want will happen in the future. Second, act as though the result you seek is already happening now. The third principle is to act calmly, with positive expectancy. In a sense, this principle is really an extension of the first two, but it focuses in on how you feel as you act. As we will see below, to a very large degree, how you feel determines how well you do.

Trust that if you are clear in your intention, positive in your expectation, and willing to persevere, the results you seek will manifest. Think about it. If you knew for sure that your goal was going to manifest, how would you feel? Would you be tense or anxious about it? Would you worry or fret? Would you hurry or rush about in a dizzied frenzy? Would you get angry or frustrated at the first sign of difficulty? Of course not. You would remain calm throughout, because all the while, you would know that in the end, your success is assured.

When we go to the movies and watch the exploits of our favorite superheroes, we don't get overly concerned. We know that no matter what happens in the interim, everything will turn out all right in the end. Knowing that it will be all right allows us to remain calm. In the same way, acting calmly, with positive expectancy, telegraphs to your subconscious mind that you know you will succeed. Like James Bond, you can remain cool under pressure, with a touch of humor—and always get the job done.

Nearly forty years after first appearing on the international scene, the music of the Beatles is as fresh and original as ever. For years, critics have tried to explain the secret of their prolific creativity. Perhaps the best explanation comes from Derek Taylor, their former press agent and an intimate observer of their creative process. Taylor asserts that the magic of the Beatles resulted from the extreme positivity of the group—the relaxed, confident, and playful way they approached their work. Though they were often under the pressure of contractual obligations (starting from scratch, they wrote and recorded the *Sgt. Pepper* album in five months), the Beatles were always confident of their ability to get the job done and have fun doing it. When working together became more of a struggle and less fun, the Beatles were soon undone. The lesson: have fun and play with your new roles.

How You Feel Determines How Well You Do

It has long been known that feelings of guilt held over a period of time can produce depression and fatigue and that chronic anxiety can produce nervous exhaustion. For better or worse, how you feel determines how well you do. As James E. Loehr, a psychologist who has done extensive research on sports performance, wrote in an article for *Sports* magazine ". . . an athlete's performance is a direct reflection of the way he or she feels inside." He goes on to say that "acting toward the upper range of one's potential is a natural consequence of the right kind of feeling."

Fear just doesn't make it as a motivator for the sustained long-term effort required to achieve important life goals. David Kauss, a professor at the UCLA School of Medicine puts it well: "The main problem in using fear as a source of energy is that it tends to completely dominate the mind, making other, necessary thought processes next to impossible." What we fear, we fight with or flee from. It's hard to think straight when you are in a dogfight or running scared. Like all negative emotions, fear impairs your ability to focus and therefore to excel in your performance.

Give me a man who sings at his work.

THOMAS CARLYLE

Yet fear is but one of the negative emotions that can keep you from receiving your goals. For example, while you hate or resent the rich, it is highly unlikely that you will become wealthy yourself. Your subconscious mind will resist making you a part of a group that you detest. Similarly, while you are jealous of people who are accomplished musicians, have good people skills, or are extremely well-organized, you will have difficulty perfecting these abilities yourself. Until you are willing to accept and enjoy the success of others in a given area of life, you block your own development in that area. This may not be a matter of divine justice, but it is a matter of fact. As we can see, a big part of the "Receive It" principle is removing any subconscious resistance you may have to achieving your goals. This subconscious resistance manifests in the form of negative emotions such as anxiety, jealousy, anger, hatred, etc. Transforming your emotional energy cancels out the subconscious resistance.

In their book *Beyond Bio-Feedback*, Elmer and Alyce Green state that "every change in the physiological state is accompanied by an appropriate change in the mental-emotional state." It works the other way around as well: a significant change in your emotional state affects your physiological ability to perform. Top sports trainers know and use this principle. They instruct their athletes in proven techniques for generating the positive emotions that facilitate maximum performance. Yet often when we think of our goals, we tense in fear. If we could apply the kind of techniques used by top-level athletes to induce positive feelings, we too could dramatically improve our performance. Fortunately, we can. Below you will find some powerful techniques for inducing the *feelings* of success.

Relaxation: The Key to Top Performance

Top athletes know that emotional distress translates into physical stress and poor performance. The ultimate remedy, of course, is the attainment of complete emotional mastery. In the meantime, you may want to use physical relaxation techniques to help you approach your goals, and the action necessary to achieve them, in a relaxed and calm manner.

For years, behavioral psychologists have known that it is impossible to feel physically relaxed and emotionally agitated at the same time. These therapists often instruct their clients in techniques for achieving physical relaxation in order to abate or eliminate negative emotional reactions to specific events or stimuli. These methods have been used with great success in the treatment of phobias. By inducing deep physical relaxation and then gradually introducing elements of a fearful stimulus, the emotional reaction to this stimulus is reduced until finally it is gone entirely. In this way, many people have overcome their fears of heights, snakes, riding in airplanes, and a variety of other situations and things.

One of the reasons why so few of us ever act, instead of react, is because we are continually stifling our deepest impulses.

HENRY MILLER

The same techniques can assist you in achieving your goals. Again, since the subconscious mind does not know the difference between real and imagined events, you can use these techniques in the comfort and privacy of your own home. Let's say, for instance, that one of your goals requires that you do a considerable amount of public speaking, and you are terrified of the prospect. First, you would enter a state of deep relaxation. Then you would begin to imagine yourself engaged in behaviors associated with public speaking. Whenever you noticed yourself beginning to feel agitated or upset, you would concentrate on the relaxation technique until you again felt deeply at ease. You would continue to do this until you could imagine standing before a large audience, successfully delivering a speech without any feelings of fear.

Deep physical relaxation can be achieved through muscle relaxation and breathing techniques. For a procedure for deep muscle relaxation, turn to page 59. To further enhance muscle relaxation, you might want to get a massage or enjoy a hot bath or Jacuzzi® prior to doing the muscle relaxation procedure. In addition, you may want to use the procedure for entering the alpha state (described on page 48) to aid in relaxation and to help open your subconscious mind.

Relaxed, deep breathing also facilitates physical relaxation and relieves you of emotional distress. There are any number of breathing techniques you can use to help you relax. Perhaps the simplest is just to become aware of your breath. Make no effort to change or correct it. Simply be aware, and in time, your breath will find its own natural rhythm. This simple exercise will energize, uplift, and relax you. It's an effective form of stress management that requires no special training or apparatus. Anyone can do it, any time, anywhere. Try taking ten minutes a day to just sit still and pay attention to how you are breathing. Then, in the midst of your day, when you find yourself beginning to feel anxious or tense, take a few moments and return to an awareness of your breath. Keep this up, and in matter of weeks, you will find that you have integrated a powerful new tool for managing stress.

Feel-and-Do Cues for Emotional Breakthroughs

Often our subconscious minds associate taking action on our goals with feelings of fear and pain. These feelings slow, or even prevent, action. It only stands to reason that if we only associated pleasure with the actions necessary to achieving our goals, we would advance more rapidly and easily toward our objectives. Through a technique I call "feel-and-do cues," you can create the positive feelings and pleasurable associations that will impel you toward your goals. Feel-and-do cues are stimuli that have strong associations with particular feelings or behaviors. You may have a favorite suit or dress that you wear on days when you want to feel your best. That's using a feel-and-do cue to evoke a positive feeling.

Whether we realize it or not, we are constantly making mental associations. For example, we create associations to places, which are linked to feelings or behaviors that have occurred while in those places. Think about how the way you feel and act seems to change almost automatically as you move from a store to a church or synagogue, from a bank to a movie theater, or even from the kitchen to the bedroom. The idea with feel-and-do cues is to take conscious control of a largely unconscious and automatic process and put it to work in support of your goals. Feel-and-do cues put the power of association to work for you.

Like visualization, top-level athletes frequently use feel-and-do cues. Watch the strange maneuverings of topnotch pole-vaulters, high jumpers, weight lifters, or skiers before they compete, and you'll see what I mean by feel-and-do cues. They often use specific hand gestures, postures, or sequential movements with which they have previously linked positive emotional feelings. They are then able to summon these feelings on command, simply by repeating the movements they have associated with them.

I've used feel-and do-cues many times with good results. Author book tours can be grueling and very physically demanding. On a recent tour, I began most days rushing to be at the local television studio by 6:30 AM for a live interview. I would go on giving radio, TV, and print interviews all day long, with scarcely time to grab a snack. In the evenings, I would conduct three-hour seminars, before traveling to another city to begin the process all over again the next day. The stress of being constantly "on" while getting little sleep began to take its toll. There were times when I felt so exhausted I didn't know how I would continue.

Yet previous experience had taught me what to expect. I brought along a small tape recorder and some of my favorite inspirational music. I had conditioned myself to respond with great energy to this music. I found that no matter how weary I was, if I sat down, closed my eyes and listened to Mozart's *Requiem* for even five minutes, things would start to turn around fast. I would not only find the wherewithal to carry on but also do so with such energy that my audience never suspected that I was anything but fresh.

In the same way, you can use feel-and-do cues to psych yourself up before taking action on one of your goals, to alter your mood or boost your confidence in dark moments, or as triggers for new habits you are trying to develop. Your cues might be words, smells, sounds, movements—any stimuli that trigger positive feelings or constructive actions. By consciously constructing and using positive associations, you will be able to create positive feelings at will. These positive feelings will not only keep you motivated but also ensure that you give your best performance.

Above all, try something.

FRANKLIN D. ROOSEVELT

Receive It

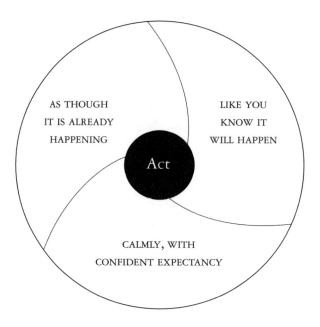

AS THOUGH
IT IS ALREADY
HAPPENING

LIKE YOU
KNOW IT
WILL HAPPEN

Act

CALMLY, WITH
CONFIDENT EXPECTANCY

Fortune favors the audacious. —ERASMUS

I will act as though what I do makes a difference. —WILLIAM JAMES

If one asks for success and prepares for failure,
he will get the situation he has prepared for.
—FLORENCE SCOVEL SHINN

The beginning is the most important part of the work. —PLATO

He who hesitates is lost. —ENGLISH PROVERB

Chapter 14 Exercises

❦

Acting Your Way to Success

Title a sheet of paper: Act Like You Know It Will Happen. Next, make a list of all the actions you are prepared to take that will demonstrate your belief that your goal will, in fact, be achieved. In what ways are you prepared to dig your ditches, ask for what you want, burn your bridges, and in other ways act like you know it will happen? See pages 211–215.

Title a second sheet of paper "Act As Though It Is Already Happening." Now list the actions that you are prepared to take to demonstrate to your subconscious mind that you believe your goal is already happening. For example, if your goals include greater financial wealth, how can you now act more prosperous? If your goals include owning your own business, in what ways can you take a more entrepreneurial approach and assume greater responsibility now? (If you don't believe you can do so in your existing job, you may want to start a small part-time business.)

"Getting the Feeling" Exercises

The following exercises will help you to access your kinetic sense to generate the positive feeling of receiving your goals. You may want to use the relaxation technique from "Relax into a World of Ideas" in chapter 5 (page 59).

GETTING INTO THE FEELING

Totally relax. Now allow yourself to experience the good feelings associated with the completion of your goal. See the completion of the goal, and as you see it, pay attention to the good feelings you have. What is happening around you? Who is there? What are they feeling? What sensations are you aware of in your body? What are your emotions? Let yourself experience the excitement, the joy, the triumph, the contentment, the exhilaration—or whatever positive emotion characterizes the achievement of your goal as a manifest reality. This is the time to express your feelings.

Now write the goal as though it were complete, including all of the good feelings you just experienced—good feelings you had about yourself, good feelings you had about others, good feelings others had about you. (Do this for each life area you are addressing.)

GOAL #1

GOAL #2

GOAL #3

GOAL #4

GOAL #5

GOAL #6

ASSOCIATE FEEL-AND-DO CUES

For each of your goals, select a color, number, keyword, a short piece of music, or gesture or movement that will serve as a feel-and-do cue.

	Color	Number	Keyword	Music	Gesture
GOAL #1					
GOAL #2					
GOAL #3					
GOAL #4					
GOAL #5					
GOAL #6					

Use your feel-and-do cues to put you in a positive emotional state just prior to taking action on your goals.

AN ACTOR'S METHOD: FEELING TRANSFERENCE

Many actors use a technique called "sense memory recall" to prepare themselves emotionally for big scenes. By recalling an experience from their own past, they can access the emotional state necessary to effectively convey the action in the scene. In the same way, you can use sense memory recall to prepare for the big scenes in your life. Here are some examples of experiences and associated feelings you might like to recall:

1. Remember a time when you felt extremely confident, as though you were on top of the world.
2. Remember a time when you were successful at something that was difficult.

3. Remember a time when you were the center of attention and it felt good.

4. Remember a time when you felt like somebody really understood that you loved them.

5. Remember a time when you felt somebody really loved you.

6. Remember a time when everyone said you couldn't do it, but you knew you could, and you did it anyway.

7. Remember a time when you stood up for yourself and were successful, and it felt good.

8. Remember a time when you did something thoughtful for someone anonymously.

9. Remember a time when you felt really good about your body and its ability.

10. Remember a time when you figured out how something worked all by yourself, and it felt good.

BRINGING YOUR FEEL-AND-DO CUES ALL THE WAY THROUGH

Combine "An Actor's Method" with "Feel-and-Do Cues." Use the principles of memory and association to propel you into making good feelings automatic.

Step One: Think of a feeling or behavior you want to manifest.

Step Two: Pick a cue to associate with that feeling or behavior. Make it something that is not a part of your normal routine.

Step Three: Do the cue, close your eyes, and recall a time when you felt the feeling or exhibited the behaviors you now want to access. Now open your eyes and test by checking whether or not you have brought the feeling here. If not, repeat. This time, see the past experience in greater detail. Repeat until you get it.

Step Four: Now repeat the cue whenever you want the associated feeling.

Value It: Reward Your Progress 15

It is the nature of man to rise to greatness
if greatness is expected of him.
JOHN STEINBECK

The "See It," "Believe It," and "Receive It" principles are power-ful tools for gaining the cooperation of your subconscious mind and putting its potent creative energies to work on your goals. The final step to maximizing and sustaining desire is to use the "Value It" principle. By focusing your attention on your positive efforts and rewarding yourself for them, you confirm your progress and renew your desire to keep moving forward on your goals. This chapter explores how you can make the most of all your constructive efforts by giving yourself the credit you deserve.

Making a point of valuing your positive efforts actually doubles their effective power. You get the benefit of the action itself, plus the motivational lift that comes with recognizing and acknowledging your efforts. You create a feeling of positive momentum, a sense of inevitability about the attainment of your goals. Too often we view our goals in black-and-white terms—we have either reached them or not. Employing the "Value It" principle gives you an immediate experience of success, even while pursuing goals that may take many years to fully realize or accomplish. It helps you to enjoy the *process* of accomplishing your goals as much as their eventual attainment.

Imagine you are hiking up a mountain trail. You climb for a time and then rest at a lookout. While climbing through dense brush or under tall pines, it's difficult to see the progress you are making. You may wonder if you are making any progress at all. When you reach a lookout, you stop and look at the landscape below and realize how far you've come. It's clear that your efforts are paying off. The resulting feeling of exhilaration provides the motivational lift needed to climb still higher and, perhaps just as importantly, to thoroughly enjoy the climb.

Like the hiker on a mountain trail, we often lose sight of the progress we've made. We see clearly how far we have yet to go, but tend to downplay the steps we've already taken. Like the hiker, we need a lookout, a way of appreciating the progress we have made, as well as the courage and effort it took to make it. That's where the "Value It" principle comes in.

"Value It" Techniques

YOU VALUE WHAT IS BY ACKNOWLEDGING:	YOU VALUE YOUR PROGRESS BY APPRECIATING:
1. Who You Are	4. Your Process
2. What You Do	5. Help You Receive
3. What You Have	6. Records of Your Progress

Acknowledgment

Remember the master formula: *Whatever you focus on you become.* Putting the "Value It" principle to work for you is a matter of training your mind to focus on the good and praise it. By focusing on the good in life, yourself, and others, and on the constructive efforts you are making to achieve your goals, you get the power of attention working for you. When you feel stuck or are having difficulty moving forward, stop, step back, and appreciate where you are now. Value and acknowledge even the smallest steps you have taken to accomplish your goals. This will provide far greater motivation than judging or condemning yourself for where you are now or panicking about how far you have yet to go.

"Value It" Technique #1: Value Who You Are

One of the greatest impediments to accomplishing your dreams is taking the attitude that you are somehow a lesser human being until you achieve them. Achieving your goals will not make you a better person any more than failing to achieve them will make you are a lesser one. People who equate their self-worth with material success, the achievement of social status, or the approval of others, set up within themselves a deep psychological resistance to the very goals they are trying to achieve.

The part of you that doesn't feel loved or accepted as it is tends to resist the very things that you have determined will make you a "better" or "more worthy" person. An inner conflict develops between the part that says, "I must do this to be okay" and the part that says, "I shouldn't have to do anything to be okay." It is not only more pleasant but also far more effective to move toward your goals from a place of self-respect and self-acceptance than from inner coercion. Beating up on yourself for not making greater progress will only slow you down.

Your essential value is in what you are as a human being, not in what you do, the positions or titles you hold, the money you make, or

A man who dares to waste one hour of time has not discovered the value of life.

CHARLES DARWIN

231

The talent for being happy is appreciating and liking what you have, instead of what you don't have.

WOODY ALLEN

the people you associate with. Placing your sense of value on these shifting sands will only leave you feeling insecure. Take pride in your efforts and accomplishments, but don't equate these with your value as a human being. The more you value who you are at the deepest level, the easier it will be to take risks and do the things necessary to accomplish your goals.

People who value and accept themselves as they are, are willing to take risks because they know no matter what the outcome, they can always count on their own love and support. Those who don't value themselves place undo emphasis on the approval of others. They also tend to be very self-critical. They fear to risk even a small portion of their meager stock of self-esteem by attempting anything they might fail at or be criticized for. Their whole approach to life becomes one of playing it safe, which usually means more of the same.

> *Every second we live is a new and unique moment of the universe, a moment that never was before and will never be again. And what do we teach our children in school? We teach them that two and two make four and that Paris is the capital of France. We should say to each of them, "Do you know what you are? You are a marvel. You are unique. In the millions of years that have passed there has never been another child like you."*
> —PABLO CASALS

To think thoughts such as "When I get the degree or the great job, when I make the big bucks or buy the house on the hill, when I get married or have kids or find the cure for cancer—then I will have amounted to something" is highly destructive to your self-esteem. That is not to say that any or all of these aren't worthwhile goals—only that to base your estimation of your self-worth on their attainment is dehumanizing *and* counterproductive. People who think to themselves, "After I do such and such, then I'll be okay, worthy, important, etc.," also tend to think, "After I have such and such, then I'll do so and so." This sets up a cycle of avoidance and delay arising from a deep-seated fear of not being good enough.

The internal verbalizations go something like this: "I'm lacking. I won't be good enough until I do whatever it is that I think I must do in order to be okay." "The situation is lacking. It's not good enough because I can't do what it is that I must do, until I have what I now lack." Overcome this double bind of psychological paralysis by accepting yourself as you are and recognizing that you can always do something to improve your situation. Accept yourself as you are and recognize that every step you take, every bit of progress you make, moves you that much closer to your goals.

Take Time for You: One way to acknowledge your intrinsic worth is to make a point of spending time alone on a regular basis. Don't distract yourself by watching television, reading magazines, chatting on the phone, or surfing the Internet. Just be—with yourself. How do you feel when you are alone? It's a good test of how you feel about yourself.

A wise man once said that the difference between solitude and loneliness is attitude. Spending time alone with an attitude of self-awareness and self-acceptance puts you in touch with your basic goodness, with how much you like, value, and respect yourself. It also provides the opportunity to become aware of the places where you judge your-

The Benefits of Solitude

1. Getting to know yourself—what you want, what you feel—a chance to really listen to yourself.

2. Rest from the pressures and concerns of daily life.

3. Perspective. An opportunity to reflect on where you are in your life, make constructive changes, and acknowledge the growth you have made.

4. Increased gratitude for relationships with others and the simple pleasures of life.

5. Rejuvenation and renewal and the heightened creativity that results from these.

self or blame others for your unhappiness. Solitude offers the opportunity to confront these places and find a way to love yourself more deeply. A stroll on the beach, a walk in the woods, even a quiet bath, can do wonders for the soul. Treasure the quiet times that are just for you. Don't neglect to put them in your schedule.

"Value It" Technique #2: Value What You Do

While striving to accomplish your goals, don't forget to enjoy the ride. Value what you are doing in the here and now, while continuing to work for something better. No matter how challenging and exciting the pursuit of your goals may be, you can't live in the future. Prepare yourself for greater success by putting yourself totally into what you are doing now, even if it isn't your "ultimate." Fully engaging yourself in the present not only helps you to enjoy what you are doing but also prepares you mentally to handle the greater challenges and responsibilities that will come with the attainment of your goals. We put our stamp on everything we do, and far more than we may care to admit, the way we handle our current responsibilities says a lot about the way we will handle future ones.

Andrew Carnegie put himself into every job he ever had. He began working for $1.20 a week in a hot and dirty textile mill. Still, he was proud of his work, saying later, "I have made millions since, but none gave me as much happiness as my first week's earnings." When he got a chance to work in the office, he jumped at it. He began taking night classes in bookkeeping to make himself a more valuable asset. Having trained himself out of the factory, Carnegie's next move was to get a job as a telegraph operator. As such, he gained an intimate knowledge of the local business scene, which facilitated his securing a responsible post with a railroad company. He soon became a vice president. After many years of valuable on-the-job training, Carnegie began working for himself in the steel business. The rest, including funding a chain of public libraries across America, is, as they say, history. Rather than condemning the situations you are in, outgrow them by throwing yourself into them and learning to master them.

Sleep on It: You show yourself that you value what you do, by taking daily stock of it. One of the easiest ways of doing this is by putting your sleep to work on it. Just before falling asleep, begin to recount the activities of the day, starting with the very last thing you did, and moving all the way back to awakening that morning. Most likely, you will fall asleep before you have completed all the day's activities. This is not a problem, as your unconscious mind will carry it through to completion, once you have gone to sleep. If you get all the way through, and you're still awake, try it again, but this time go more slowly. This process is called "retrospection." Try it for even a couple of weeks, and you will be amazed by the results.

Too happy would you be, did ye but know your own advantages!

VIRGIL

It's impossible to observe the activities of the day without automatically improving them. All of us have had the experience of "sleeping on it" and waking to find a better way of doing things, a new way of looking at things, or the solution to a difficult problem. Obviously, the subconscious mind was working on the issue while you were sleeping. Daily review of the day's activities helps you to use this power in a more consistent and effective way. Many people report improved memory as a significant by-product of the regular use of retrospection.

"Value It" Technique #3: Value What You Have

"Thems that's got shall get; thems that's not shall lose." Certainly, this timeworn saying applies to the attitude of gratitude. The more you value what you have, the more you will have to value. Successful people understand that, in any situation, what is missing is never as significant as missing the opportunity to use what is at hand. Focusing on what you don't have actually causes you to lose the opportunity to make the most of what you do have. Though it may seem a simple thing, cultivating the attitude of gratitude is an easy and simple way to increase both your happiness and your effectiveness. You'll feel better and you will be better able to take advantage of opportunities that come your way. On the other hand, feeling sorry for yourself will slow you down more than any lack of skill or any outer obstacle. Of course, you can't feel grateful and sorry for yourself at the same time. Taking time to acknowledge what you have will help keep you on track.

Count Your Blessings: Remind yourself of all you have by literally counting your blessings. Make a list. Be sure to include your talents and natural gifts as well as the special qualities of character, or personality traits, that you possess. Include the important people in your life and relationships of all kinds. The work you do and skills and experience you have gained in doing it are something to be grateful for. How about your material possessions, the physical objects you own or use? How often do you appreciate your physical abilities—the fact that you can see and hear, walk and talk? What about the beauties and wonders of the natural world? How about the everyday marvels of technology that turn night into day and keep you warm in the winter and cool in the summer? If you have good health, put it on your list. In a world with millions of starving and malnourished people, you are fortunate if you have three square meals a day. List the activities, recreations, arts, and entertainments you enjoy. Include the knowledge and wisdom you have already gained and the opportunities you have to learn still more, and so on, and so on. There are so many things to be grateful for. Reminding yourself of them from time to time helps you not only to treasure all you have but also to take full advantage of it.

Appreciation

Appreciate the efforts you make to achieve your goals. One definition of the word *appreciation* is "to raise in value," as in the appreciation of a home. As you appreciate the efforts you are making, you raise their value in your own mind, prompting still greater effort. For example, when you are cleaning your house, you are motivated by the recognition of the difference that your efforts make. As you think to yourself, "The kitchen looks so much better," you are motivated to tackle the next room, and so on. So it is with all your work, including the "inner work" of improving your self-image.

"Value It" Technique #4: Value Your Process

Since what you want is vital to you, the process of getting it must become equally so. Valuing your process means taking pride not only in final results but also in all the steps that go into achieving them. Organizational psychologists and management consultants have long known that consistent constructive feedback is the most effective way for managers to motivate their subordinates. Giving yourself immediate, consistent, and constructive feedback not only gives you a motivational lift but it also puts you in control.

Too often we are dependent on the praise and acknowledgment of others. We make an effort and wait for someone to notice. If we don't get the response we are looking for, or if our efforts are criticized, we give up. Of course, we all want the attention and praise of others. Yet if we're going to become self-motivating, we must become self-acknowledging. When you set out on a new endeavor, you naturally lack the confidence that comes with experience. Yet you can avoid a good deal of stress and discomfort by valuing and appreciating yourself for having the courage to tackle something new. If you take one constructive step today, and focus your attention on it, you will do more good for yourself than you will by worrying about all the things you have yet to do.

The way to love anything is to realize that it may be lost.

G. K. CHESTERTON

Three Kinds of Rewards: You can reward yourself with things (e.g., having a snack, buying yourself a gift) or experiences (e.g., watching a movie, taking a hot bath). These can be appropriate and effective strategies for motivation. You can also reward yourself simply by giving yourself attention for the constructive efforts you make. Attention rewards provide a direct boost to your self-esteem. By attention rewards, I mean anything that draws your attention to the constructive efforts you are making. Behavioral psychologists tell us that the key to conditioning a new habit or response is to mete out rewards as soon as possible after performing the behavior you want to adopt. Generally speaking, the longer the lag time, the less likely the conditioning is to "take."

Attention rewards are quicker and less dependent upon other people or circumstances than physical or experiential rewards. For example, if one of your favorite ways of rewarding yourself is to take a swim, you need a pool, a lake, or an ocean—maybe even a swimsuit. But satisfaction for a job well done requires nothing except your attention. Attention rewards reduce the time between action and reward. Your rewards can come at the speed of thought, with the focus of your attention. When you are doing well, taking risks, moving forward, learning and growing—bring the matter to your attention. And praise it!

"Value It" Technique #5: Value the Help You Receive

Value all the help you receive, whether it comes in the form of the assistance of people, fortunate circumstances, or unexpected opportunities. Whether we appreciate it or not, we all receive so much help from other people. The more you genuinely appreciate what others do for you (and let them know about it), the more ready and willing you will find that others are to help you. Again, anything that you appreciate tends to expand in your life. Take time to recognize and appreciate what others do for you. It will make them feel valued and make you feel happy. It will also help you appreciate a simple fact of human nature: People, all people, want to feel as though they are being helpful and useful to someone. When you let others help you, you are giving them a chance to fulfill that desire. Let others help you, and let them know what their help means to you.

Although it is one of the most useful kinds of help we can receive, the feedback that others give us tends to be one of the most unappreciated. Of course, none of us likes to be criticized or to have our personal or professional shortcomings pointed out to us. Yet if we can come to recognize how helpful this kind of feedback can be in accelerating our own process of growth, we can not only make the most of it when it comes but learn to actively seek it out. Professional dancers and musicians toil under supervision for endless hours and subject themselves to the embarrassment of relentless critical evaluation in the quest to improve their technique. Why? Because they appreciate

Who does not thank for little will not thank for much.

ESTONIAN PROVERB

An Earnest Lesson

Long ago, there lived a very pleasant young peasant named Ernie Besant. One day, while at the village square, Ernie saw a most marvelous thing happening there. It was a traveling minstrel show, with singers, dancers, and props in tow. Ernie was dazzled by what they wrought and to himself most sincerely thought, "This is what I want to be." So every day, he studied the players, carefully. When they left town, poor Ernie was terribly down. Yet more resolved than ever was he, to learn the craft of making glee. Thought Ernie, "I'll join the troupe when they return." But alas, never again did they make their sojourn. Years of farmer's toil brought an early old age and unexpressed talent, an inner rage. While lying on his deathbed, he finally got the story that this beloved troupe had returned in all its glory. "Alas," said Ernie, "All my life I've been waiting for opportunities I should have made, and now, all too soon, I'm ready for the grave." The moral of the story: Move to Hollywood and get an agent; or, don't wait too long to act on opportunities or inspirations that come your way.

the opportunity to learn from those who know more than they do in their fields of interest. They value the experience! Faced with critical feedback, a young musician at The Julliard School doesn't throw down her instrument in disgust and go storming out of the room. She recognizes that growth is often a painful process, and she values the expertise of her instructors. Besides, she is determined to get full value for the high price she is paying and the long hours she is playing. Since she wants to be her best, she values the opportunity to improve her performance.

Often the difference between those who excel and those who don't is the way they view such opportunities for growth. While the average person feels threatened by high standards and tough competition, and avoids these at all costs, top performers know such disciplines are vital to the mature development of their talent—the difference between merely adequate and really first-rate work. Consequently, they don't just accept these rigors; they actively pursue them. They thrive on chal-

Let no feeling of discouragement prey upon you, and in the end you are sure to succeed.

ARBRAHAM LINCOLN

lenge, value critical comment, and most of all, are committed to growth. They know that, as William Butler Yeats put it, "happiness is neither virtue nor pleasure, nor this thing nor that, but simply growth. We are happy when we are growing."

Take a page from those who love to grow: brainstorm a list of people and environments that are likely to challenge you. Next, develop strategies for how you can arrange to spend time with those people and in those environments. Ask for suggestions from people you know and respect about how they think you can grow. Ask them to list your strengths and weaknesses. Solicit feedback and appreciate it when you get it, whether it is good, bad, or downright unflattering.

Value Opportunities: Demonstrate to yourself that you value opportunities, by capitalizing on those that come to you of their own accord, and by deliberately creating additional ones. Taking advantage of unsolicited opportunity requires a 360-degree awareness. Don't tie yourself to any one way of making things work; remain flexible and be on the lookout for unexpected opportunities. You now know what you want; just be sure to remain open and flexible about how you get it. Create additional opportunities by putting yourself around people and situations that stimulate and challenge you.

Get the most out of unsolicited opportunities by expecting them to come, staying alert for them, and leveraging them when they do. Look for opportunity. Often, you'll find that the help you require is all around you. It's just a matter of being open enough to see and value it. Part of what keeps us from receiving all that we could is that we don't value it when it comes to us easily. Things don't have to be a struggle. The bootstrap model of success doesn't tell the whole story. As illustrated by the Andrew Carnegie example above, recognizing and seizing opportunities that come your way is just as important as working hard. Sure, effort and persistence are essential, but don't neglect to value the opportunities that come easily or unexpectedly. They could be right in front of you.

When opportunity comes along, grab it by the tail and make the most of it. Sports writers, coaches, and professional athletes are always emphasizing the importance of taking advantage of the breaks as a key to consistent winning. It's the same in the game of life. Carnegie capitalized (literally) on his opportunities because he valued them. So can you. Pluck and luck—it takes both to be successful. You can increase your luck by looking out for opportunities and seizing them when they come.

A man bought a painting for a few dollars at a second-hand shop. The owner of the shop told him that it was a copy of a painting by a famous French Impressionist. Yet the man who bought the painting had the sense to have it evaluated by an art dealer. It turned out that the painting was an original, and the new owner sold it for well over a million dollars. Both men were equally "lucky" to have the painting in their possession, but only one took advantage of his luck. Seize this day and the opportunities it presents. "Do not," as Chamfort put it, "suppose the same opportunity will knock twice on your door."

"Value It" Technique #6:
Value Records of Your Progress

Compare yourself with yourself, not with others. Records of success help you see the progress you are making and challenge you to do *your* best. Diaries, journals, logbooks, scrap books, awards, mementos—these are just a few of the ways you can measure and treasure your progress. These mark significant milestones on your road to success. They help make your progress tangible and provide a sense of positive momentum. It takes a lot of concentrated and persevering effort to achieve major lifetime goals. You don't want to wait until the entire goal is realized before you get a sense of accomplishment. You want reinforcement along the way. Regular records of progress give you just that. Be sure to see and do the exercises at the end of this chapter. The Daily Logbook, in particular, will serve as an indispensable tool in keeping you motivated and moving forward.

Value It

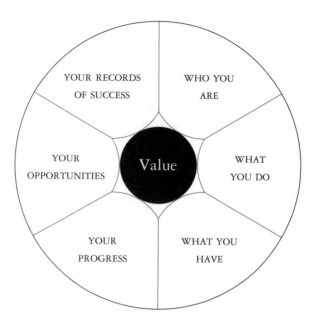

The people who get on in this world are the people who get up and look for the circumstances they want, and, if they can't find them, make them.

—GEORGE BERNARD SHAW

Think not so much of what thou hast not, as of what thou hast.

—MARCUS AURELIUS

All life is an experiment.

—OLIVER WENDELL HOLMES

Rest satisfied with doing well, and leave others to talk of you as they will.

—PYTHAGORAS

If the only prayer you say in your whole life is "Thank you," that would suffice.

—MEISTER ECKHART

Chapter 15 Exercises

❧

Count Your Blessings

Count your blessings: You have heard that expression many times. Now take the opportunity to do so, literally. List all the things you are grateful for, and refer to this list often. It may sound corny, but taking the time to count your blessings can not only lift your spirits but also put your life in a whole new perspective.

Value Your Process: Personal Reward Strategy

1. For each goal, brainstorm a list of ways you can reward yourself for incremental accomplishments on the road to achieving it.

Then select the way you will reward yourself.

When I complete _____ ,
I will reward myself by _____ .

2. Determine behaviors you want to reinforce, or increments of success you want to celebrate, and select appropriate rewards.

BEHAVIORS   REWARDS

Then for each, connect the behavior with a reward.

Every time I _____ ,
I will reward myself by _____ .

Your Daily Logbook

A Daily Logbook can help keep you motivated as you progress toward your long-term goals. Your Daily Logbook is like an encouraging friend. It always has something good to say about you, for in it, you will only find records of your successes. The process is easy and takes no more than fifteen minutes a day, with an additional forty-five minutes per week for review. By using your Daily Logbook, you will engage in and acknowledge activities that demonstrate to your subconscious mind that your success is inevitable and imminent.

If you choose to construct and use a Daily Logbook, here is what you will do. (Of course, you needn't do the entire program—choose those elements that will work best for you.) In the "See It" section of your Daily Logbook, you will translate your goals into positive images that represent their successful completion. Then every day (preferably at night, just before retiring), you will visualize these scenes. In the "Believe It" section, you will reinforce belief by writing and saying positive affirmations about your goals. In the "Receive It" section, you will identify goal-supportive actions, assign them relative values, and reward yourself for doing them. The "Value It" section puts your attention to work in rewarding your progress; it gets you in the habit of consistently valuing your positive efforts.

Your Daily Logbook is at once an application of the "Value It" principle, as well as a tool to assist you in using the "See It," "Believe It," and "Receive It" principles. By using the Daily Logbook, you are giving yourself positive feedback for staying on track with your success agenda. The daily records of success contained in your Daily Logbook keep you moving forward at an accelerated pace. The personal satisfaction and sense of accomplishment that comes with appreciating the many little steps you take will keep you moving down what can be a long and sometimes difficult trail. Tangible records of your progress prevent old negative beliefs from discounting your efforts and causing you to give up. Perhaps most important of all, your Daily Logbook helps you to internalize the "See It," "Believe It," "Receive It," and "Value It" principles so that, in time, you learn to use them automatically, without the need for any kind of structured process.

1. **Activity Value Sheet:** The first step to making your Daily Logbook is to make Activity Value Sheets for each of your goals. Using a separate sheet of paper for each goal, write the goal at the top of the page, and list the activities that will move you toward that goal. Assign each a numerical value.

2. **Daily Log Sheet:** Again, using separate sheets of paper for each goal, write the goal at the top of the page, and list the activities from the Activity Value Sheet down the left-hand side of the page. Write the days of the week across the top.

DAILY LOG SHEET

Activities	Sun	Mon	Tue	Wed	Thurs	Fri	Sat
1.							
2.							
3.							

In the evening, before retiring, record the numerical value corresponding to the activities that you have completed. At the end of each week, add these together for a total score. Repeat the process for each week.

PART IV

Commitment

Commitment:
Going the Distance

——

Discipline:
Mastering Distraction

——

Daring: Overcoming Fear

——

Diplomacy: Gaining Cooperation

——

Detachment: Learning to Grow

Commitment: Going the Distance

16

There are costs and risks to a program of action,
but they are far less than the long range risks and costs
of comfortable inaction.

JOHN F. KENNEDY

Commitment is the outcome of intense desire. When desire becomes full, you declare with resolve, "I want it! I am determined to have it!" When you want something so much that you are willing to do whatever it takes to make it happen, you have reached the point of commitment. You've crossed the threshold from the realm of ideas into the realm of action. You've resolved to turn your dreams into realities. The commitment section explores what it takes to develop and maintain the commitment necessary to realize your goals.

As part of making a commitment, it's a good idea to make a realistic assessment of the obstacles that could potentially block you from achieving your goals, and determine how you will overcome them. Obstacles include *distractions* that might lead you astray, *fears* that could cause you to delay or avoid action, the *resistance* you may encounter from other people, and a sense of *overwhelm* about all you must learn and do to accomplish your goals. In this section, you will have the opportunity to confront these potential barriers and develop strategies for overcoming then. In so doing, you will demonstrate to yourself that you are totally committed to your goals.

Commitment: A Way of Life

The ultimate commitment is the one you make with yourself: to take responsibility for your life and to make the most of it. This lifelong commitment is born from a sense of urgency, a recognition that time waits for no one and that the choices we make and the actions we take today determine our tomorrows. Living in commitment sets you apart. It means saying goodbye forever to the blasé indifference in which so many hide. It means never again contenting yourself with sour grapes or wallowing in might-have-beens. It means you are ready to claim what you want and ready to do what it takes to get it. It means that you are ready to be and assert yourself and that you won't settle for less.

Making a commitment to follow through with a specific goal is making an agreement with yourself to grow. It represents a decision about a specific direction of growth and a determination to pay the price. The lessons won and the confidence gained from committing yourself to and accomplishing one goal are directly transferable to other goals. More than providing the personal satisfaction of fulfilling your commitments to yourself, achieving specific goals expands your horizons, enabling you to envision even greater possibilities. This is why, as William Blake put it, "Sooner murder an infant in its cradle than nurse unacted desires." To abandon your desires is to abandon growth. Indeed, it is to abandon life itself.

People who avoid commitment invariably have self-esteem issues. If you have difficulty making and keeping commitments, it is because at some point, you denied your capacity to make a difference in your world. You came to believe that you were unimportant and that what you did or didn't do didn't really matter—so why commit yourself to anything? Before you can make any really significant commitments to yourself or others, you must come to believe in yourself and value what you have to give. You must accept responsibility to act like the important person you are.

Whoever told you you weren't important anyway, and what did they know? They thought they were unimportant too, didn't they? You may say, "Well, I'm not important, because I haven't done anything important." But perhaps the reason you haven't done anything you think is important is because you don't think you are. Ultimately, your importance lies not in what you do but in what you are as a human being. As Nathaniel Hawthorne put it, "Every individual has a place to fill in the world and is important in some respect, whether he chooses to be so or not."

If, at some point in the past, you stopped believing in yourself, don't despair. You *can* get your self-confidence back. Begin by admitting when, how, and why you gave up on yourself. Though this admission may at first seem too painful to confront, recognize that there is tremendous psychological power in this act of emotional self-honesty. It releases a vast store of psychic energy. Energy long tied up in resentment, bitterness, and disappointment can now be channeled into the pursuit of your goals. Put this newfound energy to immediate use. Making realistic commitments to yourself, and following through on them, will quickly restore your self-confidence.

To a committed person, *now* is the time for action, and actions count. They make a difference. We can be committed only because we have stopped demanding or hoping that others will give to us or do for us what we can only give to and do for ourselves. We accept that the power of choice resides with us, and we are determined to follow through on these choices. Commitment requires that we live in the present instead of bemoaning the past. It requires that we work toward our futures, not just wait for them.

To play it safe is not to play.

ROBERT ALTMAN

251

Commitment means doing what you are doing as though it were the most important thing in the world, as though everything depended upon it. When you are acting from commitment, body, mind, and soul are totally engaged. Watch young children at play on a beach. They have this kind of total commitment. Whether splashing in the water, playing in the waves, or building a castle in the sand, they are totally engaged. Nothing is more important to them. Nothing is held back. Do you still do anything like that? If you can honestly say yes, that's good. If you can honestly say that you are that committed to your life's work, that's fantastic! And if you can honestly say that you are that committed in your life's work and in your personal relationships, then you are a happy person and an asset to all you meet and know.

The first step in making a commitment is to analyze the cost of making it versus the cost of not making it. Commitment comes with a price. It will certainly cost you time and energy. Some commitments will cost you money or the risk of disapproval. There are always trade-offs and sacrifices involved in the pursuit of any worthwhile goal. Make a realistic assessment of these costs and weigh them against the costs of not making a commitment. (See the exercises at the end of this chapter.)

The Costs of Not Making a Commitment— Giving Up on You

While the costs of making a commitment are usually only too obvious, the costs of not making a commitment, though less immediate and apparent, are often even greater. Failure to make a commitment that's right for you will cost you the loss of belief in yourself. To stop believing in yourself is so damaging to your happiness and well-being that nothing could possibly be worth it. If you do, your career may go to pot, your health suffer, your relationships turn sour, your creativity dry up, your lifestyle become a trap, your mood become irritable and despondent, your outlook become critical, bleak, and hopeless. You'll feel drained of vital energy, adrift without purpose or direction. You may even suffer from severe depression. Failure to make a commitment that's right for you will not only rob you of self-respect, but it may also cheat you of the respect you desire from others. One thing is for sure: if you fail to make a commitment that's right for you, you will lose the chance to act in a particular set of circumstances that will never be the same again.

The Costs of Commitment:
The Will and the Willingness

Commitment means that you are ready to put yourself on the line for something, to get off the fence, take a stand, and act. Commitment means paying a price, and, of course, the price for each goal is going to be different. Yet we could say in a general way that commitment is made of will and willingness—the will to do whatever it takes to realize your goal, and the willingness to let go of whatever gets in the way of achieving it. If you were totally committed to an outcome, you would be willing to do anything to realize it, and you would be willing to give up anything that stops you from getting it. When you have that kind of commitment, you become invincible. While you are still in doubt, you take adversity as a sign to quit. Once you are committed, you take the same adversities as opportunities to test your resolve.

Confusing interest with commitment can get you in trouble. You may think that it would be nice to be a great painter or pianist, to have a fulfilling marriage or dedicate yourself to some worthwhile humanitarian cause, but that is hardly a commitment to the continuing work necessary to realize any of these aims. Your commitment is not to a particular outcome so much as it is to the *process* of achieving that outcome. Of course you want the exciting outcomes, but if you are to realize them, you must make the commitment to the often difficult process of growing toward what you have envisioned.

Don't expect to win your goals without a price, without sacrifice. The greater the goal, the greater the price. You will have difficulties, defeats, and disappointments along the way. There will be times when you want to quit, but if you persevere through the rough spots, you

The trouble is, if you don't risk anything, you risk even more.

ERICA JONG

253

will win, even if you fail to reach your goal. The character that you build by standing up for what you believe in and refusing to quit will serve you well for the rest of your life.

The Willingness to Let Go of Distractions and Fear

As strange as it seems, many people are unwilling to succeed. More accurately, their low self-esteem and negative conditioning keep them from believing they deserve to succeed. Because they don't believe they deserve to succeed, they don't believe they can. Instead of pursuing meaningful goals, they get caught up in distractions, or paralyzed by fear. Even if you are ready to succeed, at some point on the road to achieving your goals, you may be tempted by distractions and haunted by the nagging voice of fear. The first test of commitment is your willingness to let go—to deny attention to the distractions and fears that might pull you off track. Distraction wants to take you here, fear wants to take you there; yet it is up to you to stay the course and follow the call of your dreams.

Distractions: Distractions are out-of-control attempts at gaining control. Distractions keep you spinning around in circles, like a dog chasing own its tail—a lot of motion, not much progress. The more you pursue them, the further they take you from your goals. To let go of distractions, you must be willing to admit the truth, namely that you are using them to avoid confronting your goals. Remember, when you look behind any distraction, you will find the fear it hides. Chapter 17 will examine the psychological roots of chronic patterns of distraction and provide specific strategies for overcoming distractions of all kinds.

Fear: To grow is to risk, and to risk means that failure is a possibility. Fear is the expectation of future loss or injury. Fear stops us when we allow our imaginations to dwell on possible negative outcomes. Expect fears to come, but don't let them put you on the run. Fear is often a sign that things are working, not a sign to quit. We are afraid because we have left behind the narrow comfort zone of the familiar and are moving into new, uncharted territory. Yet we discover that as we face our fears, they begin to lose their power over us. Chapter 18 examines a number of specific and powerful techniques that you can use to stop fear in its tracks.

The Will to Go for Cooperation and Learning

The second part of commitment is the will to go for it. You can measure your will to go for it by looking at how ready you are to learn new skills, attitudes, and behaviors and to seek out the cooperation and support of others. If you are too proud to ask for help, or to go through the awkward stage of learning, you're not ready to go for it. Remember, anything worth doing is worth doing poorly at first. Don't be afraid to look a little silly and don't expect yourself to learn everything at once. Similarly, you may feel foolish asking for help, yet how much more foolish to let your goals slip away, simply because you are protecting your ego from a few moments' embarrassment.

Resistance: Resistance is an energy that impedes or retards forward movement. When we set out to achieve our goals, we often meet resistance from others. Sometimes this resistance is a deliberate blocking; more often, it's mere inertia or resistance to change. When it comes to overcoming the resistance of others, it is vital that we consider their viewpoints and motivations. Then we can develop effective strategies to either gain their cooperation or find ways around, under, or through their resistance. Chapter 19 will explore how you can do this.

Overwhelm: We feel overwhelmed when we view ourselves as inadequate to the project before us. We feel overwhelmed because we are confused about how to proceed. We may lack the wisdom, information, skills, or organization necessary to realize our objectives. We need the patience and detachment to step back and see what it is that we must learn and do, and then break down these activities into bite-size chunks. When we commit ourselves to challenging goals, we realize how much we must grow to achieve them. The process of growth is often a humbling one. We may want to pretend that we have it all together, but there is always more to learn. Chapter 20 will explore how you can develop the skills and attitudes necessary to make lifelong learning an integral part of your growth process.

I hold to the doctrine that with ordinary talent, and extraordinary perseverance, all things are attainable.

THOMAS BUXTON

Distraction, fear, resistance, and *overwhelm,* then, are the obstacles that must be overcome if we are to achieve our goals. In confronting these barriers, it helps to think of yourself as a warrior. In fact, every warrior must overcome precisely these obstacles. The great samurai warriors of medieval Japan developed the discipline of single-minded action. They prided themselves in being able to remain unperturbed in the face of any and all distractions. They learned to master fear and act decisively. They knew that fear leads to doubt, hesitation, and paralysis and must be overcome. A true warrior knows that alone, he doesn't stand a chance. He needs allies. Therefore, he expands his power by skillfully enlisting the support of others. Finally, a warrior must be wise and detached. He must learn from his successes and defeats, as well as from those of others.

Never Give Up

Commitment means never giving up on your goals just because things are difficult. Quit your goals if they lose meaning for you. Never quit just because it seems too hard. We all respect people who won't quit. Picasso painted every day, until he could paint no more. You can bet there were days he didn't feel like it. Beethoven conducting the *Ninth Symphony* when he was stone deaf—that's commitment. Pat Griscus completing the grueling Iron Man Triathlon with an artificial leg— that's commitment. In the end, it *is* how you play the game. It's what you do with what you've got. Everyone who does the best he or she can with what he or she has is a winner. You will have your dark moments, your times of doubt and despair, but if you are committed, like all real winners, you will hang in there.

Not long after the Second World War, Sir Winston Churchill was called upon to deliver a commencement address. You can imagine the anticipation of the students as this international hero was about to address them. They were hanging on every word. What would this great orator have to say? Churchill lumbered to the platform and proclaimed the thirteen words that comprise one of the great speeches of the twentieth century: "Never give in, never give up, never, never, never, never, never give up." Then he sat down. Enough said.

Looking Ahead: The Four D's of Commitment

The chapters that follow will explore the four D's of commitment: Discipline, Daring, Diplomacy, and Detachment. It will take *discipline* to let go of the distracting negative habits and thoughts that slow you down. It will take *daring* to move forward in the face of fear. It will take *diplomacy* to overcome resistance and gain the support you need. Finally, it will take *detachment,* because it is the key to continued learning and growth. As you successfully master the obstacles to commitment, you'll build confidence in yourself. You'll come to know that you can be, do, or have anything.

The Four Barriers to Commitment and How to Overcome Them

WHAT THEY ARE	HOW THEY GET YOU	WHAT TO DO ABOUT THEM
1. Distractions	Diverting your attention away from the goal.	Discipline yourself to substitute constructive behaviors for compulsive distractions.
2. Fear	Paralyzes you, stops you in your tracks.	Dare to risk past fear.
3. Resistance	Any individual or group that blocks your advancement toward a particular goal.	Diplomatically develop trust and gain cooperation.
4. Overwhelm	Not doing what you know you should do because you don't have a clear enough idea of how to proceed.	Detach yourself emotionally, and learn what you need to know.

The Energy of Commitment

Manifestation is the process of converting a mental vision that exists in the realm of ideas, into a physical reality that exists in the realm of things. In order for a manifestation to occur, energy must be generated, transformed, and directed. Commitment is the make-or-break point in the Manifestation Formula. It's the point where the energy generated by the Vision and charged with the mental and emotional energy of Focus and Desire is transformed into physical action. The strength of the commitment necessary is determined by the scope of the vision. The greater the vision, the stronger the force of commitment required to realize it.

Once your vision has been charged with the energy of Focus and Desire, it is imperative that this energy be conserved and directed into action. Do not allow it to be dissipated or leaked through Distractions, Fear, Resistance, or Overwhelm. You can plug these potential leaks with sufficient Discipline, Daring, Diplomacy, and Detachment.

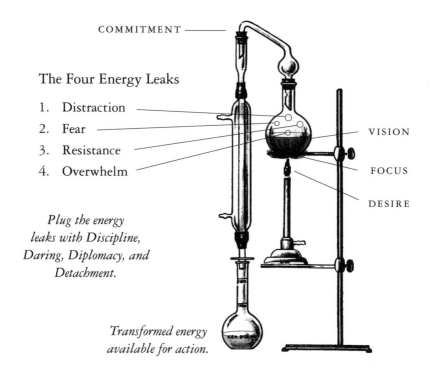

COMMITMENT

The Four Energy Leaks

1. Distraction
2. Fear
3. Resistance
4. Overwhelm

VISION

FOCUS

DESIRE

Plug the energy leaks with Discipline, Daring, Diplomacy, and Detachment.

Transformed energy available for action.

Commitment

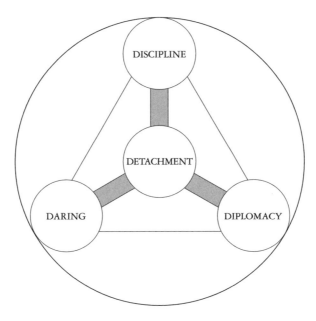

Either do not attempt at all or go through with it.   —OVID

There is nothing which persevering effort and unceasing and diligent
care can not accomplish.   —SENECA

Great works are performed not by strength, but by perseverance.
     —SAMUEL JOHNSON

So long as there is breath in me, that long will I persist, for I know one
of the greatest principles of success; if I persist long enough, I win.
     —OG MANDINO

Endurance is nobler than strength, and patience than beauty.
     —JOHN RUSKIN

Chapter 16 Exercises

❧

Affirming Your Commitment to Your Goals

Answer the following questions for each of your goals.

1. Why you are determined to meet this goal? What does it mean to you?

2. What opportunities will achieving this goal allow you to take advantage of?

3. What will you miss out on if you fail to achieve this goal?

4. In what ways is this goal especially suited to you? (Interest, talent, enjoyment, etc.)

5. What have you got going for you that suggests you'll make it?

Assessing Potential Barriers

Make a list of your goals and answer the following questions for each.

1. Which statement below best completes the following sentence? My biggest obstacle is likely to be:_____

    a) getting distracted by more immediate gratifications.
    b) being paralyzed by fear.
    c) being unable to ask for and obtain the cooperation, help, and support I need.
    d) getting overwhelmed, feeling like there are too many new things to learn, and having difficulty deciding what to do next.

2. Next write the percentage of confidence you have in your goal's completion vs. potential barriers. For example, one of Jim's financial goals is to buy three new income-producing properties by January 1, 2003. It's a realistic goal for him, and he feels about 80 percent sure he will actually finish it on time. So he writes 80 percent for assurance, and 20 percent for barriers.

Indicate the confidence you have in your goal's completion vs. the doubt you have about overcoming potential barriers.

Goal	Confidence	Doubt
1.		
2.		
3.		
4.		
5.		
6.		
7.		
8.		

3. Next, divide the barriers into Distractions, Fears, Overwhelm, and Resistance, and indicate a percentage for each. For example, Jim feels that if he doesn't accomplish his goals, it'll most likely be because he got distracted and watched his favorite television shows every evening instead of watching the newspapers for good deals. He marks 45 percent for Distraction. Jim feels comfortable with his social skills, and he has a background in sales. He has little fear about putting together deals. His main fear is that he might make a poor choice that will lose him money, so Jim marks 20 percent for Fear. Jim's wife Roberta is very supportive and is going to help Jim with this project. The only resistance Jim will have to face is that of the sellers who are selling their homes, and he is trained to handle that kind of resistance. Jim marks 10 percent for Resistance. Jim already knows much of what he must know in order to accomplish his goal, but he will have to learn more about real-estate law. He will also have to make sure that he follows his plan step by step. He marks 25 percent for Overwhelm.

Divide the barriers into Distractions, Fears, Overwhelm, and Resistance, and indicate a percentage for each.

Goal	Distractions	Fears	Overwhelm	Resistance
1.				
2.				
3.				
4.				
5.				
6.				
7.				
8.				

Discipline: Mastering Distraction 17

Perhaps the most valuable result of all education
is the ability to make yourself do the thing you ought to do,
when you ought to do it, whether you like it or not.

THOMAS HUXLEY

Many people are put off by the word *discipline*. For some, it conjures up painful images of childhood punishments. For others, it brings to mind slavish submission to a rigid routine. Still others associate it with emotional or sexual repression and stoic self-denial. If we think of discipline as something painful, mechanical, or stiff, we can hardly be blamed for resisting it. If we think of it as a coercive force imposed from the outside, it's not surprising that we shrink from it. Yet there is another, more constructive way to view discipline. This chapter will explore how we can develop the kind of discipline necessary to master the distractions that might keep us from our goals.

Genuine self-discipline is essential to a free and creative life. I define self-discipline as "the purposeful direction of mental, emotional, and physical energies toward the achievement of definite, self-selected objectives." Discipline, then, is simply acting on purpose. Any purposeful, meaningful action is a disciplined action. Anything that takes you off purpose is a distraction.

Discipline requires the ability to put decision ahead of fleeting feelings in determining action. You've used your intuition and reason to determine your path. Yet, as you move down that path, there will be times when your feelings will rebel against your decision. You may not feel like taking an action that is necessary to achieving your goals, or you may feel like you would rather do something that will take you off track. You simply can't rely on your feelings to move you where you need to go. You must act from decision.

Often, the more important the step, the less we feel like doing it. In fact, at the moment of truth, we may feel like doing anything but what we need to do. The professional actor with stage fright, the groom with the last-minute jitters, and the job seeker before an interview are classic cases of feelings in conflict with decision. Often, the good feelings come only *after* we've taken action. Develop the discipline to follow through with your decisions, and the good feelings will take care of themselves.

Discipline has value to the degree that it helps you get what you want out of life. As a practical matter, discipline means mastering distractions. You get distracted when you take your attention off your objectives and your desire to accomplish them, and allow it to drift. You get back on track by reminding yourself of your goals and what it means to you to achieve them. Act on the belief that you *will* master the obstacles before you, by aggressively confronting them.

Distractions: Attention Hijackers

Modern life is full of distractions. It seems that something or someone is always trying to take us off track. We can think of distractions as attention hijackers. You have in mind a point of focus, an objective, or destination. Then something comes along that grabs your attention and steers it in an entirely different direction. As all disciplines are finally a result of mental discipline, so all distractions result from a lapse in mental concentration.

A certain amount of distraction is unavoidable. Despite our best efforts, we will always be subject to interruptions from others and the minor nuisances of everyday life. The best way of dealing with these kinds of distractions is simply to accept them as inevitable and get back to work as quickly as possible. Becoming upset by them is futile and counter-productive. Our own irritation or emotional reaction is likely to cost us far more time and energy than the initial interruption itself. As worrying about not sleeping will keep you awake, so worrying over the time you spent dealing with minor interruptions will only cost you more time.

When we are honest, we must admit that the biggest distractions are the ones we bring upon ourselves. These distractions result from our own inner psychological turmoil and ambivalence, rather than any outside influence. They are patterns of avoidance that both cover and reinforce feelings of fear. For example, one of Amy's career goals is to become a vice president in the large corporation she works for. Yet Amy is overly concerned about what people think of her. In her efforts to get everyone to like her, Amy loses sight of her primary goal. She lives in constant fear of being criticized and appears needy and overly deferential.

From a purely technical standpoint, Amy does her job well enough. Yet her need for approval keeps her from advancing into a managerial position, where leadership and an ability to command authority are required. Her emotional insecurity and dependency affect the way others see her. She just doesn't come across as management material. She can't understand why she is passed over in favor of less experienced people who don't put in the hours she does. Her need in the present to get the approval that she lacked as a child is distracting her from her goal.

This example illustrates several important points about distractions.

1. **Distractions arise out of secondary motives.** (In this case, the compulsive need for approval.)

No man is free who cannot command himself.

PYTHAGORAS

2. **Distractions cover fear.** (She fears criticism and rejection if she asserts herself.)
3. **Distractions are out-of-control attempts at gaining control.** (In this case, she attempts to gain control by being overly dutiful and "nice.")

Patterns of Distraction

The most insidious distractions are the habitual thoughts, feelings, and activities that repeatedly pull you away from your stated intentions. I call these "patterns of distraction." (Some of the more popular ones are listed below.) While patterns of distraction take many forms, they are all out-of-control attempts at gaining control. In other words, when we are anxious or feeling out of control, we resort to one or more of these patterns in an attempt to gain a sense of being in control. Yet, ironically, giving in to these distractions only leaves us feeling more out of control. You will probably recognize yourself in one or more of the patterns described below. Becoming aware of your patterns of distraction is the first and most critical step to overcoming them.

Perfectionism

"I can't do it until. . . " You think that everything must be perfect before you can work on your goals. You straighten your desk or organize your files instead of writing the report. You intended to spend the day doing research on your new business idea but instead found yourself reorganizing your closet or cleaning out the garage. You decide you can't take any action on X because you're waiting on Y. Perfectionists fear being criticized or evaluated for their performance. Because they equate their performance with their worth as human beings, they tense up under pressure—often to the point of paralysis. Then, in an effort to relieve their tension, they often turn to compulsive sorting, cleaning, organizing, or similar pursuits that give them a feeling of being in control.

Remedy for perfectionism: Accept that no human being is perfect and that no human activity is ever done to perfection. Don't let the perfect become the enemy of the good. Suspend judgment of yourself; put aside your fears about what others will think—and act! Recognize that you can always do something constructive to further progress toward your goals and that everything you do will motivate you to do still more.

Seduction

"First, I'll do this one little thing, and then I'll get down to business. First, I'll chat on the phone, surf the Internet, read a magazine, watch part of a television show, or go and get some snacks, then I'll get to work on my goals." You take the seductive bait. Before you know it, "a few minutes" has become an hour or more. Then you might get caught up in yet another distraction. Pretty soon, the thought creeps in: "Oh well, it's already too late now. I'll get started on this tomorrow." Most people are used to working for someone else and on someone else's timeline. Even individuals in very responsible positions, who are extremely disciplined at work, often have difficulty staying on track on their own time.

Remedy for seduction: Learn to value your time as much as you do the time someone else is paying you for. You can't get away with goofing off at work. Don't do it when you are your own boss. Work on your goals when you feel spontaneously motivated and inspired to do so *and* when you have scheduled time to do so. If you feel you need a reward, make sure that it comes *after* you have done your work. Put the seductive thing in front of you as something waiting for you when you have finished. In time, you will find that you need less and less of this kind of motivation. The satisfaction of doing the thing itself will be reward enough. Meanwhile, enjoy your rewards *after* you have completed what you have set out to do.

There never has been, and cannot be, a good life without self-control.

LEO TOLSTOY

Creating Conflict

"It's your fault that I can't make any progress." You're anxious about your goal. You start an argument with your mate or with a co-worker, spend the day fighting or being upset, and make little or no progress on your goals. Then you blame the other party because you failed to get anything done. This pattern is a favorite of those who have difficulty asking for support or receiving help from others. They tend to view asking for help from others as a sign of weakness. Often they attempt to do everything themselves until they reach a breaking point; then they lash out at those around them—claiming that others are not being supportive or are actively sabotaging their efforts.

Remedy for creating conflict: If you recognize yourself in this pattern, admit your frustration and fear. Be willing to ask for the help you need, and even more important, be willing to receive it. You might be surprised at how much support is there for you right now, if you are ready to receive it. Also, recognize that while the support of others is important, the most critical steps to achieving your goals must be taken by you and you alone. We only feel the need to blame others when we feel defeated ourselves. When we recognize that all failure is simply the failure to concentrate, we can shake off the sense of defeat and get back in the hunt. When we demonstrate our commitment to our goals by taking decisive action, we attract the support of others. It really is true: the more we are ready to help ourselves, the more others will be ready to help us.

Creating Chaos

"When things settle down, I'll get started." Life is a play, which is to say, a drama. If you're not actively involved in creating your drama, you will feel like you are the victim of one. The creative drama of your life is framed by your desire to fulfill your destiny by realizing and expressing the best of who you are. The creative conflict or tension is supplied by the obstacles that must be overcome on the way to actualizing your full potential. When we fail to embrace the creative drama of our lives, we can easily get caught up in peripheral ones. In the vernacular, we call it "making mountains out of molehills."

Remedy for creating chaos: There is a Czech saying, "Trouble comes in a door left open." You close the door on an army of troubles when you decide to take responsibility for the direction of your life. Embracing the creative life and accepting responsibility for it has its costs and demands, but nothing is more painful or futile than allowing our lives to drift into pettiness or meaninglessness. Problems are a fact of life from which we cannot escape. We can, however, decide whether most of our problems will be the result of confronting or avoiding the important issues in our lives. Remember, nature abhors a vacuum. *If you are not actively choosing your problems, problems will come looking for you.*

Majoring in the Minors

"I'm so busy, I can't do it now." You load up your schedule with so many activities that you don't have time to get to the important things. You tell yourself, "I'm so busy, how can I be faulted for not making progress? I just don't have the time." In today's fast-paced society, a lot of people take pride in being busy for its own sake. Yet we can't compare frenetically running around in circles to making even a little progress toward our lifelong goals. As Thoreau put it, "It is not enough to be busy, so are the ants. The question is, what are we busy about?"

Remedy for majoring in the minors: Often, the most constructive step we can take to make progress on our goals is to do absolutely nothing. When we pause to catch our breath, we can begin to see that the real problem isn't lack of time but our fears about confronting our goals. Remember, a goal is a goal because it requires us to stretch ourselves beyond our current comfort zones. It is often easier to keep ourselves occupied with the familiar than to face the fears associated with new challenges. Busyness can become a form of psychological defense. It takes courage to stop running long enough to admit your fear. Only then can you take action that will really make a difference.

Perseverance is a great element of success. If you only knock long enough and loud enough at the gate, you are sure to wake up somebody.

HENRY LONGFELLOW

In his best-selling book *The Seven Habits of Highly Effective People*, Stephen Covey distinguished what he called the "urgent" from the "important." Don't let the urgent things, like paying your mortgage or bills, keep you from the important things, like doing your life's work or creating fulfilling personal relationships. Make a habit of prioritizing your day's activities. Be sure the most important ones get not only your time but also your best effort and energy.

Wavering

"I'm not sure I want this after all. . ." At the first sign of difficulty or resistance, you begin to doubt the validity of your goal. Perhaps you decide to abandon it altogether in favor of a new idea that "sounds more exciting." While there may be times when it is appropriate to change direction, often it is just a matter of facing the fact that it is going to take a lot of work to achieve your goals.

Remedy for wavering: Don't fall victim to the grass-is-always-greener fallacy. A writer working on a book, an entrepreneur starting a new business, a runner preparing for a marathon, anyone working on maintaining a long-term loving relationship is likely to run into blocks, obstacles, and difficulties. The tests of character come in how we meet these challenges. Do we give up? Do we decide that jumping to something or someone else is the answer? Or do we stay with it until we break through to new levels of competency, strength, and understanding? The sense of personal power and self-confidence you gain in mastering one challenge will help you tackle the next. On the other hand, walking away from difficulties can become a habit that deflates your self-esteem and limits your world.

Impatience

"This is taking too long. I'll never get there." This pattern recalls Aesop's fable of the tortoise and the hare. You start out all fired up and tear after your goals like a mad dog in heat. You make a good deal of initial progress but soon become exhausted by an unrealistic pace. In your drive to achieve your goals, you neglect other areas of your life, for example, your health or relationships. Then you decide that the pursuit of your goal just isn't worth the toll it is taking on the rest of your life.

Remedy for impatience: Taking a more balanced and realistic approach to begin with would have spared you from the pain of defeat. Learning to pace yourself is critical to going the distance. Impatience also defeats us when we fail to value the progress we are making. Our modern culture is obsessed with immediate results and instant gratification. Those in more direct contact with nature understand the value of process. Any growing thing starts slowly. A planted seed is growing, even before it breaks the surface of the soil. It often takes a good deal of time to lay a foundation that will allow for rapid growth later on. You are right to be eager for results, but it helps to value all the steps you're taking along the way.

Rescuing

"It's selfish to focus on my goals when so-and-so is obviously so much worse off than I am. . ." Some people get so caught up in rescuing others that they never seem to have the time or energy to get around to dealing with the important issues in their own lives. Often those with this pattern attract dysfunctional people who gobble up endless hours of their time. While the people they help may appear grateful, they seldom (if ever) act on the advice they receive or follow up on the help they are given, by taking the next step on their own.

Remedy for rescuing: People who make a habit of trying to rescue others are looking to escape from their own lives by becoming entangled in the dramas of others. They also gain a sense of superiority in the bargain. They say to themselves. "Look, this person is obviously worse off (or a bigger mess) than I am." This is not unlike the perverse satisfaction that many derive from watching daytime TV talk shows featuring confessions of the sad and dysfunctional. Recognize that the need to feel superior comes from a deep-seated belief that you aren't good enough. Put your energy where it will yield fruits. Work on your

Everybody, soon or late, sits down to a banquet of consequences.

ROBERT LOUIS
STEVENSON

own goals, and help people who want to help themselves and who will do something constructive with the energy you give them.

Distractions Arise Out of Secondary Motives

All of these debilitating patterns of distraction arise from secondary motives. In chapter 9, the terms "primary" and "secondary motives" were first introduced. At that point in the process, it was important to evaluate your motives for selecting specific goals, ensuring that each would be backed by a reliable and energy-rich primary motive. Yet even when you've chosen your goals for the right reasons, secondary motives may still creep in and thwart your efforts to achieve your objectives. Chronic distractions are defense mechanisms that not only divert attention away from your goals but also keep you from confronting the secondary motives that sustain them. While distractions may take an endless variety of forms, their purpose is always the same—to cover a sore spot.

Distractions Are Out-of-Control Attempts At Gaining Control

Often we turn to distractions when we begin to feel afraid. If you find yourself frequently giving in to distractions, recognize that you are getting something out of them. That "something" is a false or limited sense of control. Your patterns of distractions are devices you've created to keep you from confronting the insecurity, anxiety, or the fear of failure or rejection you feel. You lose real control when you refuse to face and overcome these fears. You regain control by confronting your fear and making a constructive effort to act into the situation.

Of course, in the short run, it's easier to maintain patterns of distraction than to overcome them. Yet the easy way is seldom the most fulfilling. It's easier to open a can of soup than to cook a gourmet meal, but you can't expect it to taste the same. The effort you put into facing your fears and overcoming debilitating distractions will pay off. You will find that you not only accomplish your goals with greater speed and less inner conflict but that you also feel better about yourself.

It's useful to distinguish between goal-specific and chronic distractions. Goal-specific distractions are triggered by the fears we feel in regard to executing a particular task or dealing with a particular situation. A salesman who devises distractions as a way of avoiding making cold calls is one example. The specific distractions that he comes up with to avoid making these calls may not be a problem in other areas of his life. On the other hand, chronic distractions cut across all areas of your life, robbing you of self-confidence and energy. Like hungry ghosts, chronic distractions gobble up tremendous amounts of your time and energy, yet leave you feeling empty. Chronic distractions are your "bad habits."

Distractions only become an issue when you take your focus off of your objective and your primary motive for accomplishing it. In facing your distractions, it helps to address both elements of the problem: (1) your fear of the effort and possible failure associated with moving toward your goal, and (2) the benefits you gain from the distraction.

Discipline is learnt in the school of adversity.

GANDHI

How to Overcome Distraction: The Methods of Self-Discipline

Below, you will find two general strategies for overcoming distractions: *bulldozing* and *dovetailing*. To employ the bulldozing strategy, identify your objective and your primary motive for accomplishing it. Admit what you're afraid of; then move through the barrier. This is the formula one popular psychologist calls "feel the fear and do it anyway."

To employ the *dovetailing* strategy, begin by stating your goal and your primary motive for accomplishing it. Next, identify your principal distractions and the payoffs you get from them. Finally, determine how you can get similar benefits from behaviors that will move you forward on your goals. Bulldozing is a direct method, dovetailing a more roundabout one; yet both are equally effective. Sometimes you will go right through an obstacle; at other times, you may want to find a way around it. Bulldozing is generally more effective in dealing with goal-specific distractions; dovetailing, with chronic distractions. Let's follow an example of each all the way through.

Goal-Specific Distractions

Tim and Jo Ann are a married couple in their early thirties. One of their goals was to improve the sense of intimacy and harmony in their relationship. Tim and Jo Ann had a distracting habit of getting involved in heated arguments over petty issues. They recognized that this habit had to go if they were to achieve their goal. Both were well-educated and articulate professionals who had no problems relating to others socially or at work. Yet at home, they often fought like cats and dogs. They played a destructive game of verbal one-upmanship and hurt each other deeply with cutting insults.

Later, they would regret the things they had said. They would even make plans for what they would do the next time they felt the urge to raise the verbal hatchet and start hacking away. Yet their best-laid plans would soon go awry, and once again, the fur would start to fly. They claimed that they just couldn't control themselves and were at a loss about what to do about these fighting spells.

In talking with Tim and Jo Ann, one thing was clear; they were ambivalent about fighting. As Jo Ann put it, "I like to argue," yet she lamented the hurt it brought. Tim felt much the same way. At this point in their lives, Tim and Jo Ann's compulsive "need" to be right or "win" was blocking their stated intention of improving their relationship. Each had read books on communication, and together they had even attended a class on communication in relationships. Their problem wasn't the result of a lack of knowledge or skill but a lack of self-awareness.

Now let's look at how Tim and Jo Ann (almost without realizing it) used bulldozing to overcome the distracting pattern of heated arguments. Again, the formula for bulldozing is:

1. Focus on your objective and your primary motive for accomplishing it.
2. Admit your fear.
3. Tackle the task at hand.

Goal:	Tim and Jo Ann's goal was to increase harmony and intimacy in their relationship.
Primary Motive:	Their primary motive was love.
Distraction:	Overheated arguments and the exchange of insults.
Fear:	They feared opening to deeper levels of emotional vulnerability.
Positive Action:	Reestablished connection through touch.

Admit the Fear

One day, in the midst of yet another heated conflict, Jo Ann suddenly stopped and said, "You know, Tim, this is not getting us anywhere. I feel frightened... Would you hold me?" Tim was baffled and surprised by the abrupt change in Jo Ann's tone. Tentatively at first, and then with a sense of relief, he reached out his arms. Holding her tight, Tim said, "I love you; I know what you mean. I'm afraid of what we're doing to each other." Admitting their fears allowed Tim and Jo Ann the opportunity to move forward and confront their problems. Despite their volatile past, Tim and Jo Ann knew they loved one another deeply. Eventually, they recognized that when one of them feared being abandoned or when either of them feared being misunderstood, they tended to get defensive and raise the volume.

Tim and Jo Ann were afraid of moving to the next level of intimacy, the deeper level of trust that arguing distracted them from. They had clung to the fighting habit because they were afraid of feeling out of control *and* afraid of admitting it. Both had been raised to view emotional vulnerability as a sign of weakness. Yet to love deeply is to place your heart in the hands of another, and that can seem frightening.

If you don't stand for something, you'll fall for anything.

MICHAEL EVANS

275

Though arguing was painful for them, it was familiar and gave them a sense (even if a false sense) of being in control. The energy that could have gone into nurturing their relationship, and deepening the sense of intimacy in it, went into fighting instead. Arguing had distracted them from the fear they needed to move through in order to get closer.

Note: If you are unaware of what you are afraid of, you may gain some insights by reading the next chapter. If you are honest and your intention to understand is strong enough, this will probably be enough. If not, you may want to seek the aid of a professional therapist to help you clarify your fears. (Most of us know what we are afraid of. And if we are willing to admit it, we can speed up the process immensely, whether we work with a therapist or not.)

Tackle the Problem

Tim and Jo Ann decided that whenever they felt themselves beginning to get into a verbal fracas, they would stop and hold each other. By stopping and communicating through touch, where misunderstanding is less likely to be a problem, they were able to reestablish emotional rapport before things could get out of hand. More importantly, knowing that they could always come back to this connected place gave Tim and Jo Ann the confidence they needed to begin addressing some of the more emotionally sensitive issues they had previously avoided. They found a way to discuss these issues from a framework of "us" rather than "you against me." As strange as it may seem to apply the word *bulldozing* to something as warm and fuzzy as a hug, it fits the formula for this reason: Tim and Jo Ann admitted their fear and moved directly to solve the problem.

Chronic Distraction

Dale has two important goals. He wants to change careers and to develop a meaningful intimate relationship. At a certain point, Dale realized his television viewing habits were holding him back. One night, he got up after watching five solid hours and decided he'd had enough. He said to himself, "That's it! There are better things I could be doing with my life." He unplugged the set, told himself, "No more," and lumbered off to bed. The next night after dinner, he remembered his promise to himself. He couldn't help but remember—the television was still unplugged. Yet he wasn't quite sure what else to do. He read the newspaper extra well and then sat down with a novel. Still, in the back of his mind, he wondered what was happening on his favorite television program.

Since he hadn't made the effort to plan activities that would move him toward his goals, before the evening was out, the tube was back on. Dale felt like a failure for lacking the will power to break the TV habit. Yet the reason he hadn't overcome this habit wasn't a lack of will power but a lack of clearly defined alternatives. Let's look at how Dale used dovetailing to overcome his addiction to television viewing. Again, the formula for dovetailing is:

1. State your goal and primary motive.
2. Identify the distraction.
2. Identify what you get out of the distraction.
3. Find a way to get the same things in a way that will move you toward your goal.

Dale's goal:	To change careers and develop an intimate relationship.
Distraction:	Watching television.
What he gets out of it:	Relaxation, easing his loneliness, entertainment, and belonging. (The people where Dale works also watch a lot of television, and discussing shows gives him a way of participating in the group.)

Dovetailing Activities

1. **Easing Loneliness:** By taking evening classes that help to prepare him for his new career, Dale furthers both of his goals simultaneously. Besides the career knowledge he gains from them, evening classes give Dale an opportunity to meet women with similar interests.

2. **Relaxation:** Dale finds that it reduces stress to run for a couple of miles every other day. It gives him more energy, helps him to stay trim, and gives his self-esteem a boost. To keep himself motivated and to make it more fun, Dale joins an early morning running club.

3. **Belonging/Approval:** Taking classes three nights a week and joining a running club provide Dale with opportunities to make friends with people who share his interests. Even if he doesn't meet the woman of his dreams, he has still gained a more rewarding social life.

4. **Entertainment:** Dale now wants to participate in his life, not just watch it go by. He realizes that even something as simple as having coffee with one of his classmates is a lot more interesting and rewarding than an evening of television sitcoms.

The compulsive nature of chronic distractions can leave you feeling exasperated and out of control. Their effect on your efforts to achieve your goals can be devastating. It's not just a matter of wasted time. It isn't just that Dale couldn't work toward his goals while addicted to watching television. The demoralizing effect that this compulsive behavior had on his self-esteem and confidence was even more problematic.

As Dale's example indicates, when it comes to chronic distractions, "don't do it" is not enough. If we want to change, we must *replace* distracting behaviors with positive alternatives. Epictetus said, "If you would make anything a habit, do it; if you would not make it a habit, do not do it, but accustom yourself to do something in place of it."

Look for ways you can get the same kinds of benefits you receive from habitual distractions—only while doing activities that will move you closer to your goal. Once you decide to eliminate a chronic distraction, you will find that the number of effective alternatives is virtually limitless.

It may take considerable effort to make a change. As strange as it sounds, you may unconsciously believe you need a given chronic distraction in order to feel comfortable or even secure in your identity. (If I'm not visible by my accomplishments and self-expression, then at least you can recognize me by my distractions.) Constructive, goal-directed actions may seem to threaten the sense of identity that we create through attachment to chronic distractions. Yet, if we are to achieve our goals, these distractions must go. Mental and emotional self-awareness are vital. Ask yourself, "Am I choosing my goal or am I choosing a distraction by this particular thought or action?"

Amy, Tim and Jo Ann, and Dale all had to do some trimming before they could reach their goals. Most likely you do, too. A gardener prunes withering branches from a tree so that the healthy ones can receive all of the tree's nutrient resources. In the same way, trim the dead branches of distraction from the tree of your life, and you give budding new possibilities a chance to thrive. Take out the pruning shears and cut away decaying distractions that lead you away from your goals and desires.

Chronic distractions may include any of the following:

Alcohol Abuse	Drug Abuse	Pandering
Arguing	Gambling	Promiscuity
Blaming	Idling	Reading
Collecting	Isolation	Rebelling
Comparing	Judging	Shopping
Complaining	Moping	TV Viewing
Daydreaming	Overeating	Talking

Self-Pity: The Ultimate Distraction

One of the biggest distractions is the habit of feeling sorry for ourselves. We can bemoan the difficulties and problems that attend everyday life and the quest to achieve our goals, or we can embrace them as challenges and opportunities to grow. Your goals represent aspects of yourself that are seeking greater expression. Rejoice in the opportunities for growth they afford, *and* in all the tests and challenges that come with them. Many of us are so used to struggling that we struggle even when it comes to doing things we really enjoy. When you admit how much you love something, you eliminate the need to make a problem out of getting it.

In order for Louise to accomplish her career goal, it is essential that she frequently speak before large groups. Louise is a competent speaker who has been speaking before groups for several years. Yet she has a nasty habit of going through near hysteria before every speech. Even though her material is well-organized and prepared, she makes such a production out of the process that she is nearly impossible to live with forty-eight hours prior to giving a speech, and completely burnt-out afterwards.

Louise makes a big point of telling everyone how much she hates public speaking and how difficult it is for her. The truth is, she loves it. She never feels more like herself than when she's in front of a group. But to hear her tell it, you would think she was a calf being lead to slaughter, rather than a competent woman expressing herself in a dynamic way. Louise just isn't willing to admit how much she enjoys being the center of attention and expressing herself in a dynamic and powerful way. Moreover, since she tells everyone, including herself, that speaking is difficult for her, she makes it so. Louise has to let go of her false humility in order to make her dreams really come alive. Everybody has a little ham in them. We all want to be stars in our own lives. It's insincere to pretend that we don't. It's okay to really love what you are doing and to get off on doing it. It goes without saying that you can't feel sorry for yourself and proud of your accomplishments at the same time. Get into it!

Discipline

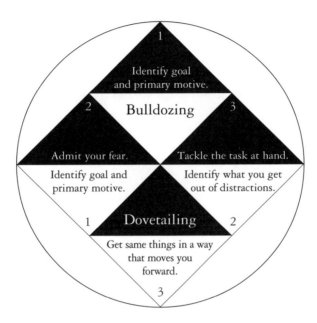

He who cannot obey himself will be commanded. This is the nature of living creatures.
—FREDRICH NIETZSCHE

Strength doesn't come from physical capacity.
It comes from indomitable will.
—MAHATMA GANDHI

To the degree that we become enemies to the highest and best within us, do we become enemies to all.
—RALPH W. TRINE

If people knew how hard I worked to get my mastery, it wouldn't seem so wonderful after all.
—MICHELANGELO

Chapter 17 Exercises

❧

Bulldozing

1. State one or more of your goals. Then answer the following questions for each goal.

2. What is your primary motive for accomplishing this goal?

3. What is likely to be the biggest ditraction that will slow your progress toward this goal?

4. What fears lie behind this distraction?

5. How will you confront and overcome these fears? What specific steps will you take to power through this distraction?

Dovetailing

1. State one or more of your goals.

2. After each goal, list the distractions that are likely to pull you off course from achieving it.

3. For each distraction, list three benefits that you get out of the distraction.

4. Next, list five ways you can get similar benefits through activities that will move you closer to the accomplishment of your goal.

Chronic Distraction Analysis

List your chronic distractions.

Then, for each chronic distraction, answer the following questions:

MAINTAIN STATUS QUO

1. What do I like about it?

2. What stake do I have in maintaining this distraction?

3. What is the compulsive need behind this distraction?

INITIATE CHANGE

1. How does this distraction limit me?

2. Why do I want to change it?

3. What will I replace it with?

Daring: Overcoming Fear

*Has fear ever held a man back from anything
he really wanted, or a woman either?*

GEORGE BERNARD SHAW

Making the commitment to get married, to move to a new city, to change careers, to start your own business, to paint, to write, or to learn a new skill—all of these decisions involve risk. Risk implies danger, the possibility of loss. Where there is danger, fear is usually in hot pursuit. The thought of acting on your decisions can put your hair on end. To remind yourself that others who were probably just as scared as you faced these dangers and overcame them can be a comforting thought. Yet, if it doesn't leave you entirely reassured, you may want to take a more studied approach to fear. That's what this chapter is about. It's designed to help you better understand fear—and give you the tools to master it.

Fear Is a Natural Part of Taking a Risk

In order to win in the game of life, it helps to recognize that fear is a natural part of taking risks. Once you accept fear, you have the power to overcome it. Of course, accepting fear doesn't mean dwelling on it. A dwelling is a place you live in; don't dwell on fear unless you want to live in it. On the other hand, avoiding or suppressing fear can get you into big trouble. To suppress awareness of a danger signal just because it is unpleasant to look at or feel is to invite disaster. Many who abuse alcohol or drugs do so to suppress the fear they feel. The best approach to taking risks is a balanced one that neither denies nor coddles fear. Fear can be either a friend or an enemy, depending on the situation and how you respond to it.

When Is Fear a Friend?

Fear is a friend when it springs from real dangers *and* you listen to what it is trying to tell you. Often, fear is simply a self-protective instinct, a surge of physical energy alerting you to the fact that you are facing danger. It's your body's way of warning you that you need to act—immediately. If you're standing in the middle of the freeway and cars are coming at you at sixty-five miles an hour, the fear you feel is a message to get out of the way. At other times, fear is a message from your subconscious mind, warning you to pay attention to some situation that you're denying or avoiding on a conscious level. If you are about to be laid off from your job, the fear you feel is a message to do something about finding another one. If your relationship is on the skids, the fear you feel is telling you to sit down with your partner and take an honest assessment of the situation. In the examples above, fear is a messenger whose warnings you ignore at your peril.

When Is Fear an Enemy?

Fear is an enemy when it is based on erroneous assumptions. For example, a person may be hypersensitive to criticism and thus fear that others are trying to snub or put her down when no slight or malice is intended. You can distinguish between rational and irrational fears on the basis of how real or immediate the danger is. When you become aware of fear, ask yourself, "Is this a rational fear? Are the dangers real?" If so, take corrective action to mitigate the danger—respond to the message that the fear signals. If not, use the techniques described below to gain mastery over it.

Even when fear arises from rational and legitimate concerns, it becomes counterproductive once you have recognized a problem and begun taking corrective action to overcome it. In this case, use the techniques below to keep fear from interfering with your constructive efforts. Using these techniques will ensure that what was once your friend won't become your enemy. When we recognize that we can respond to fear—without denying or repressing it on the one hand or being paralyzed by it on the other—we gain confidence that we can master it.

Men are not influenced by things, but by their thoughts about things.

EPICTETUS

Preparation Kills Fear

The better prepared you are for a potentially risky situation, the less you will be troubled by fear. For example, let's say you have a presentation to make in front of a group, or an important test to take for a degree program you are pursuing. Procrastinating until the last minute will tend to make you anxious and tense. On the other hand, if you take the time to carefully organize your thoughts and rehearse your presentation, or study well for the test, you greatly reduce fear. Preparation not only increases the probability of success but also greatly reduces the stress you feel along the way.

The same applies to long-range goals. If, for example, your goal involves starting a new business, taking the time to prepare a detailed business plan can reduce your fear by helping to acquaint you with potential problems. They won't sneak up on you or surprise you. You will have the opportunity to develop strategies for overcoming these obstacles well before you actually encounter them. (This is one reason why a business plan is a good idea, even for those who have in mind smaller starts-ups that don't require the support of outside investors or lenders.) For each of your goals, make a list of the steps you can take to reduce fear, by preparing to meet potential difficulties. Be aware that fear most often surfaces in conjunction with doing new things and learning new skills, knowledge, or behaviors. Chapter 20, and especially the exercises at the end of it, will help you to address these issues in a systematic and strategic way.

Choose Your Response

No matter how well-prepared you are, fear may still arise from time to time as you move toward your goals. Yet you needn't let it get the best of you. Below, you will find five techniques you can use to move out of fear. (A sixth method is discussed in chapter 14, namely, using relaxation techniques to change the physiological symptoms of fear.) Choose the techniques that suit you best, depending on the situation and your personal preference.

The first four techniques can be used on the spot to immediately reduce fear. The fifth technique requires the analysis of long-term patterns of losing out to fear, as well as frequent spot-checking to ensure that you don't allow these patterns to creep in and sabotage your efforts. Each of the techniques below involves making some kind of change. Changing any of the components or attributes of fear will begin to give you a sense that you are in control of it. Once you gain experience in controlling fear, it need never rule you again. As you consider the techniques below, it will be helpful to keep in mind the following definition of fear: *Fear is the anticipation of future loss or injury.*

Techniques for Mastering Fear

1. **Change the anticipation:** Think of gains, not losses.

2. **Change the time frame:** Move out of the future and into the past or present.

3. **Change the name:** Reinterpret the energy.

4. **Change the proportion:** Blow it up and watch it blow away.

5. **Change your awareness:** Become aware of and change the ideas that feed fear.

Fear Mastery Technique #1: Change the Anticipation

It is often said that we fear the unknown. Yet this unknown is not so much an empty void as a kind of blank slate onto which our imaginations project possible scenarios of the future. Often, it's the anticipation of dreaded consequences that makes us feel afraid. For example, when you see a suspense or horror film for the first time, your fear is greatest as you anticipate the terror that lurks around the corner (right before the ambush, just before the heroes are captured, on entry into the haunted house, or just before the appearance of the dreaded . . .) After you have seen the film and know where the "scary" parts are, your fear is greatly diminished. It is not the scene itself that is frightening but the anticipation of it. So it is with life. It is the anticipation of what lies ahead that either makes us feel excited and eager to move forward or makes us feel afraid and reticent to act.

Remember your emotional responses can support or thwart your efforts to get what you want. Change your feeling toward an activity or goal by changing what you are anticipating. In every situation, there is the potential for loss and gain. Train your mind to focus on what you can win, gain, and accomplish. Whenever you begin to feel afraid, stop thinking about what you have to lose and focus on what you can gain by moving forward.

Fear Mastery Technique #2: Change the Time Frame

Again, fear is the anticipation of future loss or injury. Just as you can move out of fear by changing your anticipation, so you can leave it behind by changing your "mental" time. Fear evaporates as you shift your thinking out of the future and come back to the present. When you're having a bad dream, you feel reassured as you begin to wake up and realize where you are. You're not in this horrible place you have imagined but safe and secure in your own bed. Recognize that in order for your mind to be free to generate negative scenarios about the future, you have to be safe in the present. People who are literally face-to-face with death may see their lives pass before them, but they certainly aren't worried about what's going to happen tomorrow. The fact that you have the time and energy to worry about the future suggests that you are safe now. You can stop fear at any time by bringing your awareness back to the present or by recalling past successes. Go back to the future when you are ready to think about it in a constructive way.

Fear Mastery Technique #3: Change the Name

Researchers in biofeedback have long known that the physiological markers for fear are virtually identical with those for positive excitement. Elevated heart and respiratory rates, increased perspiration and adrenal secretions accompany both. Those who consistently succeed tend to interpret these physiological cues differently from those who don't. Those in the first group say to themselves, "I'm really excited!" or "I'm so thrilled and keyed up for this!" While those in the second group tend to interpret the same physiological cues as fear and so respond with avoidance or aggression.

The way we name and interpret events often determines how we respond to them. Watch a child learning to walk. She falls down–kerplunk on her rear—then waits and watches. The people around her smile or laugh, so she begins to smile or laugh. Yet, if the people around her react with fear and a gasp, the child will start to cry. The child is learning how to interpret the event and thus how to respond to it. In the same way, you have learned to interpret the physiological cues that you call fear or excitement.

When working to accomplish things you've never done, you're trying on new roles, playing new parts. It's natural to have a few butterflies while you're waiting in the wings. After all, now it's your turn to sing. Just remember that butterflies aren't a sign to give up; they are a sign to get up. Put that excited energy to work for you. (Note: If you want to change the physiological correlates of fear, use the relaxation technique described in chapter 14.)

Fear Mastery Technique #4: Change the Proportion

Another way of dealing with fears is to exaggerate them out of all proportion. Fear thrives in the shadows and feeds on resistance. The fear of fear increases fear. That's what former president Franklin Roosevelt was getting at when he said, "The only thing we have to fear is fear itself." If, when you feel fear, you deny or resist it, you will feel more afraid. Try really hard not to do something and you'll find yourself doing it. Try hard not to scratch a poison ivy rash and you'll be in an itch. Try hard not to think of a pink elephant and you won't be able to get it out of your head. Try really hard not to be afraid and you'll feel afraid.

On the other hand, when you try too hard to do something, your ability to do it actually diminishes. The famed psychologist Dr. Viktor Frankl calls this phenomenon *hyperintention*. Test this for yourself; try really hard to feel afraid about something that is bothering you. Come on now . . . try harder . . . really hard. You will find that it isn't possible to feel intense fear for extended periods of time. If you really feel it, it exhausts itself quickly. Take your fears out of the dark. Make a list of them and then exaggerate each until it becomes totally ridiculous. Imagine consequences that are so dire and extreme that you have to laugh. Humor is a powerful antidote to fear.

I believe that anyone can conquer fear by doing the things he fears to do . . . .

ELEANOR ROOSEVELT

291

Fear Mastery Technique #5: Change Your Awareness

It is easier to deal with the fears you know about than the ones you don't. If you are afraid of cramped spaces or snakes or flying in an airplane, you know it, and you can use a variety of techniques to master these fears. Yet there is another category of fears that are far more destructive. These fears creep up on you without your awareness. Like vining weeds, they tangle themselves around the tree of your life, choking off the vital energy you need to achieve your goals. These deep-seated fears originate in the context of our early childhood experiences and are a natural part of human development. For example, the fear of being abandoned is natural to the infant and young child. Yet these fears often persist into adulthood, long after the circumstances from which they originally sprang have changed.

How is it that these fears remain hidden from awareness? Well, of course, they don't remain entirely hidden. From time to time, we *do* become aware of them. Yet for the most part, they remain below the surface because we've developed coping patterns that divert attention from the fears. As children, we began to adopt patterns of behavior and thought for coping with the fears we were unable to effectively deal with at the time. Whatever usefulness these coping patterns may have once served, as adults we've outgrown them. While it may not be pleasant to recognize the havoc these deep-seated fears wreak in your life, it can be very liberating and empowering. Gaining awareness of your deep-seated fears and the coping patterns you have developed to avoid them can greatly increase your effectiveness.

Remember, what you don't know *can* hurt you. So long as we remain unaware of these fears, so long as we are unwilling to confront them, we are stuck with the coping patterns we've adopted in order to avoid them. Because these patterns are both by-products of, and vehicles for, suppressing awareness, they necessarily lead us away from the lives we have intended. When we face our fears, we eliminate the need for these coping patterns, as well as for the chronic distractions discussed in chapter 17. We cut off, at its source, the energy supply that sustains them.

When you identify a fear, its grip on you begins to weaken. You begin to assert control over it. To help you better recognize these fears, they are described below, together with eight of the more popular coping patterns used to avoid them. My purpose in presenting these patterns of losing out to fear is to arm you with self-awareness, so that you can make a change. You don't just want a new label for an old problem; you want to be able to act more effectively. You don't have to merely cope with your fears; you can confront and release them. The stories that follow are somewhat extreme examples of the strategies for coping with the fears they represent. You may recognize similar patterns in your own life, even if they manifest in less dramatic ways.

Insecurity

The most basic fear is insecurity. As infants and young children, we went through a period of total dependency. Quite naturally, this experience produced a profound feeling of insecurity. We rightly felt inadequate to life and unsure of our abilities to survive. Because we lacked the cognitive skills we needed to understand our situation, and the verbal skills necessary to articulate our feelings about it, we suppressed our memory of the experience, as well as our feelings about it, in the subconscious mind.

When, in the course of our daily adult lives, we begin to doubt our abilities to get we what we need and want in life, these suppressed feelings may come rushing to the surface. They have the power to totally overwhelm all reason, destroying our ability to objectively see the situations we are in. The problems or tasks before us loom large, while we feel tiny and inadequate in comparison. Often, it is precisely when we are advancing into greater competency and self-reliance that old feelings of insecurity are triggered. It is at this point that we most need to maintain self-awareness.

Below are examples of two patterns for coping with insecurity: *daydreaming* and *insulating*. Daydreaming occurs when we disassociate ourselves from our environments and construct a fantasy view of ourselves and/or our lives in an attempt to avoid confronting reality.

Nothing is terrible except fear itself.

FRANCIS BACON

Insulating is an attempt to retreat from the world of adult pressures and responsibility, and return to a womblike existence.

Daydreaming: Suzanne is daydreaming. She's living with a man she doesn't love, yet she tries to pretend that they are the perfect couple. Actually, she stays where she is because she's afraid she can't make it without a man. Suzanne feels self-contempt for making this compromise and resents her boyfriend because she feels dependent on him. It's not that he is really doing so much for her, but she has convinced herself that she can't live without him. It's a destructive relationship, and deep down inside, she knows it. Yet she isn't willing to take a risk. So far, she hasn't even admitted the truth to herself. Instead, she is daydreaming that being in a relationship without love is better than being alone. Her unwillingness to face up to her life and rely on herself is causing Suzanne to lose out to fear.

Insulating: Brenda is twenty-three and still lives with her parents. She hides behind a hundred pounds of excess weight. Her fat insulates her from the fear that she can't make it in the world. She quit college and hasn't been able to keep a job. About the only time she gets out of the house is to get something for her weight problem. Her mother is also obese, and her parents indulge her in her obsession and avoidance. Brenda doesn't believe she can make it on her own. She barricades herself behind walls of fat and the walls of her parents' house, postponing the day that she will have to face the real world. Brenda is losing out to fear by allowing it to keep her trapped in a tiny little world where she feels safe.

Remedy for Insecurity

In a word, the remedy for insecurity is self-reliance. Recognize that you are a complete and autonomous individual and have the power and the responsibility to act accordingly. You have outgrown the dependency of childhood. While from the standpoint of the conscious mind, your adult status is obvious, it may not be clear to all levels of your subconscious mind. It is here that deep insecurities may linger, and it is here that they must be overcome. Be aware of an unconscious desire to escape from decisions and avoid responsibility for your life.

Typically, we think of self-reliance in terms of action. This, of course, is an important aspect. Yet it is even more important that you rely on yourself to understand the context of your life and decide for yourself the course of action you will take in it. It's up to you to make your life all you want it to be. Trust that you have the strength to face your life head-on and overcome patterns of dependency that you have allowed to control you in the past. You have the power to decide; use it.

To overcome *daydreaming*, give up the fantasies in your head, opt for the truth instead. If in your life you want to be a star, you have to deal with things as they really are. It may seem painful to open our eyes and take a good look. Yet pretending things are better than they are won't get you off the hook. Make reality your friend. You'll have to deal with it in the end. Better soon than late. Postponing things will only complicate. Don't just sit there like a bump on a log. Shake off this hazy mental fog. You have the power to decide. Claim it and you won't have to hide.

To overcome an *insulating* pattern, get yourself out the door! Boldly go where you have never gone before. Come on, little birdie, out of the nest. Go on, put your wings to the test. Don't let yourself be overwhelmed by all you need to do. Start small and see it through. Break down what you need to do into tiny little segments. Master your fear in increments. Build your confidence one step at a time, and you will find there is no mountain you can't climb. Keep moving forward just a little at a time, and by and by, your fears will be left far, far behind.

Our doubts are traitors and make us lose the good we oft might win by fearing to attempt.

SHAKESPEARE

Anxiety

Anxiety is the fear of losing control. Again, this fear has its roots in our childhood development. As young children, we couldn't rely on ourselves. Since others had what we needed to survive (food, shelter, knowledge, protection, etc.), we decided that we must somehow control them. After all, they might just decide to leave us, or they might not show up when we need them. Yet, because we were unable to control

He who fears he shall suffer, already suffers what he fears.

MICHEL DE MONTAIGNE

others in any predictable way, we could only make ineffectual attempts. Temper tantrums and screams, coos and tears were all we had to work with. Quite naturally, then, we felt anxious and out of control. As a reaction to these feelings, we formed coping patterns. Often these reactive patterns are carried into adulthood.

One of the most popular reactive patterns is to become a "control freak." The more we try to exert control over externals beyond our range of control, the more out of control, or anxious, we feel. If you want to prove this to yourself, start worrying over what people think of you, or about tomorrow's weather. There is, then, a vicious cycle of anxiety. The more anxious we feel, the more we feel the need to control externals; and the more we try to control them, the more anxious still we feel. In popular culture, we refer to people who are extremely anxious as "worrywarts" and tell them to "mind your own business" or "tend to your own knitting." Those who feel a great need to control others are seldom good at controlling themselves. In psychological parlance, they are called "other-directed" or it is said they have shifted the "locus of control" away from themselves. Another popular reactive pattern to the issue of control is to shut down our feelings or to try to order our lives in such a way that we never have to respond in a spontaneous way.

Below are examples of two general patterns for coping with anxiety: *dominating* and *defaulting*. Dominating is an attempt to control others in an active or aggressive manner. Defaulting is an attempt to maintain control by remaining passive and emotionally aloof. Of course, we only feel the need to utilize either of these strategies when are already feeling out of control.

Dominating: Don plays the overbearing, domineering father. He doesn't feel in control of his life in general, and of his work in particular. Don feels frustrated and trapped in a job he hates, and overwhelmed by his responsibilities as breadwinner and parent. He doesn't like or respect himself for the abuse he takes at work. Instead of standing up for himself on the job (or getting a better one), he rules his home like a tyrant. He is constantly on his kids about little things, undermining their self-esteem and initiative at every turn. Don feels threatened by practically everything and everyone in the adult world. He's not much fun to be with, and he knows it. What's worse, he feels that his kids hate him for the way he treats them. Don is losing out to fear, pretending that lording it over those whom he views as weaker than himself will somehow make him feel better.

Defaulting: We tend to feel anxious when we don't control what we can. Like Don, Brad also feels trapped in a dead-end job. Even though he has just gotten another raise and is reasonably well-off financially, he is afraid of getting trapped in a job that bores him stiff. Trouble is, he hasn't done anything about it. Like all of his feelings, Brad holds his fear of getting trapped deep within. On the surface, he demonstrates no worry, hostility, or belligerence—just a strange detachment from life. It's his way of maintaining control. Brad's inability to deal with feelings keeps him emotionally remote and distant from the people in his life. Brad is getting old before his time, At twenty-nine, he acts like he's fifty-nine. He blocks not only his pain but any sense of joy or zest for life. His whole life is lived in muted tones. To ease his anxiety, Brad must let go of his hold on his not-so-comfortable comfort, admit the pain he feels, and go for building the kind of future he really wants. Brad's unwillingness to deal with emotions and confront his pain is causing him to lose out to fear.

Remedy for Anxiety

The basic remedy for anxiety is to step back and examine the situation from the standpoint of real control. Ask yourself, "Who or what am I trying to control that is beyond my ability to control?" and "What *can* I control that I am not?" Understanding what you can and cannot control, and then aggressively attacking the former and letting go of the latter, frees you from the vicious circle of anxiety. Focus your attention on your own thoughts, feelings, and actions. These are within your control, and they provide all the creative power you will ever need. Attempting to control what you can't will only make you more anxious.

You can't control:	**You can control:**
How other people think	How you think
How other people feel	How you feel
What other people do	What you do

To overcome a *dominating* pattern, recognize that over yourself, *you* are the master. Trying to control others will lead to disaster. Admit that your fear of losing control is at the root. Bullying others will only leave you feeling more anxious, and guilty to boot. Inside every bully there is a wimp—fleeing from a giant, picking on an imp. Face your own demons and put them on the run. Come on, life can be a lot more fun. Admit your fear and take control of your own life. Go for what *you* really want; give up this unnecessary strife.

Overcome a *defaulting* pattern by taking responsibility to make your own decisions. Look at what's not working in your life and make some revisions. Admitting your pain is the way to begin, expressing your feelings is not a sin. Assert your desire, stoke up the fire. Make a choice, and give it your voice. You know what you've got to do—no one is coming to rescue you. Don't put your life on hold. Make the decision to go for the gold.

Fear of Failure

As we progress through our childhood development, new demands are placed on us. There are many instances where we are called on to perform new and difficult tasks that require us to exert greater control over ourselves and our environments (toilet training being the classic example). We learn that we must perform in order to get the approval of others. Since we associate the approval of our parents or caregivers with survival, and view their disapproval as life threatening, we come to view failure as potentially catastrophic. Thus is born the fear of failure.

The fear of failure is a nagging feeling that what you are doing will not come out right, that you will somehow mess it up. The fear of failure manifests within our minds in the form of self-critical statements.

These statements may be internalized recitations of actual criticisms we have received from others in the past, or they may be criticisms that we imagine others are making of us. Typically, we respond to these criticisms by either trying to prove how good we are, or trying to prove how bad we are—in an effort to divert attention away from our specific shortcomings. We struggle to prove that we are okay, or we rebel by not playing the game at all, so no one can criticize us for failing.

We live in a performance-oriented society. Put up or shut up. Put out or get out. The pressure to perform is enormous. We either concentrate and focus our energies from a place of deep self-acceptance, or we let the pressure get to us and succumb to the fear of failure. Below are examples of two general patterns for coping with the fear of failure: *proving* and *rebelling*. Proving is an attempt to demonstrate to others that we are worthy of love and acceptance, while doubting it ourselves. Rebelling is an attempt to demonstrate that we are beyond redemption, while clinging to the hope that someone will think otherwise.

Everyone who got where he is had to begin where he was.

ROBERT LOUIS
STEVENSON

Proving: Marlene works as the office manager of a local title company. She takes on an enormous amount of work, far more than what any one person could possibly do in an eight-hour day. So there is Marlene, processing papers on into the night, every night—Saturdays and often Sundays. Marlene feels a need to prove how indispensable she is. She makes herself irreplaceable by doing the work of at least two people, but for the price of one. Because she's such a workaholic, her superiors feel they can't afford to promote her. They'd have to hire two people to replace her. Marlene's need to prove that she's indispensable has boxed her into a corner. People who are constantly trying to prove themselves don't feel adequate. Marlene is losing out to fear, stuck on proving that she's worthy instead of following her own dreams. After all, how can she be a failure when she is doing so much?

Rebelling: Allen never knew his father. His mother was an alcoholic. When she was drunk, which was nearly every night, she would frequently verbally abuse him, telling him he was a worthless no-account like his father and that he would never amount to anything. A couple of her many "boyfriends" had physically abused him as well. Allen grew up in a tough neighborhood, permeated with fear and violence. He did poorly in his overcrowded school and, by thirteen, was frequently cutting classes. When he was sixteen, he joined a neighborhood gang and soon thereafter dropped out of high school. Today, he both uses and deals cocaine. At nineteen, he has already seen friends of his killed by members of rival gangs. Allen doesn't believe that he can make much out of his life and doesn't expect to live long. He has no dreams. Attacking himself and others are the only options he thinks he has left. Rebelling is really another way of proving. Allen's not rebelling for himself, but to show "them"—his parents, teachers, and society in general—how independent and tough he is. Allen is losing out to fear by making his whole life a reaction against the love and approval he didn't get as a child.

Remedy for the Fear of Failure

The remedy for the fear of failure begins with greater self-acceptance. Turn off the hypercritical voice inside of your head and appreciate yourself for who you are. Recognize that when it comes to achieving your goals, the only failure is a failure to concentrate. Clearly, it's difficult to concentrate when you are running around trying to prove to everyone that you are a worthwhile human being or, alternatively, that you are an unredeemable jerk. These patterns move you away from your authentic self, the source of your power and motivation. Inevitably, they divert vital focus and energy away from your goals.

To overcome a *proving* pattern, take an honest look at yourself. You may be busy, but you've got yourself in a tizzy. You can get what you want with much more ease. Look at how much you are being controlled by your need to please. Trying to prove your worth will only leave you feeling scattered and fragmented. This proving business is really demented. Stop letting your head rule your heart. Come on now, make a fresh start. On what you want, put your focus; or you may end up feeling hopeless. Not for show, but to grow, that's the way to go.

To overcome a *rebelling* pattern, recognize that you're stuck in a kind of adolescent agony, compulsively reacting against authority. You're trying to prove you don't give a damn. Yet this rebellion is really a sham. Under that tough exterior there's a little lamb who doesn't think he can. Recognize that you're letting yourself be controlled by the need to prove you're tough. Believe in yourself; you're enough. Participate, it's not too late.

Fear of Rejection

Returning to our consideration of the developmental process. The child's ultimate fear is to be rejected and abandoned. The child fears that failure to please and perform might leave him or her without the support of those upon whom his or her existence depends. (Again, this is a pre- or subconscious determination, awareness of which is largely suppressed.) As adults, the events or circumstances of our lives may trigger these deep-seated fears, prompting feelings that are out of proportion to our actual situations.

For example, we may fear losing a job or being abandoned by a mate, despite the fact that there is no rational basis for these fears. The fear of rejection can make us hypersensitive to the moods or actions of others. We might take an innocuous look from a mate as a sign of disapproval or hear in the remark of a friend a put-down that was not intended. We might hear in a boss's tone of voice a sign that we are about to be terminated, when she is simply irritated or frustrated in the moment. If we allow it to, the fear of rejection can totally control our lives. We may try to structure our lives so as to avoid risking rejection or criticism of any kind.

Below are examples of two general patterns for coping with the fear of rejection: *possessing* and *clinging*. Possessing is an attempt to overcome the fear of rejection by holding onto others by playing on and affirming their weaknesses. Clinging is an attempt to overcome the fear of rejection by playing on the pity or sympathy of others.

Possessing: Vicki is extremely possessive. She tries to keep the people in her life on an emotional leash. She plays a rescuer, the role of concerned helper and comforter to those whom she views as needy and weak. She draws out the most vulnerable in people without ever opening up herself. Because she has the emotional goods on them, she manages to convince those whom she is "saving" that they need her. Yet instead of challenging them to grow, she reinforces their sense of themselves as helpless victims. She lives vicariously through their drama and suffering. She avoids those who might challenge her to open up or grow. Her fear of risking rejection keeps her emotionally isolated and aloof. By exposing the feelings of others while covering her own, Vicki reinforces the illusion that she is superior and untouchable. She plays nice, but she's really cold as ice. Vicki is losing out to fear. Her terror of opening up and risking rejection is keeping her from having really meaningful relationships from which she and others might grow.

Clinging: Arthur plays the proverbial wimp. He'll take anything from anybody, never stand up for himself, or confront anyone. He's scared of being rejected, and it shows. Arthur is called the "Klingon" and the "leech" by his college classmates. He follows them around and accepts their taunts and insults with little complaint. Arthur is a bright young man and does very well academically. Yet his neediness and lack of self-confidence make him a social misfit. While he is tolerated within a certain circle, there is not one person in the group whom Arthur could really count on as a friend. He is playing the game of being inferior because he thinks he is worthless on his own. His fear won't allow him to see that others might actually like him better if he didn't act like he needed them so desperately. Arthur is losing out to the fear of rejection—and losing all self-respect in the bargain.

Remedy for the Fear of Rejection

The remedy for the fear of rejection is to focus on your own growth. Do what you need to do to be and express your best. Anyone who loves and cares for you will support your growth. Anyone who doesn't is *not* someone you need in your life. You're no longer a dependent child. You have the opportunity and the responsibility to *choose* the people in your life. Choose people whom you know will support you in being your best, because they are committed to being the best they can be in their own lives. Develop quality relationships, and don't worry so much about what people will think. After all, you're the one who has to live with what you do or don't do. Live a life that reflects your values and sense of integrity. Let others think what they will.

To overcome *possessiveness*, admit your desperation. Your neediness is causing suffocation. Let go; give others room to grow. Chain them to you by playing on their weaknesses, and you they will resent. Your energy can be better spent. Help people to be their best. When you try to control others, *you* are possessed. Setting them free affirms your own worth and dignity.

To overcome *clinging*, recognize that you're afraid to say good-bye because you haven't created anything exciting enough to say "hello" to. Take a look at yourself. Your neediness is showing. You're so afraid to be alone because you haven't made friends with yourself. As soon as they start to leave, you become aware of all the feelings you've been stuffing below. Be alone for awhile. It's not the end of the world. You may even get to like yourself. When you like your own company, you will be in business with others.

What all the people in the examples above have in common is an obsession with the fear of losing. I once heard the following comment applied to a sports legend. "He is a winner because he isn't afraid of losing." If you've ever played tennis, or even just watched, you have probably noticed the difference between a strategy of playing to win and a strategy of playing not to lose. Given equal ability, the person who's thinking "win" has the advantage over the person thinking "don't lose" every time. The guy who's trying to avoid losing is in a defensive posture. His tension and fear will keep him from playing at his best. On the other hand, the person who is playing to win is bolder, more relaxed and confident in her approach.

The same is true in the game of life. What makes a loser a loser is his obsession with the fear of losing. What makes a winner a winner is the way she masters fear and manages to carry on and persevere. It is not that a winner never loses, but she wins more than she loses because of her approach. Winners take calculated risks. Winners aren't afraid to fail. Winners focus more on what they have to win than on what they have to lose. Winners admit their shortcomings without dwelling on them. If you allow yourself to become dominated by fears of losing, you will become a loser, going nowhere, resigning yourself to the hope

No one can make you feel inferior without your consent.

ELEANOR ROOSEVELT

that something or someone will come along and fix the mess you have made of your life. Don't let this happen to you. Determine to master fear!

At times, it can seem as though there's a battle going on within you. The battle is between the immature you, with its infantile fears, and the mature you, with its winning love. Remember, in every moment, you are choosing whether to assert mastery over fear and win— or to succumb to it and settle for what might have been. Pay attention to what is going on inside of your head. Learn to distinguish between the voice of the mature self and the voice of the immature self. Listen to the mature self, the voice of the winner; it has your good at heart. For a summary of the major fears, and their remedies, see pages 306– 307.

Break the Cycle of Fear with:

1. **Self-Reliance:** Dependency gives rise to feelings of insecurity, and insecurity is the beginning of the fear cycle. Therefore, reduce dependency as much as possible. Think for yourself. Make your own decisions and accept the consequences.

2. **Self-Control:** Anxiety is the fear of losing control. Control what you can, forget the rest. Not to worry. Just be your best.

3. **Self-Directed Attention:** The pressure to perform spawns the fear of failure. This fear breaks your concentration. Develop the ability to keep your attention focused on your goals and the actions that will help you realize them. Then let success or failure take care of itself.

4. **Self-Acknowledgment:** When you place your assessment of your worth in the hands of others, you fear their rejection. Give yourself the permission, praise, and correction that you require to achieve your objectives. Make your evaluation of yourself the one that counts.

Daring

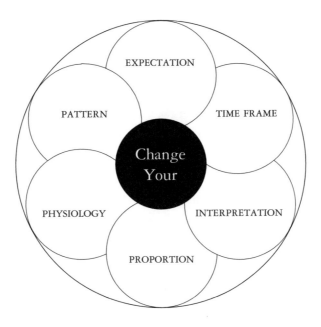

Courage is resistance to fear, mastery of fear, not absence of it.
Except a creature be part coward, it is not a compliment to say he is
brave; it is merely a loose misapplication of the word.

—MARK TWAIN

Courage is not the absence of fear, but rather the judgement
that something else is more important than fear.

—AMBROSE REDMOON

If your life is ever going to get better, you'll have to take risks.
There is simply no way you can grow without taking chances.

—DAVID VISCOTT

Eight Patterns of Losing Out

AGGRESSIVE

REMEDY

Insecurity

1   *Daydreaming:*

A maladaptive approach to Insecurity, wherein the individual blocks out aspects of reality necessary for survival and enjoyment.

Wake Up:

Shift your attention from the picture in your mind to your immediate experience. Communicate out of the hypnotic trance. Talk, move, dance.

Anxiety

3   *Dominating:*

A maladaptive aproach to Anxiety, wherein the individual attempts to mitigate his sense of being out of control by attempting to control others whom he perceives as weaker.

Lighten Up:

Admit that your fear of losing control is at the root. Recognize that bullying others will only leave you feeling more anxious—and guilty to boot.

Fear of Failure

5   *Proving:*

A maladaptive approach to the Fear of Failure, wherein the individual attempts to avoid criticism by being "overly busy" at tasks of marginal import.

Loosen Up:

Take a step back. Ask yourself: What do *I* want? You don't have to prove yourself to anyone else. Not for show, but to grow—that's the way to go.

Fear of Rejection

7   *Possessing:*

A maladaptive approach to the Fear of Rejection, wherein an individual attempts to control others by creating emotional dependency.

Let Go:

Give them room to breathe. Help others to be their best. When you try to control others, you are possessed.

to Fear—and Their Remedies

PASSIVE	REMEDY

2   Insulating:

A maladaptive approach to Insecurity, wherein the individual structures his or her life in such a way as to avoid any environments, people, or information viewed as threatening.

Get Out There:

Boldly go where you have never gone before. Get out of the nest, little birdie.

4   Defaulting:

A maladaptive approach to Anxiety, wherein the individual indefinitely delays making significant life decisions.

Make a Decision:

Decide. Make the changes that will make you great. Do it now, and don't be late.

6   Rebelling:

A maladaptive approach to the Fear of Failure, wherein the individual attempts to avoid criticism by refusing to participate.

Participate:

Admit your fear. Jump in. Stop trying to prove you're so tough. Believe in yourself; you're enough.

8   Clinging:

A maladaptive approach to the Fear of Rejection, wherein an individual clings to others for a sense of identity.

Keep Moving:

See that saying goodbye is in your self-interest, by looking at what you are saying hello to. When you like your own company, you will be in business with others.

Chapter 18 Exercises

❦

Overcome Fear

Make a list of the things that you frequently worry about. Then, for each, ask yourself the following questions:

1. What exactly am I afraid of? Frame your answer in specific *and* general terms. Describe in detail the fearful scenario you imagine, and also indicate whether you fear losing control, respect, love, etc. . . . .

2. Is this a rational fear? In other words, is the scenario that I have just described likely to actually occur? Is the danger real?

3. If the answer is no, move on to the next question. If the answer is yes, ask yourself, "What actions can I take to alter this scenario so as to minimize or eliminate the danger?"

4. Even if you recognize that a fear is irrational, it can slow you down if you allow yourself to dwell on it. If your fear is based on a real threat, obsessing on it can keep you from taking the constructive actions that will eliminate the danger. In either case, you need to manage your fear and concentrate on your goals. Refer to the techniques described on pages 289–293, and determine which you will use to keep fear in check. "I will manage this fear by…"

Moving Through the Fears

Write your goal at the top of a sheet of paper. Then move through the fears by asking the following questions:

1. Insecurity: What am I most afraid of losing? (Self-esteem, love, money, life, comfort, etc.)

2. Anxiety: What am I most afraid of changing? (Self-image, lifestyle, income bracket, social status, habits, etc.)

3. Fear of Failure: In what ways am I most afraid of failing?

4. Fear of Rejection: How am I afraid that I may be rejected en route to this goal? Whose rejection do I fear most?

5. Self-Reliance: How can I take greater responsibility for my thoughts, feelings, and actions in relation to this goal?

6. Self-Control: What do I need to gain greater control of, in order to accomplish this goal? What do I need to let go of?

7. Self-Directed Attention: What can I do to increase my concentration on this goal? Remember, the only failure is the failure to concentrate.

8. Self-Acknowledgment: How will I praise and correct myself en route to this goal? In others words, how can I best parent my own inner child to keep him or her excited and motivated about achieving this goal?

Diplomacy: Gaining Cooperation 19

The most important single ingredient in the formula of success is knowing how to get along with people.

THEODORE ROOSEVELT

Though we usually take it for granted, we rely on others for the things we need and want in life. If you're like most people, you rely on others to plant, tend, harvest, ship, package, stock, and sell the food you eat. You rely on others to design, manufacture, transport, stock, and sell the clothes you wear. Most likely, you relied on the efforts of others to design and construct the home you're living in, as well as the furnishings and appliances that fill it. If you don't own your own business, you rely on others to provide you with a job. If you do, you rely on your clients or customers to keep you going. We *all* rely on other people. In the highly complex and specialized society we live in, we could hardly survive, much less prosper, without their support. Your ability to gain the help of others can spell the difference between getting what you want and making do with less. This chapter will focus on how you can gain the cooperation and support necessary to realize your goals.

Everything that lives, lives not alone, not for itself.

WILLIAM BLAKE

Few worthwhile goals can be achieved without the aid and support of others. Whether it's one person or an entire organization, you're probably going to need somebody's cooperation to make your dreams come alive. Yet others may be reluctant to give you the help you require. We all have a certain resistance to lending our support, and especially to committing our time and energy, to help others. And well we should.

We are constantly bombarded with appeals for support. It seems that someone is always trying to get us to buy their product or service, or to donate time or money to this worthy cause or that. Yet with so many worthy causes and so many wonderful (and not-so-wonderful) things to buy, we must tune out most. The sheer volume of these requests overwhelms our capacity to respond. Advertisers estimate that on a typical day, the average American is exposed to some fifteen hundred commercial impressions. To protect ourselves from this onslaught, we put on a kind of psychic armor. Professional salespeople call it "buyer resistance."

Buyer resistance—we've all been on both sides of it, and of course it doesn't just apply to the sale of products or services. Every parent who has ever asked a reluctant child to clean his room or help with household chores knows what buyer resistance is. Every husband or wife who has ever tried to convince their spouse of the right vacation spot knows what buyer resistance is. Every manager who has ever tried to implement a new operational system knows what buyer resistance is. Sooner or later, we all face buyer resistance. Yet this resistance must be overcome if we are to obtain the cooperation we need. And overcome it is. Every day, we are influenced by others—and we influence them as well. The remainder of this chapter will concentrate on how you can sharpen your skills of persuasion and get the help and support you need. With regular practice of the techniques discussed below, you will become adept at recognizing, averting, and overcoming resistance.

Avoid Creating Resistance: Think Before You Speak

The first step to overcoming resistance is to be aware that it exists. Don't be naive. It's a mistake to assume that everyone wants to help you. Of course, most people are merely indifferent—too caught up in their own lives to care one way or another about your goals. Yet you may also encounter those who deliberately, or more often, unconsciously, try to block your progress. Learn to differentiate between those who can and want to support you and simply need to be convinced, and those who are incapable of providing real support or don't have your best interests at heart.

Keep in mind that, as a rule, people can only wish for others what they would be willing to receive for themselves. Happy people are much more likely to support your happiness than unhappy people. Effective people are more likely to support your effectiveness than in-effective people. People who have goals of their own are more likely to support you in achieving yours. People who are expressing their creativity are more inclined to support you in expressing yours, and so on. Associate with those who can help you achieve your goals, and try to avoid, as much as possible, those whose resistance would tend to slow your progress.

Anyone who proposes to do good must not expect people to roll stones out of his way, but must accept his lot calmly even if they roll a few more upon it. —ALBERT SCHWEITZER

There are times when even those closest to you may resist your growth. This doesn't necessarily mean that they don't love or support you. It simply means that people resist change, especially change they themselves have not initiated. When you take a step in personal growth, those who have a stake in relating to you in old, limiting, or habitual ways may feel threatened.

Becoming aware of this resistance and accepting it as natural helps you to adopt an effective approach for overcoming it. It will enable you to avoid the two major pitfalls in dealing with the resistance of those you love. You won't become angry at them for "keeping you down" on the one hand—or yield to their resistance and abandon your goals on the other. Becoming angry will divert energy away from the pursuit of your goals and will only stiffen the resistance of others. On the other hand, giving in to resistance robs you of the opportunity to realize your dreams. It's also likely to spawn resentment that could severely damage your relationships in the long run.

The best approach is to remain calm, flexible, and determined. Listen to the other party's concerns and take them seriously. Let them know that you want their support and that you are committed to creating a situation that works for everyone involved. Be flexible in terms of how your goals are to be accomplished, but don't waver in your determination to see them through. Once your loved ones understand the depth of your commitment and realize that you are not about to be deterred, the emphasis will begin to shift away from an emotional resistance to change, toward a consideration of the practical issues involved.

Ken grew up in a lower middle-class neighborhood in Portland, Oregon. For generations, his family had identified themselves as members of the working class. As his high school graduation approached, most of his boyhood chums were preparing to follow in their fathers' footsteps, working in factories and warehouses or as construction laborers. Ken, a bright kid and an exceptional student, had applied for and was granted a scholarship to attend an Ivy League university. Ken noticed that though his friends and family said they were proud of him, he felt that somehow, deep down, they didn't really want him to succeed. His success seemed to threaten many of the beliefs they held about the possibilities in life, and what people of his social class could expect. In subtle, yet painfully obvious ways, they were resisting his success.

Often we fall victim to resistance, simply because we don't recognize it. Keep in mind that it isn't always explicit or obvious. We dismiss it because we don't want to see the worst in people and because we don't want to give up our own fantasies about the way things are. If Ken hadn't been aware of the resistance he faced, he might have failed—just to ease the strain and alleviate the sense of separation he felt between himself and his friends and family. Many people sabotage themselves for similar reasons. Ironically, when Ken does succeed, the very people who are now resisting his success will be the ones to say they are most proud of him. More than likely, they will take credit for his success or, at the very least, say they knew all along that it was going to happen.

Discuss your goals with those you can count on to help you achieve them. It's best to operate on a "need to know" basis with people whose low self-esteem prevents them from being fully supportive. Unfortunate though it may be, many people find that their parents fall into this category. In this case, keep your dreams, goals, and plans to yourself. Find other things to talk about with them. Discuss your goals only after you have completed them or are well along in the process. Bear in mind that just because someone asks you a question doesn't mean you *have* to give them a direct answer. Reveal what you want, to whom you want, when you want. Remember, you are in control. Using discrimination in choosing when and to whom you reveal your plans protects you and your ideas from the doubt, fear, jealousy, and even outright hostility of others. You will avoid creating unnecessary resistance and save yourself a lot of pain and heartbreak in the bargain.

While awareness of resistance is certainly an asset, fearing it or turning it into an excuse for inaction is a great liability. There is always the danger of our becoming so distracted by the fact that people are opposing us, that we take our attention off of our goals. Don't give those who deliberately or subconsciously resist your success any more time or attention than they deserve. You have the power to concentrate and focus—don't give it away! Keep your eyes on the prize, and don't use others as scapegoats for your own failure to act.

Regardless of how others may respond to your ideas, there are times when it's best to keep quiet about your plans. This is for one simple reason: it conserves vital energy needed to make things happen. Don't let the term "all talk and no action" apply to you. Instead of blabbing it away in idle chatter, put your energy to work on your goals. The tendency to substitute talk for action has been the downfall of many successful writers. Though it was his fourth major work, the publication of *In Cold Blood* in 1965 was a watershed in Truman Capote's life. Following the phenomenal success of this book, Capote became an international celebrity. He frequently appeared on national television talks shows and was a regular and much sought-after guest at parties attended by celebrities and the social elite. Capote often spoke about his next book, and eventually, he even published small excerpts of it in *Esquire* magazine. Yet, though he lived for nearly another twenty years, he never completed this novel—or any other, for that matter.

If you can talk brilliantly about a problem, it can create the consoling illusion that it has been mastered.

STANLEY KUBRICK

The point isn't that you should never talk to strangers about your goals. On the contrary, often it may be essential that you do so. What is important is that you think before you speak. Ask yourself, "Is talking about my goals, to this person (or these people), at this time, really going to help me achieve them?" Avoid spilling the beans in idle chatter or for the sake of momentary self-aggrandizement. In the midst of heightened security concerns during the Second World War there was a popular saying: Loose lips sink ships. "Loose lips" can also deep six your dreams. Think before you speak.

Trust: The Key to Gaining Lasting Cooperation and Support

Up to now, much of our discussion has concentrated on when, and with whom, *not* to talk about your goals. Now, we'll shift our focus toward strategies for enlisting the support of those whose help *is* vital to the accomplishment of your objectives. The key to gaining and maintaining their continuing cooperation can be stated in one little word: trust. When you are seeking the support of others, you're asking them to trust your ideas, your mission, your products or services. Most of all, you are asking them to trust you. If we can call it an emotion, trust is a very elastic one. It varies even within the same individual, depending upon the issue involved, the degree of risk you are asking them to take, their mood at the time you ask, and a host of other factors.

Before you attempt to gain the support and cooperation of others, ask yourself, "What degree of trust do I enjoy with this individual or group at this time and with respect to this issue?" The answer to this question will tell you how best to approach them. Electrical engineers measure resistance in terms of ohms; in human relations, resistance is measured in degrees of trust—or rather, the lack thereof. We know from elementary physics that what is in motion tends to stay in motion, while what is at rest tends to stay at rest. We also know that resistance is that which retards or impedes motion. The idea is simply that the greater the resistance, the more energy must be applied to still bodies to get them moving. The same

Take Their Trust Temperature

TRUST TEMPERATURE	DEGREE OF CONFIDENCE	YOUR OBJECTIVE	METHODS
Cold	No Confidence	Melt the Ice	Smile, be friendly. Search for agreement. Don't push. Don't argue. Listen.
Cool	Potential Confidence	Warm Them Up	Appeal to their interests. Paint pictures they can relate to. Build bridges of understanding.
Warm	Conditional Confidence	Fire Them Up	Show them how your idea benefits them. Get their input and agreement. Show empathy.
Hot	Total Confidence	Maintain the Flame	Show them you value their trust. Be clear and direct.

principle applies in human relations. The less people trust you, the greater their resistance, and the more energy must be expended to win their confidence and get them moving with you, toward your goals.

To assist you in assessing the degree of confidence others have in you, four "levels of trust" are described below, along with suggestions for dealing with people at each of these levels. When you sense that you're going too far or too fast in terms of what you are asking others to believe or do, slow down, and back off. Revert to the steps outlined for the previous level of trust. Reestablish a sense of connection and rapport before you move on to the next level.

Trust Level #1: When They Have No Confidence

When people have little confidence in you or your ideas, begin by being friendly and building a foundation of agreement. Whatever you do, don't argue with them. Listen to others, draw them out, and search for agreement. Your objective is to help open their minds to you and your ideas. These folks are cold. Your task is to melt the ice.

Be Friendly and Smile: Mother Teresa said, "We shall never know all the good that a simple smile can do." Certainly, a smile helps to melt the ice. A genuine smile communicates warmth in a universal emotional language. It proclaims, "I'm open, friendly, and approachable." Page through issues of the *National Geographic*, and look at the faces of people from around the world. Smiling faces—be they Tibetan, Peruvian, Chinese, Slavic, Oklahoman, or Parisian—communicate an unmistakable warmth and humanity. We don't need to know a person's language or understand their culture to comprehend and appreciate what their smiles are saying. We feel as though we want to meet the people behind these smiles and as though, in some way, we already have. If a smile can help you feel close to people from strange lands, whom you will never meet, how much more will your smiles touch those you come in contact with in your daily life?

Search for Agreement: Whether you are engaging in small talk with a stranger or conducting complex international negotiations, the search for agreement is critical to advancing relationships. All small talk is simply a search for agreement. Beautiful day, isn't it? Lovely evening, don't you think? While hardly momentous, these little niceties initiate conversations that may later bear real fruit. Skilled negotiators make every effort to structure meeting agendas in such a way that the issues that have the best chance for agreement are discussed first. This helps to ensure a momentum of success that will later prove invaluable, when more thorny and contentious issues have to be dealt with. Agreement has a momentum to it (as does disagreement). Prepare for your encounters by thinking through in advance what you and the other person will likely agree on. Build a foundation of agreement, and move on from there.

Be Sensitive to Timing: While timing isn't everything, it is often the most important factor in determining how you and your ideas will be received. In our personal relationships, we know that to bring up difficult or sensitive issues when the other person is tired, not feeling well, or preoccupied can be a big mistake. We risk irritating the other party and feeling rejected ourselves—especially if we interpret their reaction as a lack of caring. When interacting with those we hardly know, we may have only one opportunity to present a proposal or appeal for support. It would be a mistake to risk a negative response simply because we were insensitive in the timing of our approach. Don't let your excitement and enthusiasm blind you to the concerns or pressures of others. When you are asking for the support or understanding of others, make sure that it is at a time convenient for *them.*

Don't Push: Recently, I heard a woman from a group called "Beyond War" being interviewed on a radio talk show. A listener called in to say that war was "just the way it is, and if we got rid of all the nuclear weapons and implements of destruction, some way or another, man would find a way to start a war anyway." He said that every neighborhood has a bully, and that nations are no different. The representative from "Beyond War" responded by saying that if enough people began thinking like those in her organization, they could *force* the rest of the planet's population to see the merits of peaceful conflict resolution. Needless to say, the caller went unconvinced. The irony of trying to force people to be peaceful was not lost on the host or, I suspect, on the audience.

Like this well-meaning woman, we often try to force people to agree with our ideas or ways of doing things. We are convinced that we are right and have the answers. We talk when it would be best to listen. We push when it would be better to ease up. Trying too hard to convince people often sends them running in the opposite direction. In sales, this is referred to as "overselling." You can actually *create* resistance in people who would otherwise be favorably disposed to your ideas, by trying too hard to convince them.

Any fool can criticize, condemn and complain— and most do.

DALE CARNEGIE

Listen to the Other Person's Point of View: Though it sounds corny, the old adage that human beings are born with two ears and one mouth makes a point: Listen more and talk less. While listening, suspend judgment. Let what the other person is saying really come through. Resist the urge to interrupt, revise, correct, or criticize what they are saying. Really listen to what the other person is saying, not the brilliant retort in your head. Whether you think so or not, they *can* tell the difference. Listening is the most important step to overcoming resistance because it provides you with information you need to gain the willing cooperation of others. If you listen, people will tell you what they want. Knowing what other people want makes it easier to get what you want.

Listening Tips

1. Be open: View listening as an opportunity to learn.
2. Concentrate: Give the other person your full attention.
3. Show interest with eye contact and body language.
4. Ask questions that demonstrate interest and understanding.
5. Be patient: Don't interrupt.

Don't Argue: Above all, don't argue. You can't get the best of an argument, so don't bother trying. It seldom works to tell anyone, especially a stranger, that he is wrong. Give him the right to be "wrong." After all, there is always the odd chance that you may be wrong at some time in the distant future. Acknowledge people's freedom to resist—it's only natural. Instead of pushing your ideas on others, listen to what they have to say. Take it in. Think about it. Then apply your creative imagination to the task of helping the other person see your ideas in the light of the way *they* see things.

Trust Level #2: When They Have Potential Confidence

When people are open-minded toward you and your ideas, they possess potential confidence, which you can develop and enhance. Appeal to their interests; paint vivid mental pictures that relate to their experience and desires. Build bridges of understanding and watch for any sign that you are "losing" them. The objective at this stage is to move them from a neutral to a favorable position. These folks are cool: Warm them up.

Appeal to Their Interests: Whether it is one person or a large group, take time to think about your audience. What are their problems, concerns, and fears; their interests, goals, and aspirations? Make a list of each. Ask yourself which of these are most important to them, and target your communication accordingly. You may be attempting to inspire them to great heights. They may be worried about making their mortgage payments. If you want others to listen to you, speak to their concerns.

Often we think we have to impress people with how charming, witty, accomplished, or successful we are. More often than not, we put people off with such a show. In a world of endless hype, people are hungry for those who demonstrate real sincerity and show genuine interest in them. If you want people to warm up to you and your ideas, show them that you are interested in them and theirs. If you try to impress others, you're likely to tie yourself up in knots—they're liable to think you're selfish or a bore. Talk about what interests them. Better yet, get them going on their favorite subject, and they'll really be impressed with how intelligent you are. Find out as much as you can about their likes and dislikes, and appeal to their interests.

Speak the Language of Your Audience: Avoid technical jargon or buzzwords. If you are going to use jargon at all, make sure that it is that of the audience and not yours. Speak in terms that your audience knows and understands, and they'll be right there with you. Talk above, below, or around them, and you've lost them.

The only gift is a portion of thyself.

EMERSON

Paint Pictures That Others Can Relate To: Aristotle said, "The greatest thing by far is to be a master of metaphor." That's a powerful statement! Let's think for a moment about how it might be true. We all depend on our ability to communicate, and there is no more powerful way to communicate than through the use of metaphor. Using concrete images, vivid mental pictures, and symbols makes your ideas, goals, and plans come alive in the minds of your audience. The skillful use of appropriate anecdotes, pictures, and symbols can help you make a more lasting impression, and make it in much less time, than the use of abstract concepts alone.

Political media strategists attempt to shape our perceptions of their candidates by painting mental pictures they think we will relate to. Take the case of a United States senator running for reelection in Iowa, a state where many voters are farmers or sympathetic to their issues. In their commercials, the media strategists want to paint a picture of the senator as a man who understands the issues and concerns of farmers. Instead of taping these commercials from his Washington office, with the senator appointed in a three-piece suit, listing his legislative accomplishments—they film the spot down on the farm, with the senator dressed in a red flannel shirt, huddled with a group of farmers, listening to their concerns. An announcer's voice-over says, "Bill X: He listens. He cares." By painting a picture the voters can relate to, the senator's media consultants are hoping to gain the cooperation he needs to reach his goal—namely votes. They know farmers are interested in their own problems, not in how much the senator thinks he's doing for them.

For better or worse, advertisers know how to build mental bridges and step across them into the deep recesses of our subconscious minds. If you want to see how to link intangible desires with tangible items, watch what advertisers do. For example, the consumer's desire to "taste power" is linked to cigarettes. The desire for spirituality and longevity is linked to a fragrance and becomes "Eternity" cologne. The desire for greater personal freedom is linked to feminine napkins and becomes "New Freedom" maxi pads. On the face of it, these links are trivializing and absurd. What does power have to do with cigarettes, eternity with cologne, or freedom with maxi pads? Clearly, nothing. Yet advertisers know that through repetition they will be able to form an unconscious associative link in the minds of many. In the same way, advertisers try to link the influence and prestige of celebrities to the products they are trying to sell. The positive feelings we have for famous people are used to sell everything from sneakers to investments, from breath mints to political candidates. Judging by what celebrities are paid for their endorsements, the gimmick works.

The ability to construct vivid mental pictures and make associative links is a great power, which, like any other, can be used for good or ill, depending on the motive for which it is employed. To be sure, it has often been used to manipulate people and exploit their baser motives. Yet we shouldn't allow the fact that some people misuse it to cause us to reject this most important communication tool. Present your ideas in vivid images that are clear and personally meaningful to your audience.

Build Bridges of Understanding: You build a bridge of understanding when you link the old with the new, the familiar with the unfamiliar. Today, we associate the theory of evolution with the name Charles Darwin. Yet through his own independent research, Alfred Wallace also came upon the idea of natural selection. In fact, Wallace wrote an articulate explanation of it one year prior to the publication of Darwin's *On the Origin of Species*. The essay by Wallace, together with an abstract written by Darwin, announced the theory of evolution to the world, at a meeting of the Linnean Society in 1858. The reason that every school kid knows Darwin's name and not Wallace's is because Darwin was better able to bridge the idea of natural selection with the existing scientific thought of the day. He went into greater detail in his explanations of the theory and provided greater supporting evidence. Darwin did a better job of placing a new idea within the context of the known and accepted. Darwin provided a link—even if it wasn't the missing one.

When you're trying to get your point across, link what your audience already knows, likes, and values, to your message, and you dramatically increase your odds of getting a friendly hearing. If you have a new product, get endorsements from celebrities (local or national). If you're starting a new company, link it with stable and enduring images. If you are introducing a new proposal, get a well-respected spon-

We awaken in others the same attitude of mind we hold toward them.

ELBERT HUBBARD

sor. If you are suggesting a new idea, show people how it relates to what they already know. Take some time to brainstorm and think, think, think how you can link, link, link.

Trust Level #3:
When They Have Conditional Confidence

When you are dealing with people who have conditional confidence in you, tell them why you want their support. Provide them with evidence for why they are wise to support you. Show them how they will benefit personally or how they can participate in a larger purpose that is meaningful to them. Your objective is to move them from a favorable position to one of complete confidence. These folks are warm: Fire them up.

Demonstrate Credibility: Abraham Lincoln gave us that wonderful line about how "you can fool some of the people some of the time, but you can't fool all the people all the time." When it comes to your veracity and integrity, you can't fool others for long—so don't bother trying. Think of your credibility as a credit line of trust that others are willing to extend to you, and remember that, like your financial credit, it's based on your past performance. If you initially lack, or later destroy, your credibility, all your efforts at gaining the cooperation of others will likely go for naught. There are no substitutes for sincerity and follow-through. Don't make promises you can't keep, and keep the promises you make.

Remind or inform people of your past accomplishments and the benefits they or others like them have received from placing their trust in you. Present others with evidence of your credibility. Be willing to toot your own horn—not in off-putting, arrogant boasting, but by recounting the contributions you've made and the services you have rendered. Let people know what you can do for them. Don't be bashful about emphasizing your strengths. Far from rejecting you, most people will think more highly of you when you share with them what you have to offer, without making them work to get it out of you.

Show Others How Your Idea Benefits Them: Whether we care to admit it or not, we all know that the most important person to each of us is the one we call "I." It's not an accident that "I" is the most frequently used word in the English language. We all want to be appreciated, acknowledged, and understood. Keep this in mind when approaching others for their help. Show the other party that you understand his needs, desires, and interests—and he will be interested in what you have to say. Let him think that your primary motive is your self-interest, and he will tune you out faster than you can say good-bye. Find out what the other person wants, and demonstrate how what you have to offer will help him or her to get it. The best way to get what you want is by helping others to get what they want.

Randi is a regional sales manager who was recently informed that the sales quota for her area had been raised by 10 percent. She was faced with the task of persuading her sales force to significantly increase their output. She identified the two things that people on her team wanted most: more recognition and more money. Accordingly, she designed a sales promotion plan that featured new sales incentive bonuses and new ways to acknowledge improvements in both individual and team performance. Randi realized that her best chance of meeting her goal was to help others to get what they wanted.

One of June's goals was to improve her relationship with her thirteen-year-old stepson, Ricky. Although it seemed like a small thing, June realized that she was upset with Ricky for failing to take care of his dog, Rex. Before his parents had agreed to buy the dog, Ricky had promised them that he would care for it. Yet he neglected to follow through, and June was left holding the bag. Every time she fed, walked, or bathed the dog, she felt irritated with Ricky. June told Ricky that she was disappointed he hadn't kept his promise, and that she resented having to bail him out. He said he felt bad about it, but he was too busy with other things to take care of Rex.

June realized that the issue was more important to her than it was to Ricky. She decided to take another approach. After consulting with her husband and gaining his agreement, she sat Ricky down and explained to him in no uncertain terms that if he didn't start taking care of the dog, it was going to cost him. For some time, Ricky had been

Talk to a man about himself and he will listen for hours.

BENJAMIN DISRAELI

325

asking for a new mountain bike. June made it a bargaining chip. She explained to him that if he wanted the bicycle, it would be a good idea for him to keep his promise about the dog. That did it. Ricky wanted the bicycle enough to alter his behavior, and he began taking care of Rex. June found what Ricky wanted (the bicycle) and used it to help her get what she wanted (the elimination of an irksome chore and a source of irritation in her relationship with her stepson). They agreed that if Ricky faithfully took care of the dog for three months, he would get the mountain bike. Ironically, once he became invested in caring for Rex, Ricky began to take pride in the task and did it willingly and well—without the need for any additional bribes.

Make a list of things wanted by those whose cooperation you seek. Select items that you feel *you* can address, and develop a second list of ways you can help them get these things. Then be sure to follow through. Try this a few times, and it will begin to become second nature. You will find that you are automatically making all your requests for support, win/win propositions for all concerned.

Get Their Input and Commitment: Management consultants know that a company's productivity can be dramatically increased by giving the work force greater input in the organization's goal-setting and strategic planning process. When they are included in management decisions and rewarded with a portion of the profits, most workers will gladly go the extra mile. The same principle applies to any kind of common effort. The more you can involve others in the preliminary planning and decision-making process, the greater their enthusiasm and commitment will be when the time comes to execute the plans.

We all want to feel important, as though our ideas and opinions make a difference. When you involve key people in the decision-making process, you get this desire working for you. On the other hand, if you fail to afford them an opportunity for meaningful input, the same desire can work against you. When an individual has a part in making decisions, he becomes emotionally involved in making sure they are well-executed. On the other hand, when you try to force him to accept your way of doing things, his ego is likely to rebel. He will try to show you how important he is and what a dummy you are for not seeing it. Given the opportunity, most people prefer to take a positive approach.

Every year for the last thirty-five years, Brownsville's chapter of the Junior League has put on an annual fund-raising event. For all those years, it was customary for the president of the group to make all of the decisions involved in planning, promoting, and organizing these events. When Patti Clairmont was elected president, she decided to try something different. A few months prior to her election, Patti and several of her colleagues at work had attended a seminar on participatory management.

Patti thought trying this new approach might put some life back into what had become rather tired and predictable affairs. She called a special meeting of the Junior League and asked how many of those attending would like to participate in planning and organizing this year's fund-raising event. She was surprised when, out of the thirty-five members present, twenty-four volunteered. She thanked the others for coming and dismissed them.

The remaining women began brainstorming ideas for making this year's event something to remember. After some considerable discussion, they decided on a theme, a Spring Fair. Next, they began to break the event down into different areas of responsibility that needed to be addressed. They settled on promotion, food preparation, entertainment, games and prizes, volunteers for the day of the event, childcare, and decorations. Next, they elected a coordinator for each of these areas and broke up into teams. Patti still maintained overall responsibility, but now the ideas, energy, creativity, and enthusiasm of twenty-five people were going into creating the project, instead of those of just one. The results were terrific. Since each team took pride in its area and devoted its best efforts to it, the resulting event was a big hit. Everyone had a good time, and they raised three times the money they had raised the year before.

While getting the input and agreement of others is initially more time-consuming and potentially more contentious, it pays big dividends when the time comes to execute the plan. Make the effort to seek out the input of those on whom the success of your goals depends. Think of it as an investment in your ultimate success.

Never be haughty to the humble. Never be humble to the haughty.

JEFFERSON DAVIS

Trust Level #4: When You Have Their Trust

When you are dealing with people who have complete confidence in you, you are fortunate indeed. Treasure their trust; there is nothing more valuable. Those who place their trust in you are giving you far more than the help you receive from them. Their faith in you provides a boost to your self-esteem, a powerful incentive for growth, and a motivation to remain strong and continue to give your best. Give those who believe in you every reason to maintain their trust. These folks are already fired up. They look to you with confidence. Don't let them down. Maintain the flame.

Show Them You Value Their Trust: People crave recognition, attention, and appreciation. Year after year, in surveys of what employees desire most from their employers, recognition and appreciation come out at the top of the list. People complain of being "underappreciated" even more than they do of being underpaid. Appreciation: Your clients, customers, and co-workers or employees want it. Your mate wants it. Your children want it. Your friends want it. It takes so little to give it; don't hold back. Let people know that you appreciate not only their efforts and performance but also what is special about them as unique human beings. In the highly complex, often frenetic and impersonal world we live in, we can all feel a bit invisible from time to time. It's gratifying for people to know that you see them for who they are and that you appreciate their special gifts and qualities.

There is magic in the two simple words, *thank you*. Few people hear it as often as they would like. Be generous with your praise (when it is due), and there is virtually no limit to what those who trust you will be willing to do for you. Especially, give praise and thanks to those whose support has been or can be significant to your success. Simple things, things like being on time, promptly returning messages, sending thank-you cards, and giving little gifts or mementos can go a long way toward making people feel appreciated and eager to help you the next time you require assistance.

Show Empathy: Be sure to consider the point of view of the person who is placing her trust in you. She may feel like a water-skier on the back of a boat. The skier has to feel confident that the operator of the boat knows what he is doing, and is looking out for her. As the driver of the boat, you're asking the other party to trust that you won't put her too near another skier or boat. She has to trust that you will be sensitive to her situation and look out for her interests. The water skier who has a great ride on the back of your boat can hardly wait for the next outing. But the person who gets repeatedly dumped or put into dangerous situations isn't going to want to ride with you again, is she? The point is simply to remember that trust is a two-way street. If you want the trust of others, you'll have to work hard to earn it—and just as hard to keep it. Don't expect blind allegiance; be worthy of continuing trust.

Be Clear and Direct: We can distinguish between personal and professional trust. You trust your plumber to fix the pipes. You trust your closest friends to be sensitive to your feelings and support you in realizing your dreams. Yet regardless of whether an issue involves personal or professional trust, it helps to be clear and direct in your communications. Spell out exactly what you want and expect from others. Don't expect them to read your mind. Psychics charge a fee. Don't expect your mate, friends, and colleagues to do it for free. If you rely on hints or subtle suggestions, don't be surprised if others fail to get your drift. Speak up and clearly articulate what is on your mind.

Making the effort to clarify your thoughts and spell out exactly what you want can eliminate potential conflict with others before it has a chance to develop. It can also save you a lot of disappointment and frustration. For example, you may feel frustrated in your relationship with your mate, disappointed that your partner isn't giving you something you want. Yet if you haven't told him or her directly, or aren't even sure yourself exactly what it is that you want, you can hardly blame the other person for not giving it to you. First, define what you want, then express it clearly.

If you think about it, it's amazing that we communicate with one another at all. Take English, the world's most popular language. Its five hundred most common words have over fourteen thousand meanings. That's an average of twenty-eight meanings per word. With so many meanings, there is plenty of opportunity for misunderstanding.

Trust men, and they will be true to you. Treat them greatly, and they will show themselves great.

EMERSON

In the best of circumstances, the communication process is difficult enough. Don't make it more difficult by being vague or sloppy in your speech. If you're sending a message that looks like the return of the blob—don't be surprised if your audience isn't seeing the roses you want them to see. A rose by any other name may smell just as sweet, but when you are communicating with others, a rose is a rose, and that's as plain as your nose.

Avoid the tendency to substitute conservation with third parties for dealing directly with the person involved. I call this the "cop out and redirect" style of communication. You know what I mean. You talk to your co-workers about a problem you are having with your boss; you discuss a conflict you're having with your mother with your sibling; you talk to your buddy or girlfriend about an issue with your mate. You never discuss the issue directly with the party involved. Then you wonder why, after all this talk, nothing ever resolves. Be direct, go to the source.

Sometimes it helps to jot down your thoughts on paper before attempting to share them with others. This is particularly true when you want to communicate complex ideas or address issues that have an emotional charge for you or the other person. In aerodynamics, you reduce wind resistance by streamlining the surface. In human relations, you can reduce resistance by streamlining your communications.

Streamline Your Communications

1. Take a positive approach.
2. Get to the point.
3. Be clear and precise.
4. Omit jargon.
5. Adapt to suit the audience.
6. Be brief.
7. Link to the familiar.
8. Use descriptive metaphors.

In the exercises that follow, you'll have the opportunity to apply to your own life the principles discussed above. Getting clear about the kind of support you want from others will go a long way in helping you get it. Most importantly, remember that the best way to get what you want from others is to help them get what they want.

Diplomacy

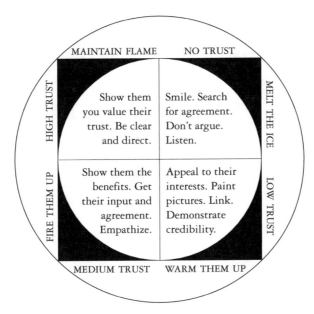

Undertake not what you can not perform,
but be careful to keep your promises.
—GEORGE WASHINGTON

Every man is a volume if you know how to read him.
—WILLIAM CHANNING

It is better to have one friend of great value than many friends
who are good for nothing.
—ANARCHARSIS

Life is to be fortified by many friendships.
To love, and to be loved, is the greatest happiness.

—SYDNEY SMITH

Chapter 19 Exercises

❧

With a Little Help from My Friends

1. Ask at least three people you know and trust, to make a list of your social strengths, weaknesses, and how they feel you can grow. In the space below, write down what you learn.

2. List all of the people and environments you can think of that will challenge you to be your best (i.e., to pursue your goals).

3. Next list ways in which you can arrange to put yourself in front of these people or in these environments (for example, joining groups, associations, or organizations of people with similar goals and interests).

Overcoming Resistance:
Knowing What You Want from Others

Write your goal at the top of a sheet of paper. Then write your answers to the questions below.

1. Whose cooperation and/or participation is essential in order for me to meet this goal?

2. For each individual or group of individuals you identified above, ask yourself: "Precisely what kind of support is it that I want from them? Do I want their..."

Time	Understanding	Influence
Effort	Knowledge	Permission
Money	Encouragement	Advice
Skill	Agreement	Mediation

3. Develop a strategy of approach for each individual or group of individuals you want support from. Ask yourself: "How will I approach this person or group?" "What will I offer in return for their support?

Overcoming Resistance: Building Trust

Write your goal at the top of a sheet of paper. Then write your answers to the questions that follow.

1. Whose cooperation is essential? List below.

2. Next, for each person or group, answer the questions below:

    a) How can I establish rapport and a feeling of mutual interest?

    b) How can I paint pictures they can relate to?

    c) How can I build bridges of understanding?

    d) How can I show them how they will benefit?

❧

Overcoming Resistance: Handling Objections

State your goal. Again, identify an individual or group of individuals whose support you need. Then list what their major objections are likely to be and how you will handle them.

OBJECTIONS   RESPONSES

Detachment: Learning to Grow 20

Most ignorance is vincible ignorance:
We don't know because we don't want to know.

ALDOUS HUXLEY

Every goal requires learning. Were it not so, it would not be a goal at all, but an accomplished fact. Simply put: To do things you have never done before, you will have to learn things you do not now know. How easily and rapidly you learn will determine how long it will take you to achieve your goals. It might even determine whether or not you will reach them at all. Throughout this book, you've been learning keys to manifesting the results you want in your life. This chapter will focus on the process of learning itself. You'll see how you can accelerate progress on your path to success by increasing the speed and ease with which you learn. In the exercises that follow, you'll have the opportunity to identify exactly what you must learn, and to plot definite strategies for gaining the information and understanding you require to achieve your goals.

Learning: The Fountain of Youth

Through the ages, human beings have searched for the secret of youth. In the Western world, we can trace our obsession with youth back to the ancient Greeks, who glorified the physical power and beauty of youth and lamented its loss as a fate more tragic than death itself. In the Middle Ages, witches and magicians invoked spirits with spells, potions, and amulets to confer the vigor of youth, while alchemists labored to produce the philosopher's stone of immortality. In the sixteenth century, Ponce de Leon traversed vast expanses of the newly discovered American continent in search of the mythical Fountain of Youth. In the nineteenth century, traveling hucksters sold "vitalizing elixirs" and "youth restoring tonics" from the backs of wagons and at carnival shows. Today, health foods and supplements, anti-wrinkle cremes and exercise regimes are touted as the keys to lasting youth.

Perhaps, as so many of our wisest philosophers have told us, youth isn't so much a physical condition as a state of mind. They would agree with Frank Lloyd Wright's statement that "youth is a quality, and if you have it, you never lose it." The secret to *this* fountain of youth is no mystery. A youthful attitude, a vibrant state of mind, is available to anyone who will commit themselves to lifelong learning and growth. In the words of Henry Ford, "Anyone who stops learning is old, whether twenty or eighty. Anyone who keeps learning today is young. The greatest thing in life is to keep your mind young."

Young children learn at phenomenal rates. Behind this drive to learn is the incessant drumbeat of one simple question: Why? Children are not afraid of asking the obvious questions and persisting until they get answers. They want to know why and are not shy about repeating the question again and again. Often, their persistence outlasts our patience, in part because their questions may force us to admit our own ignorance or challenge long-held assumptions. We can learn a lot from children about how to maintain our own mental youth.

Often our minds show signs of age long before our bodies do. As the years roll by, our mental muscles become flabby from lack of use, our mental arteries become clogged with prejudices, and our gray matter begins to calcify into rigid belief systems. We lose the questioning spirit of youth, and with it, the zest for life. We grow mentally lazy, avoiding new fields of inquiry or ideas that challenge our fundamental beliefs. We settle for answers we don't understand. After all, they sound reasonable, and who wants to make the effort to delve any deeper? In the words of Mark Twain: "The trouble is we know too much that ain't so." We regain a youthful zest for life to the degree that answering the question *why?* once again becomes more important to us than defending our ignorance or protecting any particular point of view.

What Is Learning?

My dictionary defines learning as "the act, process, or experience of gaining knowledge or skill." That's straightforward enough, yet it offers no insight into *how* to learn. Francis Bacon, author of the classic *The Advancement of Learning,* called learning "the study of truth" and, in the course of describing his own abilities, defined it with great precision in the following quote: "I found that I was fitted for nothing so well as for the study of truth: as having a mind nimble and versatile enough to catch the resemblances of things (which is the chiefest point) and at the same time steady enough to fix and distinguish the subtle differences."

Simply put, *learning occurs when we gain new understanding of the similarities and differences in things, events, or ideas.* We learn as we come to recognize what Bacon called "the resemblances of things," or the underlying patterns, within a diverse range of events. The previous chapter briefly referred to the theory of evolution and the principle of natural selection. The discovery of natural selection represented a new understanding of a similarity of process, or underlying pattern, in the evolution or development of all biological species. The recognition of this unifying principle greatly advanced the scientific understanding of the day and spawned further discoveries. The recognition of similarities in the creative process across fields of interest (discussed in the beginning of this book) is another example of this type of learning. Every time you discover similarities or patterns in the way things work, or events unfold, you are learning.

The great man is he who does not lose his child's heart.

MENCIUS

You also learn whenever you come to distinguish subtler degrees of difference between things, events, and ideas. At some point in your life, you've probably taken tests where you were asked to pick out which item in a list of words, phrases, or classifications did not fit with the rest. You were being tested on your ability to notice differences. As you gain understanding in a given field, your capacity to perceive subtle differences and to choose from a greater variety of responses increases. Most of us might be able to name one or two of the bones in the human foot; a good podiatrist ought to be familiar with all twenty-six. So it is in any field, the more expert one is, the subtler level of difference he or she can distinguish. A quick and flexible mind can see similarities in variety; a focused mind can see differences in the seemingly similar.

Practical Intelligence: Confidence in Your Ability to Learn

If learning is the ability to perceive similarities and differences, then what is intelligence? While there are many tests for, and definitions of, intelligence, this chapter will concentrate on what I call "practical," or "applied," intelligence. Practical intelligence is not measured by academic performance or by the ability to excel in performing the abstract mental operations typically measured in IQ tests. Most of us have known people who made excellent grades or scored high on intelligence tests but still had a difficult time functioning in the real world. Practical intelligence is measured by your ability to learn what you need to learn in order to achieve your goals. We can define your *practical intelligence* as nothing more or less than your *confidence in your ability to learn*.

Emerson said, "They conquer who believe they can." Those who believe they can are those with confidence in their ability to learn. They're not afraid of what they don't know because they know they know how to learn. They trust their ability to grow, change, and adapt to new environments. Understanding and applying the keys to effective learning contained in this chapter will enhance your confidence in your ability to learn, your practical intelligence.

Education is not filling a bucket but lighting a fire.

WILLIAM BUTLER YEATS

To Improve Your Learning Capacity:

1. Focus on your purpose. Keep in mind why you want to learn.

2. Admit your ignorance and accept that it's okay.

3. Gain confidence by recalling what you have already learned.

4. Increase your awareness. Improve your capacity to perceive similarities and differences.

5. Check your emotional temperature.

6. Take advantage of OPE (Other People's Experience).

7. Practice, practice, practice.

Recognize that, given ample motivation and effort, all that can stand between you and your goals is what (or who) you don't know, and what you know that "ain't so." While your understanding is insufficient or inaccurate, efforts to reach your goals will meet with frustration. You may feel as though you are butting your head against a wall you can't break through. You may feel overwhelmed—afraid that you will never grasp all that you must learn in order to achieve your goals. Always keep in mind the distinction between what you now know and what you can learn. You may not know it now, but that doesn't mean you can't learn. Don't sell yourself short or give up too quickly. Commit yourself to learning all you need to know to succeed. As you embark on the adventure of lifelong learning and growth, keep in mind the important keys highlighted above.

Define Your Purpose for Learning

Understandably, for many of us, the learning process has some rather negative associations. In school, learning was often something we had to do, a necessary chore over which we had little say or control. Much of what we were forced to learn seemed irrelevant to our real lives. It had little to do with our interests, much less with our dreams and aspirations. The purpose for learning was simply to pass a test or make a grade, and we often forgot what we learned as soon as the test was over. Many of us were never taught how to learn nor encouraged to pursue personally meaningful areas of interest. Basing our assessment of our interest in, or capacity for, learning on this kind of experience is fraught with danger. Yet it happens all the time. For example, many with less than stellar academic careers conclude that they are poor learners or even stupid. Nothing could be further from the truth!

Poor academic careers do not keep people from learning or succeeding later in life. You may have heard stories about CEOs who never went to college or who dropped out of high school. You may know that Edison, who did as much as any single person to transform life in the twentieth century, had only three years of formal education. What you may not realize is that every day, people from all walks of life, who did not excel in school, discover that they are indeed very good learners when it comes to tackling subjects that are of interest to them and that are in line with their unique talents and goals. A strong sense of purpose can also stimulate you to take on subjects that lie beyond your usual areas of interest. I know a woman who would never have dreamed of a taking a business course in college but began pouring over sales and marketing books once she determined that going into business for herself was the only way she could do the work she truly loves. The importance of having a purpose cannot be overemphasized as an essential key to effective learning.

When facing what you need to learn to achieve your goals, keep in mind your purpose for learning. Ask yourself, "Why is it important for me to learn this? Where does this new knowledge or skill fit in my overall plan to reach my goals? How will acquiring this new information, knowledge, or skill change my life?" Along the way, keep referring to your purpose or intention for learning what is in front of you.

When you increase your intention, you increase your attention— and attention is the key to learning. You might watch someone doing something hundreds of times without really noticing *how* they do it. Think of how many times a child has seen his parents driving the family car. Yet most kids don't really pay attention until they are around sixteen or so. Now learning how to drive means freedom, dates, social acceptance—and that makes it interesting.

In addition to sharpening your attention, keeping your purpose in mind helps you prioritize and organize your learning efforts. Looking at all you must learn in order to achieve your goals can seem overwhelming. Focusing on your purpose helps you sort out the essential from the extraneous and avoid getting bogged down in details. You'll find that you can greatly accelerate the learning process by breaking it down into discrete segments and tackling these in an appropriate order. With your purpose firmly in mind, you'll be able to plot an efficient course of study that will take you where you want to go. At every point, you'll know where you are on that course and why you are doing what you are doing.

George Washington Carver said, "There is nothing that will not reveal its secrets if you love it enough." This statement holds another great key for increasing your attention, and with it, your learning capacity. Love for your subject matter increases both the speed and depth of your learning. Those who excel at learning have learned to love their subject matter, as well as the process of learning itself. Your desire to achieve your goals, and your love for your subject, provide powerful motivations. Focusing on these will compel you to act, to get out there and learn all you require to be successful. Desire always leads to action, unless it is somehow inhibited. What often inhibits our natural desire to learn is judging ourselves for not already knowing.

Everyone is ignorant, only on different subjects.

WILL ROGERS

Admit Your Ignorance and Accept That It's Okay

Let's face it. It's difficult to learn anything when you're trying to prove you already know it all. None of us likes to admit our ignorance. Yet most of us will admit we don't know everything, which means we are ignorant of something. Admitting your ignorance can come after a long and difficult struggle or as spontaneously and simply as a child asks why. Once we admit that we don't know, we can do something about it. We can take responsibility to chart a course toward greater knowledge and understanding.

As strange as it sounds, we often expect ourselves to know *before* we have learned. The belief that we must know before we do creates anxiety, tension, and a sense of struggle that inhibits learning. When we admit our ignorance, we can relax and concentrate on the material in front of us. When we are concerned with protecting our ignorance, our attention is on ourselves, not the subject we are trying to learn. We can't expect ourselves to learn well while our attention is so deeply divided. Admit and accept your ignorance, and you reclaim energy and attention lost in self-conscious defensiveness. Now you can give your full attention to what you are trying to learn.

Often instead of learning, we channel our energy into various strategies for defending our ignorance. These include denying, blaming, and playing sour grapes. They have in common a psychic tension, a palpable sense of struggle. Now, let's look at an example of each.

Denying: Joan's career goal requires that she go into business for herself. Yet she knows virtually nothing about administering a business. She rationalizes her lack of understanding by telling herself that she can make sales and perform the service she is selling. She tells herself that administration isn't important. She's denying the importance of a critical area just because she doesn't know anything about it. Her denial spawns a sense of anxiety and uneasiness about her goal that she can't quite put her finger on. She is blocked from learning until she admits that what she doesn't know *can* hurt her. As long as she refuses to admit her ignorance, she blocks the perception of potential solutions (e.g., taking night classes in business administration, hiring full- or part-time help, reading on the subject, and so on).

Blaming: One of Nelson's goals is to improve communication with his twelve-year-old son, Mike. Nelson went through a difficult divorce and now sees his son only on the weekends. Nelson blames the problems he has communicating with his son on his ex-wife, whom he says has turned the boy against him. While there is an element of truth in Nelson's charge, he's using it as an excuse to avoid the pain he feels for not having learned how to communicate on an emotional level. Nelson's blaming is blocking his capacity to learn. As long as he continues to blame his communication problems on his ex-wife, there is little chance of his learning a new approach.

Playing Sour Grapes: One of Marguerite's goals is to become a cheerleader at her high school. Until recently, she wasn't ready to admit (even to herself) that she was interested in cheerleading. Last year, she watched her friends try out and told them how silly and corny it was. When her best friend Mary made the team, Marguerite realized that she had been playing sour grapes all along. Now she practices at home with Mary on a regular basis. She began learning quickly as soon as she admitted both her desire to make the team and her fear that she couldn't. Next year, she'll try out, and with all the practices she's putting in, her chances look good.

Admit your ignorance, and learning is possible. Deny, blame, pretend, and you're sure to hit a dead end. Accept yourself for not knowing, and you give yourself room to grow. Judge yourself, and you're liable to remain stuck where you are. Despite what we may have been taught in school, learning is fun. In fact, the moment of learning is always a moment of exhilaration. It isn't necessary to struggle in order to learn. When we admit our ignorance and accept that it is okay, we've eliminated most of the struggle. The next step to easy learning is to recall what you have already learned.

Recall What You Have Already Learned

Lest you feel overwhelmed, consider this: When you were born, you could not walk, talk, write, drive an automobile, comb your hair, go to the bathroom, brush your teeth, or add or subtract—yet you probably do these things every day. But these are simple things, right? Try telling that to a child learning to walk or talk. There are few things you will ever learn that are as difficult or complex as these. Taking the time to value what you're already learned gives you confidence to learn still more. You may be ignorant of many things—as we all are—but you certainly are not stupid (unable to learn).

Anyone even surviving in today's highly complex urban society has learned a great deal. Some years ago, while living in Denver, Colorado, I observed a scene that brought this point home. A young Native American man got off a commuter bus and stood alone on a crowded downtown street corner, looking utterly confused and completely out of place. After some time, I spoke with the man and discovered that

Many of life's failures are men who did not realize how close they were to success when they gave up.

THOMAS EDISON

343

If we are facing in the right direction, all we have to do is keep on walking.

BUDDHIST SAYING

this was the first time he had ever ventured off the reservation where he had grown up. He was utterly overwhelmed by the frenetic pace and the vast array of stimuli that surrounded him. This encounter made me realize how much learning we take for granted. We forget that even how to cross a busy street or how to negotiate a crowded sidewalk are things we have learned.

We tend to discount what we've already mastered and view that which is before us as the most difficult thing we've ever had to learn. To get some perspective, recall all that you've already learned. You may be surprised. If you think you have difficulty learning in general or that the material before you is the most difficult you've ever confronted, take an objective look at the evidence (see the exercise on page 353). The fact of the matter is, you have already learned a great many things, and among these, many difficult things. Leverage your learning. Say to yourself, "Since I have learned A, B, and C, there is no reason why I can't learn X, Y, and Z."

Increase Your Awareness: Perceive Similarities and Notice the Difference

As was discussed earlier, learning occurs when we come to understand similarities in things, events, and ideas. Confucian scholars referred to it as "apprehending the principle in things." In *Science and Human Values*, Jacob Bronowski concluded that it is this ability to recognize fundamental or essential similarities that is the essence of science. As he put it, "All science is the search for unity in hidden likenesses. . . . Science is nothing else than the search to discover unity in a wide variety of nature—or, more exactly, in the wide variety of our experience." Whenever we look beyond variation in form or content and penetrate to the "unity in hidden likenesses" of things, we are learning. This is the right-brain aspect of learning that requires the use of our creative intuitive intelligence. It is not a function of logic but of insight.

Learning also occurs when we notice the difference. To the uninitiated, computer-programming language appears as an incomprehensible mass. We lump it all together and say, "It's Greek to me." Yet the trained expert easily differentiates among the various languages and perceives their meanings and applications. Any area of knowledge in which you have a high degree of mastery or expertise is one in which you are able to distinguish a high degree of difference.

This is true regardless of your field of expertise. It could be designing aircraft or baking cookies, managing corporations or gardening, collecting stamps or conducting foreign policy. You are an expert because you know the subtleties of your craft. The uninitiated can enjoy the end products of your work, but not the process through which they are created. The uninitiated may say, "That was a delicious cookie," or "This new software is really incredible," but how the cookie was made or exactly how the software does what it does, the uninitiated do not know.

As we grow in understanding, our capacity to differentiate grows with us. Take the classic example of the cat on the hot stove. The cat burns its rear on the heated stove and, from then on, avoids all stoves. The cat makes the association between "stove" and "burn." It is unable to distinguish the difference between a stove that is "on" and one that is "off." A child, on the other hand, has the advantage of verbal interpretation. Her mother says "hot" or "burn." Now, when the child again hears the word "hot" or "burn," the word has become associated with the painful physical sensation. Her ability to understand the abstract symbols we call words gives the child a greater capacity to distinguish difference than that possessed by the cat. She is able to stay away from all things labeled "hot" or "burn," while the cat may avoid the stove, only to be burned by an electric iron.

Yet the young child's limited vocabulary and undeveloped cognitive skills mean that her ability to differentiate is also limited. For example, a toddler is bitten by a dog after she unwittingly pokes it in the eye. In her mind, it becomes a "bad dog" and remains one long after the incident. Her cognitive development has not reached the stage where she is capable of making a causal link between poking the dog in the eye and it biting her. It's simply a bad dog.

Even as adults (and especially when we are under stress), we sometimes revert to childlike reasoning. We make sweeping generalizations and fail to distinguish differences. Your boss, mate, or friend gives you specific constructive feedback on your behavior. You get defensive, lose the distinction between who you are and what you do, and interpret their feedback as a statement that you are wrong, bad, or inadequate. You feel guilt or shame but are none the wiser and do not alter your behavior. On the other hand, you may want to "kill the messenger," concluding that the pain or embarrassment you feel is not the result of your own fear of looking foolish but a result of the messenger's hostile intent. They're just out to get you. You get angry at the messenger and miss the opportunity to learn from their feedback. Remember: *while we are emotionally reactive, learning isn't possible.*

Detach and Learn

Emotional reactions keep you from operating at your best, *because they keep you from noticing the difference.* Often, we are emotionally blocked from learning about what matters most to us. Nelson has no problem learning about complicated computer design operations on the job. Yet he hasn't learned how to communicate effectively with his son. When it comes to computers, Nelson is emotionally detached; when it comes to his son, he's emotionally reactive. Remember, it's necessary to achieve a measure of emotional detachment before you can learn.

Tania took a public speaking course. During the first two months, she learned little, repeating the same mistakes over and over. Whenever she received feedback from her instructor or the class, she would become extremely defensive. She blocked out their input, dismissing it with, "They don't know what they're talking about" and "They're just picking on me." Near the end of the second month, the class began videotaping their presentations. While viewing video replays of her speeches, Tania was able to differentiate between the effective and the ineffective in her speaking style. Not only was she able to critique herself more objectively, but she was also now willing to accept the feedback of the teacher and class. She could see that their criticisms had been valid and that they had been trying to help her all along. As a result, she was able to detach, notice the difference, and learn.

While spending the summer on Cape Cod with his parents, Johnny, who was nearing his sixteenth birthday, tried to learn how to drive a car. Even though his father explained things carefully and was reasonably patient, it was difficult for Johnny to learn from him. With the smallest criticism, change in tone of voice, or sign of impatience, Johnny would tense up and become virtually paralyzed with confusion. Johnny became a nervous wreck. In fact, he almost had a couple of wrecks. He decided that he was a terrible driver. Yet when Johnny took his driver training class at school in the fall, he was surprised to learn that he could be a very good driver after all. With the driving instructor, Johnny's full attention was concentrated on learning to drive the car. He was no longer distracted with trying to please his father; consequently, he now learned quickly and easily.

If you are having difficulty learning anything, take your emotional temperature before you decide that it's too hard or that you are "too stupid." You may just be too emotionally involved. Detach. Cool out. Reduce your emotional temperature, and you may discover you are really pretty bright after all. In order for the transmission of a car to go from reverse to forward, it must pass through neutral. When we are learning, our lives are going forward. When we are emotionally reacting, we're going in reverse. To get things moving forward again, shift into the neutral gear of emotional detachment. Humor helps. Don't take yourself too seriously. The joke may be on you. As Ethel Barrymore said, "You grow up the day you have the first real laugh at yourself." When you are able to laugh at yourself, you let go of your attachment to ignorance and pass into the neutral or objective state necessary for learning. Now you are ready to notice the difference and learn.

Is there anyone so wise as to learn by the experience of others?

VOLTAIRE

Take Advantage of Other People's Experience

There is an easy and a hard way to learn anything. The hard way is by trial and error. The easy way is by taking advantage of OPE (other people's experience). Availing yourself of the knowledge and experience of others saves you a great deal of time, energy, and frustration. There's no point in trying to reinvent the wheel or go through an exhaustive process of trial and error when the hard-won experience of others is so readily available.

It may have taken someone fifteen years to learn the ins and outs of their business. Yet you can learn many of the essentials from them in a weekend seminar, or by reading a two-hundred-page book. By taking advantage of their expertise, you'll know where to concentrate your attention *before* you open up shop. You'll be spared many of the costly and time-consuming mistakes they have made. You'd be foolish not to seek out and learn from the experience of others. Take the attitude: "Somebody knows what I don't. It's my job to find out who, and learn from them."

Never before in human history has so much information been so readily and easily accessible. Today, you can find other people's experience in the form that suits you best. Here are just a few of the ways you can access it: conversations, live interviews, classes, seminars, books, audio- and videotapes, films, the Internet, CD-ROMs, newsletters, magazines, and newspapers. Gain maximum benefit from learning materials such as books, the Internet, or audio- and videotapes, by pausing periodically to mentally project yourself into the situations you are learning about. If you're learning a new skill, visualize yourself doing the thing described. Visualization allows you to "pre-experience" a situation, ensuring that you will deal with it with greater confidence and effectiveness when you encounter it in the real world. Remember, the subconscious mind doesn't know the difference between real and imagined experience. (See chapter 11.)

We don't all learn in the same way. Some of us learn well from books; others do much better in a classroom setting. Choose strategies that take advantage of your learning strengths. While we process information through all of our senses, we learn principally through sight, sound, and feeling. Most of us are visual learners. It has been estimated that the normal sighted person living in today's technologically advanced society processes as much as 90 percent of all incoming data through their eyes. Visual learners learn best when they can see the idea. Viewing diagrams, pictures, graphics, film, videos, slides, photographs, and live demonstrations, are examples of visual learning. Others learn best by hearing about their subject. For these audio learners, lectures, audiotapes, conversations, interviews, radio programs, and reading are excellent ways of digesting new material. Still others learn best when they can get a feel for a subject; they are kinesthetic learners. Modeling or imitating behavior, hands-on contact with objects, dance and physical movement, field trips, and dramatic enactments of the subject matter are examples of kinesthetic learning.

Identify your dominant learning style and rely on it. Reinforce what you learn through your dominant style by incorporating the others. Of course, the best of way of learning a given subject often depends on the subject itself. Whatever your dominant style, learning the skill of archery from audiotapes, or judo from books, will leave a lot to be desired.

He that can have patience can have what he will.

BENJAMIN FRANKLIN

Learn Skills and Attitudes Through Osmosis and Observation

We learn by osmosis. Ever notice how, quite unintentionally, you pick up verbal expressions or patterns of speech from those you associate with? This is an example of learning by osmosis. Simply putting yourself in the physical presence of those you want to learn from will help you immensely. Without thinking about it, your subconscious mind will pick up and incorporate ways of being and acting, of carrying and presenting yourself.

We also learn by observation. By *observation,* I mean deliberately paying attention to what those we want to learn from are doing, and making mental or written notes of what we see. Because it requires greater attention (the key to learning), observation is a more effective learning strategy than mere osmosis. Moreover, it allows us to critically assess what we are learning. Remember, even the best role models can teach what *not* to do, as well as what to do.

Do Some Modeling

Modeling is a more effective learning technique than observation because it requires still greater attention. You're not merely taking note of how others are doing things but actually imitating, or copying, them while they are doing it. Modeling brings learning all the way into the

*He who can copy
can do.*

LEONARDO DA VINCI

body. It's the classic way the great masters of art taught their pupils. Children love to model behavior. We sometimes call it "monkey see, monkey do." The monkey business of modeling plays a big part in the speed with which children learn.

As adults, we often miss out on opportunities to accelerate learning by copying, or modeling, those who are expert. In our pride, we want to think of ourselves as original, "different," and unique. We want to create *before* we can copy. Of course, once you gain mastery, you can bring in your own touch, but you will learn the basics much more quickly if you're willing to imitate. Skiing was one of the first behaviors to be systematically modeled. Observers carefully analyzed films of expert skiers and broke down the process into small components that could be easily duplicated. Then they had simply to teach the various components in succession, and the complex set of skills necessary for skiing could be easily and rapidly learned by virtually anyone. Study how others who are expert in your field approach it. How do they prepare themselves? How do they execute? Break it down into steps you can model. Make their skill your own.

Find a Mentor

When you are entering a new environment, it helps to have a guide who knows the territory. Mentors play the role of guides. A good mentor provides you with a total learning experience. The mentor shows you what he is doing; he tells you about what he is doing, and gives you a feel for it. After a short time with a mentor in a given field, you will know whether or not this is an area you want to pursue. A mentor provides not only information and understanding but also the caring and concern of another human being. Mentoring can provide an intimate and warm context for learning. You may want to have several mentors to guide you in a single area, or one for each of a number of areas. The mentor's mastery gives you a mark to shoot for—or even surpass.

What often blocks us from learning is simply our refusal to ask someone who knows. Again, this comes from failing to perceive the difference between ignorance and stupidity. I have never met a man or woman who wasn't ignorant (about something), nor yet met anyone who was inherently stupid (unable to learn). If you find yourself neglecting to avail yourself of the help you might receive by asking others, ask yourself if it is because:

- You won't admit your ignorance.
- You have a compulsive need to be right.
- You lack confidence in your ability to learn.
- You fear the other party may reject you.
- You are too emotionally involved.
- You are afraid they may ask you to work too hard.

Practice

The final step to effective learning is to repeatedly practice and apply what you learn. In fact, we could say that until you apply new knowledge, you haven't learned it at all. Practice may not make you perfect, but it will certainly make you better. Actors in Broadway plays average three months of rehearsal before a new production. Olympic athletes train for years. Great speakers practice their speeches; comedians, their jokes. You will want to practice the skills required for you to achieve your objectives. Be willing to make mistakes. If you limit yourself only to what you do well, you leave no room to grow. Don't be afraid of looking foolish. Remember, anything worth doing is worth doing poorly at first. Hang in there; practice will make you better.

Summary

In review, the attitudes best suited for creative learning can be verbalized as follows: "I have a strong desire to learn. I know what I want to learn and why. Instead of wasting my energy by judging myself for not already knowing, I will keep my attention fixed on my objectives. I can detach emotionally, penetrate to process, and distinguish differences. I will seek out knowledge and those who know. I will practice and practice—and keep a sense of humor!"

Detachment

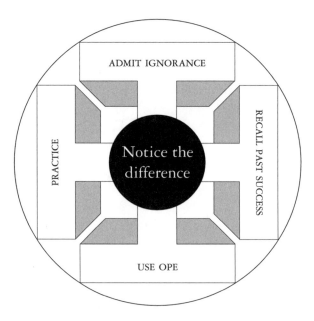

Anyone who stops learning is old, whether twenty or eighty.
Anyone who keeps learning today is young. The greatest thing in life
is to keep your mind young. —HENRY FORD

I am not ashamed to confess that I am ignorant of what I do not know.
—CICERO

First learn how to do whatever you want to do properly through
instruction... then mentally visualize yourself doing it properly...
whenever the time presents itself. —EARL NIGHTINGALE

I am defeated and know it if I meet any human being from which I find
myself unable to learn anything. —GEORGE HERBERT PALMER

Chapter 20 Exercises

❧

Recall What You Have Learned

Make a list of at least thirty things you have learned how to do. Be sure to include obvious things that you may tend to dismiss as insignificant, but which are in fact extremely important, such as: learning to walk, to talk, drive a car, read a book, and so on. Remind yourself that there were times, on the way to learning these things, when you may have felt that it was too difficult, but nevertheless, you did ultimately learn how to do them. Recalling things you have already learned will not only encourage you to learn still more but remind you that learning is a process which at times includes doubt.

1.	16.
2.	17.
3.	18.
4.	19.
5.	20.
6.	21.
7.	22.
8.	23.
9.	24.
10.	25.
11.	26.
12.	27.
13.	28.
14.	29.
15.	30.

Learn the Skills

Write your goal at the top of a sheet of paper. Then list the skills required to achieve the goal. Finally, referring to your list, organize these skills into two columns, one being the list of skills that you possess already and the other, the list of skills that you have yet to learn.

GOAL:

SKILLS REQUIRED TO ACHIEVE THE GOAL

1.	9.
2.	10.
3.	11.
4.	12.
5.	13.
6.	14.
7.	15.
8.	16.

SKILLS I POSSESS	SKILLS I HAVE YET TO LEARN
1.	1.
2.	2.
3.	3.
4.	4.
5.	5.
6.	6.
7.	7.
8.	8.
9.	9.
10.	10.

What I Need to Learn
in Order to Achieve My Goals

Write your goal at the top of a sheet of paper. List what it is that you will need to know in order to accomplish your goal. Then organize this list into four categories:

GOAL:

WHAT I WILL NEED TO KNOW TO ACCOMPLISH MY GOAL

1.	*9.*
2.	*10.*
3.	*11.*
4.	*12.*
5.	*13.*
6.	*14.*
7.	*15.*
8.	*16.*

1. The things I want to learn from instruction.

2. The things I want to learn from self-directed study.

3. The things I want to learn from observing other people and events.

4. The things I want to learn from introspection.

Creating Detachment

The purpose of this exercise is to help you recognize how your approach to a particular situation determines the range of available options. More importantly, it will help you to see that when you take the right approach, you already know what to do. First, identify goal-related situations about which you often feel overwhelmed. Then for each situation, answer the questions below.

OVERWHELMING SITUATION #1:

Next, write about this situation from an emotionally attached point of view. This is your opportunity to express all your frustrations, to whine, complain, and blame others for this situation. Go ahead and vent your feelings about how impossible this situation is. We will call this the perspective of your "little self."

Now describe the same situation from an objective, detached viewpoint, in other words, from the perspective of your "big self." Examine the statements and concerns voiced by the "little self" and respond to each in terms of specific actions you can take. Give your "little self" the guidance, support, and direction it needs to handle this situation effectively.

Beyond
Commitment

Your Master Plan

———

Tips for Time Management

———

Evaluation

Beyond Commitment

Now it's time to move beyond commitment, into the four remaining steps of the manifestation process. As you may recall, these steps are: the Plan, the Execution, the Feedback, and the Evaluation, relevant to the manifestation of your goals. This brief section will consider ways that you can begin moving forward into these final steps. With respect to planning, the key is to break down your goal into a series of concrete action steps and then assign definite deadlines to each. (See and complete the exercise on pages 360 and 361 for each of your goals.) With respect to the execution, time management is an essential. How well you use your time will determine how efficient, and more importantly, how effective, your efforts to achieve your goals really are. As important as it is to plan your time wisely, it's just as important to keep a time diary, a record of the way you actually use your time. (See *Tips for Time Management* on pages 362 and 363.)

Your goals, specific action steps, and records of time use provide the basis from which to judge the effectiveness of your efforts. In other words, they provide a framework from which you can create a system of feedback. Take the time to develop and apply systematic procedures for monitoring progress toward your goals. Schedule time to review these measures of progress and to assess what is working well and ways in which you can improve your performance. Once you have completed a specific goal, evaluate what you learned in the process and how well the final results you have achieved match with your original vision. Finally, determine where you want to go from here, what additional goals and challenges lie ahead. (See the exercise on page 364.)

All of this may sound like a lot of work, yet investing the effort to manifest your dreams is one investment you will never regret. On the other hand, if you fail to make the effort, you will always have a nagging question in the back of your mind: Could I have made it? Go on, determine to manifest your dreams and apply the effort necessary to make them come alive. Even if you don't completely realize your vision on the first try, you will have made significant progress and learned valuable lessons. Most of all, you will know that you had the courage to stand up for what you believed in. You were true to yourself.

Even if you're on the right track, you'll get run over if you just sit there.

WILL ROGERS

Your Master Plan

Review your goals (see page 157) and the milestones to accomplishing them that you identified on page 189. (After reviewing your answers to the exercises on pages 333 and 354, you may want to revise these milestones.) Write your major milestones below, and for each of these, identify four significant action steps to completing them. For each of these action steps, assign a due date, and estimate the time and financial cost involved. Also indicate who will be responsible for the completion of this task.

GOAL:

MAJOR MILESTONE #1

MAJOR MILESTONE #2

MAJOR MILESTONE #3

MAJOR MILESTONE #4

Major Milestone #1	Due Date	Est. Time	Est. Cost	By Whom
Action Step A				
Action Step B				
Action Step C				
Action Step D				

Major Milestone #2	Due Date	Est. Time	Est. Cost	By Whom
Action Step A				
Action Step B				
Action Step C				
Action Step D				
Major Milestone #3	Due Date	Est. Time	Est. Cost	By Whom
Action Step A				
Action Step B				
Action Step C				
Action Step D				
Major Milestone #4	Due Date	Est. Time	Est. Cost	By Whom
Action Step A				
Action Step B				
Action Step C				
Action Step D				

Tips for Time Management

1. **Devote sufficient time to planning.** In addition to a long-term, master plan, be sure to make daily plans. Ideally, this will be something more than a simple "to do" list. Identify high priority activities in relation to your goals and plan to do these first. Remember to allow a realistic amount of time when scheduling activities. Things often have a way of taking longer than we might hope. Divide up your day into small time blocks and try to make each one of these blocks as productive as possible. A good rule of thumb is to schedule one hour of planning for every four hours of work. Use a personal time planner or week-at-a-glance that you can carry with you.

2. **Do something toward the completion of your major goals every day.** Each new day is a building block with which you are creating the house of personal goals and dreams. As you lay each new block, keep in the forefront of your mind the house you are building. Try to take some action, no matter how small it might be, on your goal-related activities each and every day. If you find yourself procrastinating, simply writing your goals down again will create some movement. Because action creates momentum, try to schedule as many goal-related activities as you can for early in the day.

3. **Reduce big jobs into bite-size steps.** Visualize yourself doing each of the steps required to accomplish an important activity, and then, one by one, set about doing these. If the activity is a major one, make a list of the specific steps.

4. **Coordinate your activities to avoid duplication of effort.** It generally saves time to group related activities. For example, making all of the day's important phone calls in one sitting, or in a series of sittings, is a more efficient use of time than phoning on a hit-or-miss basis. A simple technique to help you group related activities is to section off a piece of paper into activity categories, for example: out-and-about errands, phone calls, appointments, work-related

projects, new ideas, etc. Keep this list at the ready, and enter activities in the appropriate sections as they come up. Then take out your list during your morning planning session, and schedule related activities in specific time blocks. Again, be sure to give priority to your goal-related activities.

5. **Concentrate on doing one thing at a time.** Avoid splitting your attention, whether by attempting to do several things at once or through mental preoccupation. Spot check yourself for alertness. Take frequent breaks to stay fresh. A change of pace helps keep you alert, but while you are actually working, stay focused.

6. **Remember the 80/20 principle.** Time-management experts tells us that, generally speaking, only 20 percent of what we do is really effective in terms of helping us to achieve our goals. That means, of course, that 80 percent isn't. Identify what the key 20 percent is for you, and give this the bulk of your time and attention.

7. **Complete what you begin.** Completing the tasks you have set for yourself (1) energizes you—freeing psychic energy (2) rids your mind of clutter, worry, and concerns (3) improves your concentration, and (4) maintains your motivation. The keys to effective time management are choosing your time-use priorities and improving your ability to complete things.

8. **DO IT NOW!** There is no time like the present. When in doubt, do something. Ask yourself, "What is the best use of my time right now?"

Evaluation

Once you have completed a goal, answer the following questions to help you evaluate the process and to determine where you now stand in relation to your continuing progress.

1. How well does the accomplishment of this goal match what you originally envisioned? In what ways did it meet, exceed, or fall short of your expectations?

2. What did you learn along the way? What surprises did you encounter along the way?

3. What, if anything, would you do differently?

4. What were your biggest challenges and disappointments en route to realizing this goal?

5. Now that you have accomplished this goal, what you would like to do next? What new goals seem most inviting to you at this time?

Appendix

Manifesting a Thing: Buying Your First Home

Vision: You have become tired of renting and have decided that the time is right for you to purchase your own home. Your vision is to buy a house that provides you with the space, comfort, amenities, and privacy you desire. You also view purchasing a home as an important key to your financial goals, providing you with considerable equity, tax, and appreciation benefits. You are also attracted to the idea of creating your space just the way you want it and being able to make the improvements you desire, without having to ask for anyone's permission.

Focus: You read books on buying a home. You begin researching the housing market in the general area in which you want to live, including price, turnover, rate of appreciation, property taxes, and so on. You research the local neighborhoods, including schools, shopping, parks, and proximity to services or facilities of particular interest or importance to you. You research financial factors, including prevailing mortgage rates, the loan amount you qualify for, down-payment requirements, creative financing strategies, and so on. You determine the criteria that are most important to you in deciding which home to buy. Finally, you set a definite goal for when you will purchase and move into your new home.

Desire: The more you focus on your goal, the stronger your desire to realize your dream becomes. Your research helps you to begin seeing yourself in your new home. Each step you take affirms your belief that you will find the home that's right for you. You begin taking pride of ownership in the home you are currently renting, giving it the care and attention you intend to give your own home. You take time to value and acknowledge all the little steps you take, knowing that each and every one is moving you closer to your goal.

In addition to these more automatic increases in desire resulting from your focus on the goal, you employ techniques described in the Desire section of this book. For example, you spend quiet time visualizing yourself in your new home. You write affirmations about easily and effortlessly finding the perfect home. You keep a logbook of your efforts and reward yourself for the steps you take.

Commitment: You have selected the specific home you want and are committed to making it yours. You are determined to overcome any and all obstacles that may arise and to see the process through to completion. You are prepared for the fact that buying your new home will take time and energy and that some financial sacrifices may have to be made along the way. You are ready to confront your fears about making what may be the biggest purchase and financial commitment of your life. You and your partner agree to divide up tasks and to give each other moral support throughout the process.

Planning: You map out all of the financial details and arrangements for closing on the house. You plan any improvements that you or the current owner will make prior to your taking possession. You plan how you will decorate your new home, including any new appliances or furnishings you will purchase. You schedule and make all of the necessary arrangements to move in.

Execution: You execute all of your plans, dealing with obstacles and setbacks as they arise. Finally, the day arrives, and you move into your new home.

Feedback: You enjoy living in your new home. You appreciate the financial benefits at tax time and when you assess your net worth. You determine to make additional improvements, such as planting fruit trees and installing a hot tub.

Evaluation: Relaxing one day on the deck of your new home, you determine that you have realized your dream. You decide that all of the thought and effort that went into it were well-spent.

Manifesting a Lifestyle: Creating a Healthy Lifestyle

Vision: You are inspired to incorporate lifestyle changes that will support optimal health, increase vitality, and control your weight.

Focus: You read books about health, fitness, and nutrition and subscribe to magazines, such as *Alternative Medicine, Health,* or *Prevention.* You research various exercise program options and determine which seems best for you. You make an appointment with a nutritionist to discuss an optimal diet for you. You make a definite goal for when you will have incorporated exercise and nutritional changes into your daily routine.

Desire: The more you focus on your goal, the stronger your desire to see it happen becomes. In your mind's eye, you picture yourself healthy, fit, and energetic. You visualize yourself working out; eating delicious, healthy food; and feeling and looking better every day. You write daily affirmations about achieving your weight goals and feeling healthier and more energetic. You buy clothes that will fit you at your target weight. You create a logbook that you will use to track your progress.

Commitment: You've become aware of the less-than-healthy habits in your life, and you are now committed to replacing them with constructive alternatives. You're ready to confront habitual reactions with awareness, strength, and a positive attitude. You realize that when you are under stress, you tend to rely on sugar and caffeine for energy, and fatty foods for comfort. You develop alternative coping strategies. An upcoming business trip could throw you off your routine unless you take steps to ensure that it doesn't. You face your fears that you will never achieve your goal. You counter your fears in a variety of ways, including reading and learning about how others have overcome. You involve your partner and/or your family in your efforts, and make the effort to gain their cooperation and support.

Planning: You work out a detailed dietary program with the help of your nutritionist. You work out the details of your exercise program, including how, where, and with whom you will exercise. You set up a regular exercise schedule.

Execution: You start to execute all of your plans—beginning your exercise program and stocking up on the appropriate foods that are needed for your new dietary program. You inform your partner or support team about your progress and record your efforts in your daily logbook.

Feedback: You feel and look better. Your partner notices the extra sparkle in your eyes and the spring in your step. At times you feel tired, but it is a satisfied feeling that makes you more determined than ever to stay the course. You remind yourself that with each passing day, you are getting stronger and healthier. You incorporate improvements and adjustments into your program to ensure that it stays realistic, challenging, and fresh. Perhaps now is the time to update your nutrition or exercise plans, or buy yourself additional exercise clothing or equipment to help keep you motivated.

Evaluation: After a few months on the program, you pause to reflect on how you felt before you began. You realize that although at times, the rate of measurable progress was slower than you would have liked, you have made real and important changes to the quality of your life. You also realize that you learned many things about yourself in the process. You've seen it grow progressively easier to stay on your program. You smile inside yourself as you reflect on how all of these results have come in only three months' time. You remind yourself not to rest on your laurels as you lace up your shoes for yet another brisk jog. There's no stopping you now!

Manifesting a Livelihood: Opening a Bookshop/Cafe

Vision: You want to move out of the large city you now live in, to a smaller town, where you and your family can enjoy a higher quality of life. You love books and have always dreamed of owning your own bookshop. Your vision is to open a community-minded bookstore in a small town. You want to include a coffee bar and to host a variety of community events, such as author signings and lectures, poetry readings, book discussions, political forums, and concerts for local musicians.

Focus: You research, first through the library and Internet, and then through visits, a variety of towns, until you find one that fits your lifestyle requirements and offers a book-buying public sufficient to make your store a success. You investigate trends in the book business, scout out potential locations, and research start-up costs and financing options. You read books such as *Growing a Business, Visionary Business,* and *A Manual on Bookselling.* You subscribe to magazines such as *Publisher's Weekly* and *NAPRA ReView.* You select a town and establish a definite goal for when you will open your new store there.

Desire: The more you focus on your goal, the stronger your desire to see it happen becomes. You choose to employ the techniques described in the Desire section of this book. You visualize yourself in your new store. You write affirmations about operating a successful bookselling business. You spend a lot of time in bookstores, mentally critiquing them in terms of the way you will do things in your own store. You order catalogues from publishers. You keep a logbook, recording all of your efforts to realize your dream, and giving them the attention and appreciation they deserve.

Commitment: You are committed to opening your bookshop, determined to overcome any and all blocks and obstacles that stand between you and your goal. You discipline yourself to adopt a regular schedule for focusing on and planning the execution of your dream. You face your fears about leaving your secure, if unfulfilling, corporate job. You continue learning about the town you plan to move to by taking frequent visits. You research and make arrangements to join local organizations such as the Chamber of Commerce and the Rotary Club.

Planning: You prepare an extensive business plan and seek funding for your project. You design the floor plan and layout of the store. You zero in on a store location and begin drawing up a profile of likely customers. You plan your inventory accordingly. You incorporate items that will appeal to the heavy summer tourist traffic as well as ancillary products and services that will attract a steady stream of local customers during the off-season. You coordinate with a small local college to carry their course textbooks and college paraphernalia. You establish relationships with suppliers, including book distributors, business equipment suppliers, and local bakeries. You negotiate with your commercial landlord with respect to the lease and improvements to the building.

Execution: You execute all your plans, taking possession of the store and moving in your fixtures, business and kitchen equipment, and inventory. You convince a noted author who lives in your area to give a lecture at your store in conjunction with its grand opening. You heavily promote your grand-opening event through local radio and newspapers. Finally, you open your doors and make your first sale. You're in business!

Feedback: Your feedback is the response of your customers. You actively seek out their advice in terms of the inventory you carry and the events they would like to see in the store.

Evaluation: On the first anniversary of your grand opening, you and your partner are sitting at a table in the cafe of your bookshop. It is early in the morning, before the store has opened, and you are reflecting on your store and all of the hard work that went into creating it. You are delighted that you have indeed made your dream come true.

THE INTEGRATED LIFE MATRIX GUIDE

The Practical You: What You Want to Own

Health: Health-related goals might include diet, exercise, or weight goals. Perhaps you want to cut down on, or give up, sugar, caffeine, alcohol, or cigarettes—or move to a healthier environment. Health issues can include:

Longevity	Energy Level	Comfort	Recreation
Strength	Appearance	Pleasure	Environment
Relaxation	Diet	Sports	Body Awareness

Lifestyle: These goals include where and how you want to live, as well as things you'd like to own: e.g., real estate, cars, electronics. (Lifestyle goals often involve the way you spend your money, while financial goals typically involve how you make, save, or invest it.) Lifestyle issues can include:

Housing	Freedom	Culture	Time Management
Travel	Community	Clothing	Interior Design
Pace of Life	Leisure	Dining	Standards of Living

The Potential You: What You Want to Be

Self-Development: Self-development goals include things you want to learn, qualities you want to develop, spiritual goals—anything that challenges you to become the best person you can be. Issues in this area can include:

Wisdom	Character	Challenge	Personal Growth
Reading	Education	Adventure	Emotional Well-Being
Values	Meditation	Spiritual Growth	New Skills and Abilities

Creative Expression: These goals could include painting, singing, dancing, hobbies, writing, arts and crafts—anything you make or do that expresses the individual you. Issues in this area can include:

Play	Cooking	Painting	Imagination
Poetry	Drama	Writing	Arts and Crafts
Music	Clothing	Hobbies	Ritual

THE INTEGRATED LIFE MATRIX GUIDE

The Productive You: What You Want to Do

Career: Career goals include the profession or professions you want to work in, and levels of achievement, excellence, or recognition you desire to achieve within your field. If you are financially secure, include contributions you want to make through volunteer work. Career issues can include:

Training	Security	Challenge	Experience
Colleagues	Recognition	Advancement	Working Conditions
Status	Responsibility	Clientele	Achievement

Finance: Financial goals include your definition of financial independence, as well as any goals concerning your annual income, investments, net worth, retirement, children's education, and so on. Financial issues can include:

Income	Investments	Expenses	Net Worth
Budget	Security	Debt Service	Philanthropy
Retirement	Insurance	Savings	Tax Planning

The Personal You: What You Want to Share

Social: Social goals include your relationships with a wide range of individuals, participation in groups, clubs, associations, churches, business associations, etc. Issues in this area can include:

Friends	Self-Confidence	Parties	Hobbies
Cooperation	Health Clubs	Social Clubs	Professional Associations
Image Projection	Tolerance	Acquaintances	Political Organizations

Intimate: Intimate relationship goals include goals for improving your relationships with your spouse, family, and closest friends. Issues in this area can include:

Intimacy	Respect	Children	Openness
Trust	Marriage	Family	Commitment
Support	Honesty	Sex	Tenderness